EMILIO AMBASZ

INVENTIONS

THE REALITY OF THE IDEAL

Published to coincide with an exhibit of the work of Emilio Ambasz
at the Institute of Contemporary Art at Tokyo Station.

東京ステーションギャラリーに於けるエミリオ・アンバーツ展に際し、同時出版。

EMILIO AMBASZ
INVENTIONS
THE REALITY OF THE IDEAL

ESSAYS BY

TADAO ANDO

FUMIHIKO MAKI

FOREWORD BY RYUICHI SAKAMOTO

OVERVIEW BY PETER BUCHANAN

First published in the United States of America
by Rizzoli International Publications, Inc.
300 Park Avenue South, New York, N.Y. 10010

Return of the Entire Humankind to Earth © 1992 Ryuichi Sakamoto
Amplitude's Promise Fulfilled © 1992 Tadao Ando
Primary Architecture © 1992 Fumihiko Maki
Emilio Ambasz: The Relevance of Resonant Ritual © 1992 Peter Buchanan

Library of Congress Cataloguing-in-Publication Data

Emilio Ambasz, inventions : the reality of the ideal / foreword by
   Ryuichi Sakamoto : overview by Peter Buchanan

       p.   cm.
     Includes bibliographical references.
     ISBN 0-8478-1607-9. -- ISBN 0-8478-1608-7 (pbk.)
     1. Ambasz, Emilio--Criticism and interpretation.   2. Architectural
   practice, International--New York (N.Y.) 3. Architecture,
   Modern--20th century.   I. Ambasz, Emilio.   II. Buchanan, Peter.

   NA839. A66E47   1992
   720' .92--dc20   92-14686
                                                                CIP

Technical editor: Andrea Truppin
Consulting editors: Darl Rastorfer
                     Daniel Brown

Design and composition: Anistatia R. Miller, New York, N.Y.

Printed and bound in Japan by Toppan Printing

Front cover illustration: Fukuoka Prefectural International Hall, Japan
Back cover illustration: Handkerchief Television

Contents

FOREWORD

RYUICHI SAKAMOTO

LUCILLE HALSELL CONSERVATORY,

SAN ANTONIO, TEXAS

Return of the Entire Humankind to Earth

Ryuichi Sakamoto

Mr. Ambasz's architecture. Why is it so appealing to us?

Is it because it suggests a new state of "Cohabitation with Nature"? Why the " "?

Is it because the history of the few, albeit very long, last thousand years teaches us that, since the destruction of nature is not limited to industrial agents, we cannot easily believe that we can reestablish the pact of reconciliation with nature?

Notwithstanding all the above, in Ambasz's architecture nature appears almost everywhere, around and within. See, for example, the Nishiyachiyo Station Master Plan for the new town of Nishiyachiyo in Japan (page 192).

The nature that emerges in his architecture is there not simply to give some color to the taste-lessness of empty spaces.

When one sees photographs and drawings of Ambasz's work one is stricken by the considerable amount of "thought-heavy" green.

Why?

After all, isn't an architect a person who draws detailed designs for great pylons, steel beams, glass panels, or concrete blocks?

Certainly, there are other architects who have been successful in skillfully integrating natural conditions into their own architectural plans.

Or to say it differently: there are other architects who have expressed their architectural philosophies by adapting their work to the forms of animals and plants.

But, there is a very definite difference in Ambasz's inventive architecture.

And it reminds me of something.

What?

LUCILLE HALSELL CONSERVATORY,

SAN ANTONIO, TEXAS

For example, a gigantic space station, endowed with desert and savannah areas, where ten million people dwell. Of course, in my evocation I am not retracing the bright scenarios of the conquest of space that were dreamed in the late fifties or mid-sixties.

To me such a space station stands as a inconsolable emblem for the desolation of our "Mother Earth." Mankind, who has not yet been able to elucidate fully the mysteries of photosynthesis, certainly should tremble at the dangers of living in space.

Nothwithstanding all of this, if we are forced to think about space stations, it is entirely because we feel a longing for escape from the crises that we feel will emerge in the coming years.

In short, Ambasz is an architect, that rare one, I suspect, who does not merely think in terms of just one building but, rather, always bears in mind an entire culture, who thinks of his buildings in the context of an entire planet still possessing many areas to be explored.

If I were the chairman of the committee for the Return of the Entire Humankind to Earth, I would first go to Mr. Ambasz and ask him to be our architect.

There is a ritualistic element to the *promenade architecturale* of Le Corbusier, whose houses and apartments were also temples to sacramentalize daily life and several of whose late works include much more explicit barrows than anything by Ambasz. But the intensification of experience characteristic of Ambasz's projects is quite counter to that of more conventional modern architecture, which tends to be shaped for convenience and as a minimally impinging background. Postmodernism's reaction to the utilitarian banalities that modernism had been progressively reduced to, whether it be of the classicist (Michael Graves and Robert Stern) or neo-modernist (Richard Meier and Peter Eisenman) sort, is a formal flurry of little experiential consequences. To these Ambasz's work stands as an alternative, reminiscent of that of Giambologna and Buontalenti's to the mannerism that succeeded a run-down Renaissance. Yet it is an alternative that draws on another reaction to a moribund modernism—that of abstracting yet further into minimalism.

In contrast to mannerism and postmodernism's desperate play with distorted and disjunctive forms, what Giambologna and Buontalenti did (at Pratolino and the Boboli Gardens) and what Ambasz, too, does is to try to help man make peace with the world and himself by entering into a regeneratively nurturing compact with nature. Following the Land Artists, he marries minimalism with nature. Yet if minimalism's strategy was to provoke perception so free and fresh as to be entranced by only primary form and color, Ambasz adds whole other dimensions. But instead of formal complexity or semiological conundrum, he adds or draws attention to the primordial elements of nature—sun and sky, earth and grass, water and wind. And in contrast to Land Art's bald and brutal (to nature that is) statements, Ambasz, for all his actual manipulations of nature, pursues a much softer and more ecological vision, less acting on than with nature.

Yet the most crucial dimension to Ambasz's work that distinguishes it from minimalism and most modernism stems from his belief that "architecture and design are acts of the myth-making imagination": his architecture is then a self-conscious attempt to resurrect and reach the resonance of the mythic. Again though, Le Corbusier comes to mind, for his architecture too is underpinned and overlaid with myth. But with Le Corbusier this involves a very complex mapping of private themes on sev-

BANQUE BRUXELLES LAMBERT,

MILAN, ITALY

eral occult systems simultaneously. Elaborated through the paintings, these themes were then encoded as signs and metaphors in the forms of the buildings. Yet for all the power of the resulting architecture the mythical messages remain, to all but a few scholars, utterly hermetic. For Ambasz, the myths are not so much encoded in form as unfolded, almost as a narrative, along the ritualistic route where they are readily experienced and relatively transparent. And evoked might be such universal myths as that of the Eternal Return, as with the Castelli house, or a fable that Ambasz himself created to help generate the design, as with the Columbus Bridge. It is this use of myth and self-generated fable as not just an overlay on a design but as it germinal core, underlying even function, that is both unique and so timely in Ambasz's architecture.

The initial design process for Ambasz's architectural projects now seems largely instinctual and immediate. He trusts that images arising in his imagination will not only be engaging to others too, but will also have the mythic resonance he seeks. Yet his confidence in this is founded in his experience of generating his earlier architectural projects in a more self-conscious process, with image and informing fable elaborated together in a deliberately sustained reverie. Indeed, he has said that he did not trust a design to be truly compelling until he felt that the fable was so resonant that he could relate just it to several artists or draftsmen and they would all conjure and draw the identical thing. And the fable would not only provide the narrative and structure of the processional ritual, but also ensure the resonance of these events as well as all the formal elements of the design.

At its most elementary, the fable might be the story of an enchanted visit to the realized project. And sometimes this might result in the marrying of an archetypal myth with an archetypal form—as with the house for Leo Castelli. Here the myth of the Eternal Return is focussed on the court that exactly recalls its archetypal essence as evoked in the Borges poem "Patio," which is included in Ambasz's "Working Fables" (*Emilio Ambasz: The Poetics of the Pragmatic*, page 33).

>With the evening
>the two or three colors of the patio grew weary.
>The huge candour of the full moon

BANQUE BRUXELLES LAMBERT,

MILAN, ITALY

no longer enchants her habitual firmament.
Patio, channel of sky.
The patio is the window
through which god watches souls.
The patio is the slope
down which the sky flows into the house.
Serene.
Eternity waits at the crossroads of stars.
How beautiful to live in friendship with the shade
of a porch, eaves and a well.

If the Castelli house uses archetypes to satisfy generalized longings for reconnection to self and cosmos, other fables and designs are more specific to the particulars of a place. The Banque Bruxelles Lambert in Lausanne (page 32), for instance, seems to satisfy subliminal local longings by reinstating to view the surrounding mountains once visible from the city center and now dismayingly obstructed. And the Houston Center Plaza (pages 34 and 36) supplies what is missed but has never been in that sweltering city—cooling mists and cascades, and shady, scented, and secret bowers for intimate trysts. Also, the gridded layout of the bowers is both a miniaturizing and intensification of the city grid, thereby both symbolizing it and becoming the heart it intrinsically lacks.

Startling in imagery and originality, yet both immensely apt to place and thoroughly pragmatic in its exploitation of contemporary technology and financing, the Houston Center Plaza is one of Ambasz's most compelling projects. As such, it is also a convincing vindication of the power of his design method. What he has achieved is a place that everyone, not just architects and artists, would find as magically potent as those, both natural and deliberately man-made, that earlier cultures recognized as sacred. Again it would evoke an awed alertness in which experience is intensified and along with it the sense of one's self and one's actions.

Places of such potency are of course not often apt. But a similar approach has generated a series of other less intense and often larger projects that would be every bit as intrinsic to the identity of the

MUSEUM OF AMERICAN FOLK ART,

NEW YORK CITY, NEW YORK

host city. Frankfurt Zoo (page 94) is such a project, a wonderfully appropriate and pragmatic solution that is both highly integrated as a design yet richly various in the conditions it provides. Other such projects would not only immensely enhance but intrinsically transform the city they were part of. Examples are the Rimini Seaside Development (page 238) and Seville World Exposition (page 88) projects. With Seville's Expo about to open, it is sad to think of the huge opportunity it missed in not committing to this competition gold-medal prizewinner. Five hundred years after Columbus sailed west in his three frail ships, a flotilla of exotic craft would have returned from all corners of the earth to dock in the lush new world now on Seville's threshold. And when these craft had gone, Seville would be as permanently enhanced as it has been by the remnants of the 1929 World's Fair, while the new lakes, giant fountains, and mist-sprayed pergolas would do much to temper permanently the fierce, dry heat of the city's summer.

At a smaller scale, and all included in this volume, projects that add a new dimension to their city and its identity are the reworking of the Convent of the Holy Infant Jesus in Singapore (page 152), the Fukuoka Prefectural International Hall (page 100), and the Phoenix Museum of History (page 140). The last two add to the city's resources by, among other things, extending existing parks. The Fukuoka project also reestablishes, from the top of it, a view to the sea; and the Phoenix Museum (like the bank in Lausanne) returns to the city center some sense of the surrounding countryside while the curving walls of its courtyard recall something of the original adobe settlements of the area. In a complimentary strategy, the town center of the new town of Nishiyachiyo (page 192) intensifies the character of the surrounding countryside so that the town will never be divorced from it, while also gaining a potent and unique identity. Here it is a pair of yoked office blocks that straddle the station like a gargantuan version of a Shinto temple gate, both announcing arrival and recalling an element of local traditional architecture.

All these projects prove how Ambasz's design approach can achieve a certain reenchantment and reintegration of the world. If the more powerful projects still the soul and evoke awe, then the

MUSEUM OF AMERICAN FOLK ART,
NEW YORK CITY, NEW YORK

appropriately less intense projects are not only pleasant and practical, but make or repair more obvious connections across space and even sometimes across time.

The reenchantment and reintegration, which happen in other ways too, are an urgently needed antidote to the desiccation and fragmentation of our world. This has been caused not only by modern architecture and town planning but also by the whole instrumental world view of modern society, especially as endorsed by science and economics. Myth was reduced from being an ennobling truth of higher order than mere fact to being debunked as silly superstition. But believing everything to be explicable only in terms of mechanical cause and effect, and valuing everything only in terms of the bottom line, has robbed, or at least denied, the world of its magic and mystery. And with them have gone the more subtle experiences and the larger meanings that engage and sustain us as complete and fulfilled human beings. Now the planet seems drained of the vital juices that made everything lushly sensuous and radiantly sacred and of those symbolic and energetic bonds that once held it all together and included us so that we felt we belonged and were at home in the world. And the modern city is the most perfect symptom-symbol of how everything has dried up and fallen apart.

Most of us now have a sense that our modern scientific culture has failed us, that there are whole parts of our personalities and psyches that are not sustained and offered succor. Alienated, we distract ourselves from our feelings of dissatisfaction and insubstantiality by compulsive overindulgence—in work and entertainment, drink and drugs, sex and food. The more sentient, as is confirmed by where they prefer to holiday, long at some level for the sort of world where they can quietly open up to its splendors and satisfactions, and experience again a deep connection between themselves and their settings. And they are rediscovering that myth is not mumbojumbo, but the most powerful means of reinstating meaning, direction and a sense of connection at both the cultural and personal level. Ambasz's long-standing advocacy of the mythic in architecture now seems less and less eccentric even to the skeptics and instead particularly prescient—as proven by visiting bookshops and noticing the boom of new books on mythology.

Other pressures make the resurrection of the mythic even more urgent. Ecological crises and AIDS in particular, but many other things too, tell us that we cannot continue to trash our world and our

GRAND RAPIDS ART MUSEUM,

GRAND RAPIDS, MICHIGAN

relationships, quickly moving on from places, products, and people when deemed profitably exploited and obsolete to us. Among the most crucial of contemporary cultural challenges is to learn how to establish deep, long-lasting, and genuinely affecting relationships with the world and people around us. And increasingly central concerns in architecture and product design (with Ambasz in the forefront in both areas) are with the various ways we relate to building and objects, and with how design can enhance the quality of the relationships—with the physical environment and between people, too. Ultimately, as more and more people are realizing, the most potent way of immeasurably intensifying and elevating these relationships is by mythologizing (or re-mythologizing) them so we become more self-conscious about and deeply committed to them. However this is done (whether through evoking essential archetypes and choreographing rituals as Ambasz does, or some other way) it would have significant consequences. It would resensitize us to the magic in things, ennoble our intentions in interacting in them, and add to the latter an expectancy that these will unfold and change over time—always revealing new dimensions to both our settings and ourselves.

The ongoing re-mythologizing of the world can be seen in many areas, especially in the arts, advertising, ecology, and self-help. Green issues, for instance, appeal not just for their obvious urgency to our survival. They also offer us, in our scientific and secular age, an inclusive and ennobling ethical, spiritual, and even mythic dimension to our relationship with the planet and everything and everybody on it. And the Gaia hypothesis, in which the planet is seen as almost conscious and in control of its evolution, is only one facet of the mythic Mother Goddess that is arising everywhere, including in the celebration of all sorts of feminine archetypes that encourage more nurturing, non-exploitative relationships between people, and between people and planet.

The intensifying awareness of our need for myth coincides (as neatly preprogrammed by Gaia?) with our deeper and more widespread knowledge of mythology and how it functions. We are, then, in a historically unique situation of being able to self-consciously select or even elaborate and synthesize the myths that will best suit us and our times. We are, after all, inheritors of the work of Frazer, Levi-Strauss, and Mircea Eliade, as well as of those two patron saints for the nineties, Carl Jung and Joseph Campbell. To these can be added the generally less well known understandings developed by Milton Erikson and others of how fable and ritual, myth and metaphor enrich our sub-

BANQUE BRUXELLES LAMBERT,

LAUSANNE, SWITZERLAND

conscious resources. It is for his having seen and seized such potentials some time ago, as well as for the compelling qualities of his designs, that Ambasz's work is so immensely relevant.

However, Ambasz's is not the only way of achieving the mythic in architecture. It could be argued that it is the undeniable power of the rituals he elaborates that is also their weakness: the rituals are too compelling and so, ultimately, coercive. To submit to such rituals may be fine as a special event, but too much for everyday experience. (That Ambasz is aware of this is clear in the very different handling of the ceremonial visitor's entrance to the Museum of American Folk Art [pages 26 and 28] and the more conventional one for office workers in the tower above.) An alternative approach is to evoke the mythic with representational means, using recognizable symbols and legible iconography which can be engaged with, when, and to the degree of intensity one chooses. Traditionally, of course, architecture uses the resources of both ritual and representation, and this may happen again. After all, the same factors that allow us to resurrect the mythic, and even create new myths for our time, could also justify a return to architectural iconography—though it could also be argued that electronics is now the pervasive medium we read and that it is futile for architecture to try and regain this role. Besides, most attempts in this direction have been unconvincing kitsch—so Ambasz's strategy seems the safer and shrewder. And its messages are available to anyone, as they do not need the knowledge required to read any representational system.

Yet there is more to be gained from the use of myth than to produce architecture in which it is encoded through ritual and representation. Trying to elaborate and evoke the mythic inevitably asks of architects a level of intention and focus that is integrative of their own personalities and creative powers, helping them also to dredge the resonant resources of the subconscious. More than that, myth can help to effectively shape, consciously and unconsciously, one's own persona and destiny. Jung, for instance, records that a turning point for him was when he asked himself what was the personal myth that should guide his own life.

Le Corbusier's self-created persona had multiple mythic overtones evident in his life as well as his works. It is interesting, then, to speculate to what degree Ambasz's own career and persona are consciously designed, and the latter at least deliberately given a mythic twist. Going direct from Princeton to a curatorship at MoMA and in the process cultivating colleagues, collaborators, and potential clients seems, in

HOUSTON CENTER PLAZA,

HOUSTON, TEXAS

retrospect, a brilliant bit of design. And whether or not the mysterious, quicksilver, and schizophrenic persona of Emilio (the architect-poet, a gentle dreamer) and Ambasz (the designer-pragmatist, a tough realist) is simply innate or deliberately designed, he/they certainly do not fail to be shrouded in myth. In this regard, I love in particular his story, which now he claims to be fable—and who knows—that a boyhood birthday present from his father was two books, Saint Exupery's *The Little Prince* and Machiavelli's *The Prince.*

Irrespective of the truth of these speculations, they bring attention to other facets of what is topical about Ambasz. Not only does he suggest the operational advantages in designing, with or without mythic overtones, one's own career and persona, but he reminds us of two important things. One is that in most historic cultures, it was known that to serve others best the architect had to cultivate himself, particularly in the esoteric (the very architectural disciplines of reading meaning into forms)—a legacy that lingers on in very debased fashion in the Masonic Brotherhood. In short, architecture was once a Way—and well it might be again one day. The other thing Ambasz's architecture recalls for us is how desperately impoverished are the views of most modernists, especially functionalists, as to the purposes of architecture.

The originating impulses of architecture were not just to provide shelter. This accounts for neither the complexity of buildings, nor for most of that elite category that until relatively recently were the only buildings deemed to be architecture—monuments and edifices of honorific purpose. The complexities of a house, for instance, of separating kitchen from dining, dining from living, formal living from family room, and so on and so on, cannot be explained in simple functional terms. This relentless partitioning of life's activities is in response to a deep-seated psychic drive. Overwhelmed by an awareness of frailty and vulnerability and at the mercy of any distraction, mankind's response has been to compartmentalize life into manageable chunks which then could be savoured in themselves, and elaborated into all the rituals that became human culture. Thus life was given order and rhythm, intensity and serenity, and overlaid with meanings and myths. Ambasz's architecture is very much about separating out things in space and time while also connecting them through ritual, with everything appropriately placed in relation to some evocation of natural archetypes.

This brings us to another of the originating impulses of architecture, which was to map in monumental and/or microcosmic form the majesty and mystery of cosmos and nature. Such mighty

HOUSTON CENTER PLAZA,

HOUSTON, TEXAS

monuments as Stonehenge and the ziggurats were built for this purpose as were later the paradisiacal gardens of the Near East and some cities in China and India. But these works are not only microcosmic, bringing down to earth the cosmos, their parts also represent aspects of the psyche, which is projected out to be explored in moving around city, palace, or garden. Thus we gain some symbolic accord with, and become part of and at home in, nature and cosmos, while also being encouraged to explore or elaborate our full selves. Ambasz's architecture, while avoiding conventional symbol, is not without cosmic overtones, but it does not so much bring cosmic elements down to earth as raise the earth's natural and ambient elements to become potent primordial presences that play on the psyche. His ecological vision excites our response because it is sacramental as much as scientific or merely ameliorative.

In reminding us how much architecture was once a celebration of nature, abstracting and intensifying aspects of it, and also how it heightened human events by a combination of mutual isolation and ritualistic connection, Ambasz brings us back to the beginnings of architecture and culture. Yet just as he reminds us that to be original means going back to origins, so he also seems to tell us that to be truly creative the architect must encourage us to recreate ourselves daily. This we do through ritual, which opens us to connect with the cosmos and to the deeper levels of the psyche. It is in the resonance of the rituals along the processional routes he contrives that lie the real meanings of the forms and images of Ambasz's architecture. It is here he fully lives up to his boast—a timely one when our culture is so in need of regeneration—in a 1983 interview, that he hopes to become "the last man of the present culture, looking longingly to designing the house for the first man of a culture which has not yet arrived."

ESSAYS

TADAO ANDO

FUMIHIKO MAKI

HOUSE FOR LEO CASTELLI,

NORTHEAST, USA

Amplitude's Promise Fulfilled

Tadao Ando

Originally, nature and architecture enjoyed a symbiotic relationship, an integrated fusion. Modern times have seen this relationship disintegrate and architecture thrust forward into abnormal prominence. Nature has been severed from the environment of architecture and reduced to the status of a subordinate element. When, concomitantly, economic efficiency was given priority, nature came to be treated as a mere visual accent, a mere aspect of landscape, a subject of adornment, and too often it was relegated to the margin of the site.

In recent years, consciousness has indeed grown in matters regarding nature and environmental issues. It was Emilio Ambasz who first called our attention to nature and the environment at quite an early point in his career, and ever since he has striven to achieve a fusion of nature and architecture. In this regard our methods of work may differ. I have tried, using "cathartic dialogue," to achieve such an ideal fusion between nature, man, and architecture, but I think that though different in approaches, our understanding and sensibility to the problems are quite similar.

The use of abstract forms and modes of expression in architecture, while it is the most remarkable concept born of the twentieth-century modern movement, contains the germ of contradiction. I have become convinced that architecture cannot be derived from the purely abstract as long as a function is demanded of it. The concrete aspects of nature, climate, and tradition, are intrinsic to the existence of architecture and it is not possible to ignore the extremely concrete demands of daily life. By drawing nature into abstraction and giving it expression within his method of architectural creation, Ambasz, in his brilliant insight, appears to have embarked—and he brings us with him—into a realm of architecture previously unknown to human experience. To underscore this marriage, I may want to

HOUSE FOR LEO CASTELLI,

NORTHEAST, USA

call it "environmental architecture." Someday we may just call it, again, Architecture. Ambasz's quest has started a trend in the recent work of many other architects.

By using nature on a massive scale, Ambasz presents us with the entire environment as a constellation from which architecture draws its essential being. There is, I believe, no prior example of nature governing architectural creation with such power and haunting seduction.

Ambasz's work has also been concerned with postulating visions of everyday life and its ancillary elements. The lighting fixtures, office furniture, diesel engines, ballpoint pens, and many other artifacts of daily life that he has created, while refined and modern, are highly attentive to the needs of our daily lives and laden with exalted concreteness of functional requirements satisfied.

Much as the Renaissance artists came upon their insights about architecture by means of painting, so Ambasz has arrived at a large vision of the urban environment by way of familiar everyday artifacts.

The scope of his vision and the depth of his insights overcome immense differences in scale, traveling freely between poles of macro and micro, thoughtfully contemplating the intervals between the abstract and the concrete. This is especially true of his attempts to transform nature into architecture on a grand urban scale. We can see in his most recent work, like the Fukuoka project, that we are presented with ideas and images which are quite outstanding.

The journey on which he has embarked is as yet uncharted, as is always the case of original design, and it is one where he shall surely encounter immeasurable difficulties. Nevertheless, as we all now stand before the twenty-first century, I have high expectations that the results which his endeavor and findings are yielding will prove truly substantial. He has taught us to see a dimension where nature and architecture are inseparable a realm extending from the God-given to the man-made nature. His work promises an ample domain where the found and the made, the natural and the artificial, coexist joyfully. He has fulfilled the promise of his early projects and has indeed shown us the way to a re-beginning of architecture.

SCHLUMBERGER RESEARCH LABAORATORIES,

AUSTIN, TEXAS

PRIMARY ARCHITECTURE

FUMIHIKO MAKI

I first became acquainted with the work of the architect Emilio Ambasz in the 1970s and 1980s when several of his projects won a number of awards, given annually by *Progressive Architecture*. The projects for the Grand Rapids Art Museum, the Mercedes-Benz Showroom, and the San Antonio Botanical Center (pages 30, 46, 48, 8 and 10), the last one constructed several years ago, were quite original in their design and concept, and I remember being impressed by them.

What was so impressive about them? I believe it was the fact that those projects, like other projects he has subsequently made public, represent a continual search for what is primary in architecture.

Postmodernism was at its peak in the 1970s and 1980s, when Ambasz appeared on the architectural scene. The postmodernist approach is to treat architecture as signs. Signs are to be continually produced and consumed. What is important in postmodernist architecture is the differences between signs. In the 1970s and 1980s, historicism, or the manipulation of a particular set of signs, was ascendant, but today historicism has lost its hold on many architects. Postmodernism itself is now most often referred to in the past tense, but the conditions we have come to associate with postmodernism still persist, even in the 1990s.

Ambasz, however, has paid little heed to postmodernism and has always been concerned with the more elementary aspects of architecture: that is, domain and boundary. He has offered clear and bold proposals that define domain and boundary by means of walls, roof, ground, water, space, and light. For example, the inclined plane introduced between two existing classicist buildings in the Grand Rapids Art Museum project was not just an addition to a pair of old structures. The intention was to create something new through a violent opposition.

What is sought by the above-described procedure is not harmony, but, tension through opposition. The plane may be functionally a stairway, a roof, or even a cascade, but in maintaining that tension it serves as a device that transcends time and continues to generate diverse meanings. Again, in the Mercedes-Benz Showroom, a single black wall and a white, wavelike floor create a place of ceremony in the same way that the Japanese tokonoma does. The static wall and the dynamic floor are in a relationship of tension. At the same time, these basic elements create a microcosm.

MERCEDES BENZ SHOWROOM,

NEW JERSEY

Upon seeing these projects I had the feeling I had previously encountered something like them. Something about them, not so much the forms but the spirit behind them, jogged my memory of history.

In mid-eighteenth-century Europe, particularly in metropolises like Paris, the world of the bourgeoisie was gradually entering a period of maturity, and cities were characterized, as they are today, by much noise and agitation. In reaction, an urge to return to nature and to seek less fettered forms of human behavior began to be felt. Jean Jacques Rousseau's paean to nature was one manifestation of that impulse.

A predilection for things archaic became stronger in architecture as well. The idea that buildings and gardens ought to be pantheistic worlds in miniature, able to accommodate a new style of life for human beings, gained force. Architects like Claude Nicolas Ledoux and François Le Queu made their appearance.

My feeling that there was something about Ambasz's work that recalled an earlier time in architectural history became stronger when I learned that he has always had a strong interest in the role of rituals and ceremonies in architecture.

Those earlier architects had created compositions of mysterious forms that were intended to expand the consciousness of observers and enable them to transcend time and space. The forms were allusive, at times oriented toward the heavens and at other times buried deep in the earth. They existed in their own closed domains. In looking at the plan of the conservatory in San Antonio, I was reminded of cave house of Le Queu. The San Antonio Conservatory was the first of a series of realized projects by Ambasz using earth architecture. Other projects include a number of proposals in Japan now under construction, such as his projects for Shin-Sanda and Fukuoka.

Employing vegetation and earth, Ambasz has developed a new architectural vocabulary that one might call "meta-architecture."

His architecture also reveals an intense awareness of boundaries. Modern architecture gave birth to homogeneous space, which is a rejection of the notion that a building has an outer shell, particularly a shell with special significance, as in classical architecture. Ambasz denies the homogeneity of space, but he is concerned not with surfaces but with domains. For example, the Fukuoka Prefectural International Hall, which is to be constructed in the center of Fukuoka City, will be a work of earth

MERCEDES BENZ SHOWROOM,

NEW JERSEY

architecture unprecedented in the world in its scale. The park in front of the hall rises in steps at a forty-five-degree angle. The building does not have a façade in the conventional sense. This is Ambasz at work as an environmental artist.

Ambasz himself declares that his works do not fall into separate categories such as architecture, landscape architecture, product design, and sculpture, but on the contrary fall into all categories. This stance gives his message true originality and moving power.

As has already been pointed out, we are today in an age that offers many parallels to the Enlightenment of two hundred years ago. However, it should be added here that Ambasz rejects the kind of cultist stance that eighteenth-century architects were apt to assume. When Ambasz declares the need for rituals and ceremonies, he means it within the context of people's everyday actions. In that sense, he remains a humanist and populist.

Today, architects in our society must invent new programs. Contemporary architecture must not simply supply containers for conventional functions required of existing lifestyles. Ambasz appears to recognize that, on the contrary, new programs must be conceived if a new architecture is to be created. The conservatory in San Antonio is an excellent demonstration of the correctness of such an approach. Through the deeply inspirational architecture and environmental art that he has created, Ambasz continues to expand our own horizons.

ESSAYS BY EMILIO AMBASZ

NEW ORLEANS MUSEUM OF ART,

NEW ORLEANS, LOUISIANA

Fragments from My Credo

Emilio Ambasz

I have always believed that architecture, as well as design, are myth-making acts. I believe that the real task of architecture and design begins once functional and behavioral needs have been satisfied. It is not hunger, but love and fear—and sometimes wonder—which make us create. The designer and the architect's milieu may have changed, but the task, I believe, remains the same—to give poetic form to the pragmatic.

•

There is in all of us a deep need for ritual, for ceremony, procession, magical garments, and gestures. I believe it is an archetypal search in which we all partake.

•

In my architecture I am interested in the rituals and ceremonies of the twenty-four-hour day. I am not interested in the rituals for the very long voyage—a voyage which can take forty or fifty years. And what a tragedy to discover that for the sake of those long-term dreams, we have sacrificed our daily lives. No, I am interested in daily rituals: like the ritual of sitting in a courtyard slightly protected from both the view of your neighbors and the wind—looking up to the stars. Dealing architecturally with that type of situation attracts me. Because it is not in the house, the house only provides a backdrop for it.

•

The architecture I create is steeped in mysticism. On the one hand, I am playing with the pragmatic elements that come from my time, such as technology. On the other hand, I am proposing a certain mode of existence which is an alternative, a new one. My work is a search for primal things—being born, being in love, and dying. They have to do with existence on an emotional, passionate, and essential level. Perhaps, I use very austere elements to express this quest and, therefore, the gesture may be seen as an austere one also. But by doing it in this way, I believe that it may be far more durable—it is certainly a far more classical attempt. I am interested in the passionate and the emotional when they assume a timeless guise.

In one of my projects, a house in Cordoba, I actually wanted to "eliminate" architecture. The only thing to stand was the façade, which would be like a mask—a surrogate for architecture. The architecture would disappear. You would see only the earth. You might say that by this device, I rhetorically seek to eliminate architecture as a culturally-conditioned process and return to the primeval notion of the abode.

I seek to develop an architectural vocabulary outside the canonical tradition of architecture. It is an architecture which is both here and not here. With it I hope to place the user in a new state of existence, a celebration of human majesty, thought, and sensation. Though apparently quite new, there are devices—both primitive and ancient—permeating the designs. The result is an architecture that seems to stand for eternity.

•

The ideal gesture would be to arrive at a plot of land which is so immensely fertile and welcoming that, slowly, the land would assume a shape—providing us with an abode. And within this abode—being such a magic space—it would never rain, nor would there ever be inclemencies of any other sort. We must build our house on earth only because we are not welcome on the land. Every act of construction is a defiance of nature. In a perfect nature, we would not need houses.

•

If one finds the quintessence of a problem, one will have better access to an irreducible solution. The thread supporting my design quest in every area—my products and my architecture—is a single preoccupation: finding the root of the problem, its essence.

•

As for expressive means, I seek to approach a design problem in the most crystalline, austere, and graceful manner. I long for an architecture which has been reduced to essentials and which, at the same time, is an architecture full of potential meanings. Such concision is the method to achieve a multi-dimensional, epigrammatic architecture.

•

If I may paraphrase Paul Valery: my quest for the essential in architecture is not about being simple and light, like a feather; it is about being essential and concise, like a bird.

•

Architecture, is for me, one aspect of our quest for cosmological models. I suspect that such an all encompassing image, if it ever arrives, will be as simple and as dense as a point suspended in mid-space. Every one of my projects seeks to possess, at least, an attribute of the universe. The quest for that which is infinite, eternal, and ever present, I suspect, may be contained in designs of very few lines which manifest themselves with great economy of expression. In a such seemingly simple manner those lines may, hopefully, acquire the fascinating power of mythical structures. Maybe it is because I seek essentials that I love Lucretius' *De Rerum Natura* so much.

•

I am only interested in discovery, not in recovery; in invention, not in classification. In the uncharted realm of invention, taxonomy is always in the process of being yet born. In the same way as I search for essential and lasting principles in architecture, I think that in opting to write fables rather than write theoretical essays I have grasped something basic: fables remain immutable long after theories have crumbled. The invention of fables is central to my working methods and it is not just a literary accessory. The subtext of a fable, after all, is a ritual and it is to the support of rituals that most of my work addresses itself.

•

Much of my work emphasizes traditional concerns of architecture, such as the presence of light, the sound of water, the manipulation of perspective, and the humane use of space to engender feelings of reassurance and hope. I am not against striving to maintain a continuum with history, nor am I against a search for ornament. But, I believe in inventing ornament when it comes from using natural materials; when it is intrinsic to the structure of the thing being made. I value this as yet another aspect of the continuing process of discovery. Architects who return to historical sources only to utilize elements that make sense to each other, end up talking a hermetic language that can be understood only by those cult initiates. One can remain in this mode if one is content to stay within the convent, but one cannot solve real problems—such as housing—by cutting out little moldings and pasting them up to express a longing for modulated surfaces.

•

We must create alternative images of a better life to guide our actions, if we do not wish to perpetuate present conditions. I believe that any architectural project which does not attempt to propose new or better modes of existence is immoral. This task may stagger the imagination and paralyze hope but we cannot avoid it.

FROM "EMILIO AMBASZ: WORDS & PROJECTS,"

L'ARCHITETTURA, NOVEMBER, 1991.

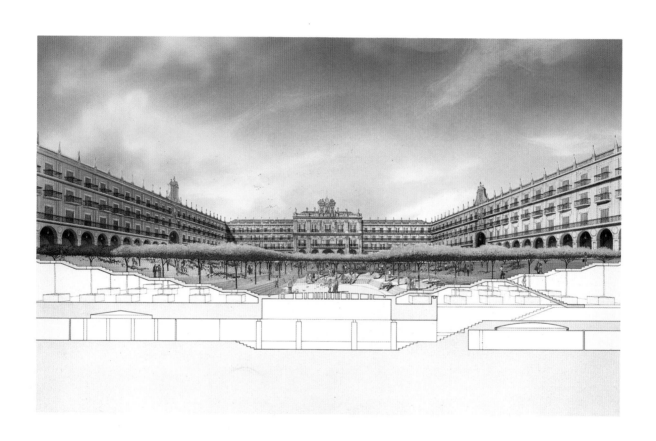

PLAZA MAYOR,

SALAMANCA, SPAIN

The Four Gates to Columbus

Columbus, Indiana, USA

Emilio Ambasz

The brochure said, "Discover the beauty and enjoy the hospitality of Columbus, the architectural showplace of America. Over forty public and private buildings, each reflecting the creativity and ingenuity of the individual architect, provide the most concentrated collection of contemporary architecture in the world." Asking friends, I learned that all this had come about through the enlightened patronage of J. Irwin Miller, for many years the chairman of Cummins Engine Co., the largest company in Columbus. Taking advantage of an opportunity to lecture in Chicago, I decided to visit Columbus, approximately 250 miles away. Landing in Indianapolis, I rented a car and headed toward the nearby city. As I drove, images of great cities I have known came to me: Lucca, with its walls and almost surrounded by water; Verona, adorned by the remnants of its grand entrance doors; Bologna, the city of porticoes; Ferrara, with its long alley of trees, planted four centuries ago to shade the seasonal movements of its court toward the summer villas.

The images were pleasant and the trip therefore short. A sign read "Columbus—6 miles." Getting closer to the city on Route 65 and then 46, I imagined on both sides of the highway two single rows of trees that seemed to have originated deep in the countryside. Slowly they grew closer and closer to the road, until they began to flank it. The trees were robust and so close to each other that they created a continuous, elevated wall of leaves. Another row separated the highway's two lanes, its foliage extending high to left and right producing a gauzy canopy above the cars. At a certain moment the road became wider, with four lanes divided by two extra rows of trees. I drove under four canopies side by side. The trees murmured in the wind and filtered sunlight on the passage. I reduced my speed, opened the windows, and let in the air. The trunks marked a ceremonial rhythm. The countryside, thus framed, acquired heightened·color. And the city, announced from afar by four green portals, had that strong meaning only memory can bequeath and the deeper reality only metaphysical gestures can evoke. The entrance ritual was complete. I had entered.

After passing the city's doors, I observed that the rows of trees bifurcated into a tree-lined belt surrounding the city. Columbus's walls, like its entrance portals, were of living matter. A gentle gesture rather than strong action. A city perimeter delineated by plows rather than blades. The health of the place was visible in this humble love of nature.

Arriving downtown, I entered a covered mall (The Commons). Inquiring, I learned that the city had four such leafy doors, each different from the rest/others. It seemed to have started some twenty years ago on the basis of a proposal ventured by a New York architect. The townspeople were at first reluctant to define the city's boundaries because they hoped for eternal urban growth. But slowly it became evident to all that the city would derive more strength from knowing its true limits than from an unfocused sense of freedom diluting its center. Once the town agreed on the need to define the city edges and mark its entrances, there were countless discussions. One faction wanted to define the city edges by means of a proudly erected construct, circling the city in a manner emblematic of its level of architectural consciousness. Another faction proposed a ring road, with overpasses, bridges, and toll entrances. A third group sustained the notion that no construction of any sort was necessary. They believed it sufficient to evidence the city limits by means of well-designed maps and street signs posted at city edges. Discussions grew in tone and temper until, the story goes, they were all humbled. How this came about is not clear. Some say it happened because the city was the victim of a catastrophic flood. Others claim the town lost its economic base. A few believe it happened because the quarrels drove the children to indifference. Whatever the cause, the fact is that all groups met and agreed, however uncomfortable at first, to return to the original proposal. By that time the architect who had made the proposal was nowhere to be found. But his designs remained.

The scheme was thoughtfully revised to meet the city's new circumstances, and the resulting plan was approved by all. Everyone was asked to donate at least one tree. School children destined their savings to planting in their parents' name, while parents donated trees to honor beautiful houses which stood no longer while private individuals planted trees in remembrance of caresses received, first loves, forgotten tastes of favorite desserts, generous deeds performed, and vengeful actions repressed.

When first planted, the trees were saplings. When I found them, they were quite grown. In some cases, their seeds had already given rise to new saplings. It seems that the townspeople are at present discussing whether to leave the saplings in place so that the emerging forest may slowly reclaim the city or to transplant them to other cities as tokens of Columbus's hard earned gift for reconciling nature with the human environment.

FROM *ARTISTS & ARCHITECTS COLLABORATION*, 1981

RESIDENCE-AU-LAC,

LUGANO, SWITZERLAND

Paris: May 1968

Emilio Ambasz

Be realists, demand the impossible. From the walls of the Censier. Columbia in April, Paris in May, Prague in August, Mexico in September—the crumbling walls speak. The poster is heard again.

Distrustful of the Marxist models and the nineteenth-century concept of change; repelled by the impermeability of Europe's political and educational institutions yet simultaneously resisting the sponginess of America's cultural and social establishment; Youth—self assured of purity by their refusal to define plans and buoyed by the tension of their own contradictions—envisions, nevertheless, an undeterministic type of social system, tolerant of emotions and designed to operate in a permanent state of reform.

The disruption of classes in Nanterre's New Faculty of Letters led by Daniel Cohn-Bendit, the supporting student demonstrations in Paris, the police invasion of the Sorbonne, the occupation of the Sorbonne and the Odéon by the students, the first and second barricades, and the government's reaction and referendum are by now well-known items for a yet unconcluded chronology of youth's rebellion. But, in contrast to the manifestoes of revolution, which have always been rooted in the future, the propaganda of the French revolt nourished itself in immediacy.

Graffiti sustained a relentless match of squash against the communiqués of the official radio and TV. Slogans were picked off the walls and brought to the limited printing facilities of L'Ecole des Arts Decoratifs and L'Ecole de Beaux-Arts, rebaptized Atelier Populaire by the students entrenched there. Students and sympathetic workers enraptured by the spirit of community experimented with participatory design, discussing and choosing together the Poster subjects and images. Anonymity was not only a consequence of this method of working but also an understandable necessity.

The first posters were printed by whatever means were at hand. As the movement became more organized and the number of those involved increased, silk-screen workshops were established. When need overcame production, the ateliers were joined by the workshops of the Faculties of Science and of Psychology, as well as by the committees of Revolutionary Action operating in each neighborhood, which restored to every available printing medium—blue print and office duplicating machines included. In solidarity, Paris' international artistic community contributed posters which although more accomplished graphically lacked the punch of the students' simplicity.

Resorting to the folklore of popular idioms and visual images was the students' way of achieving more directly the desired union of university and factory. Nevertheless, it gradually became clear that Tomorrow had many forms of commitment to reality. While the students had been proposing humanistic anarchism as natural man's Garden, the majority of the workers had been demanding the Arcadia of the Levittowns. But, then, Today understood will be the myth of history and these posters, its documents. For its actors, the reality of May dwells in the paper barricades and in the fervid hours of their collective creation.

FROM *Paris: May, 1968*, 1969

KANSAS CITY UNION STATION
Emilio Ambasz & Associates
December 1987

Union Station,

Kansas, Missouri

Some Notes on a Mental Correspondence
I Have Maintained throughout the Last Twenty-five Years
with Delfina Williams about Amancio's Work

Dear Delfina,

Your eight children have asked me to write a prologue to the book on Amancio's work. I am very touched. Perhaps they have accepted me as their ninth sibling. As an only child, my longing for extended brotherhood has been finally fulfilled.

I think you have never known it, but when I was fifteen years old, and still in high school I came to the realization that one can only learn the craft of poetry from poets, and I developed a plan to work for Amancio through a friend who, already in Amancio's studio, spoke to him about me. I came to interview with Amancio one afternoon—by that time I was already all of sixteen years—and he invited me to join his studio. In order to better attend to this new responsibility, I switched my attendance in high school to night classes, and went to Amancio's studio during the day.

So began the first warm breath of Spring.

Affectionately,

Emilio

My Dear Delfina,

I hope the book reprints some of the beautiful words said about Amancio's work by Le Corbusier, Max Bill, Mies van der Rohe, and other great artists. I have recently read those over. I am not surprised they have always been fascinated by Amancio's work. To them, he was like Argentina, also a child of Europe; like Argentina he was the one they envisioned enacting the European Utopian dreams. What had been dreamt in Europe was to be given strong poetic embodiment in a virgin place, where memories could only be recalled in libraries. It was the cleanest piece of paper and the largest unspoiled natural surface left. So far away a place that Europe could call it its mental dwelling of last resort. It has been noted that Amancio's father, Alberto Williams, introduced European modern music to Argentina. His was the result of a very refined process of assimilation and transformation. It came into the Argentine house through the main door, but when heard in its patios and gardens it felt as if it were humming from the earth. Alberto's garden was a manmade one; Amancio's garden was also manmade, but one where by *arte y oficio*, a great gardener takes seeds from other confines obtaining roses miraculously very much of his own place.

Amancio was always fascinated, or, rather should I say, bewitched, by the pursuit of escaping earth's gravity. First as a young man in the late 1930s, when he was an aviator; and then when he started inventing architectural prototypes as flowers linked to the earth by the thinnest stems—their roots in memories and their bodies high above the ground. This archetypical pursuit might to some resemble superficially that of Le Corbusier's, but Europe's land had been scarred by the march of history and lifting the building above was Le Corbusier's only way to establish a new datum. Amancio's land was pure and man had to ask permission to set foot on it. To hover high above the ground was the respectful thing to do; to let the land and building remain true to themselves, uncorrupted by context.

I know, you must be thinking that this note is unscholarly and embarrassingly too personal; and so it is; you are right. However, having tried to write this so many times, I feel that this is my most faithful and loving way to do it. I'll write to you again soon.

Emilio

•

Dear Delfina,

As I look at the panorama of this century's Latin American art and architecture, Amancio shines as one of its greatest artists. He strongly practiced his belief that architecture must contribute to human happiness; that for an architect not to search for alternative solutions to the present was unethical; that for architects to revel in historical and/or simple minded methodological references was to skirt their responsibility. He always believed in creating and inventing master examples. He constantly searched for the irreducible solution, believing that if an architectural problem could be reduced to its essentials its answer would stun evil and proclaim God's kingdom. He searched for prototypical pilot concepts. They were to be as unselfconsciously simple as many a child's answers. After all, what could be more obvious than to put Buenos Aires' airport on the water of the River Plate where it would not have created urban and traffic conflicts, where it could have been easily erected by barges effortlessly bringing materials to the site, where it would stand out in poetic contrast with the river's long brown horizon which Amancio's planes were to stitch to the blue sky.

It must be said in his defense that Amancio never spoke in romantic terms; he always explained his projects with a sometimes overbearing abundance of technical details. These were always right, even in their most extreme cases. I have always suspected that by analyzing the pragmatics of his projects to such an exhaustive degree Amancio made it possible for his explanations to become an intellectual super-structure, a shell under which dwelt the poetic core. Perhaps Amancio believed that such a blanket of technical perfection would everlastingly shield "Teknes'" marriage to "Poesis."

I have never been able to forget Amancio's splendid tall office building of 1946, the Hilleret "skyscraper," suspended from wires. It was a brilliant insight. So impeccably elegant that the only thing I could always see was not the technological bravado, but the blocks of buildings floating as if in mid-air. But, contrary to popular belief, Amancio was of this earth. I remember working with him on a project, an elegant pavilion for a swimming pool, when he was concerned about a small detail: how a steel column would rest on and inside a horizontal reinforced concrete slab, close to a swimming pool. In his sketches, Amancio laid out the concrete slab on carefully based foundations. Then, the resting location of each column was represented by a cubic empty cavity, an approximately thirty-centimeter cube. At the bottom of the cubic cavity he detailed a square piece of thick stainless steel plate, on which the I-steel column was to rest. Then, the first thirty centimeters of the steel column were to be wrapped in a copper sheeting leaving a one centimeter gap between the copper and the steel column. Afterwards, this one-centimeter interspace was to be filled with molten lead and the remainder of the cavity was to be again filled with a very rich and pure mixture of cement containing powdered marble. When, puzzled, I looked at him, Amancio assured me that this was done to ensure that the steel column wouldn't rust in contact with the concrete for at least five hundred years.

You and I know that Amancio has always been criticized for building very little, but is it such an important argument? Did he not carry his architectural ideas to the most detailed extent possible? Did he not produce hundreds of drawings and construction documents for each project? You and I are witnesses that larger historical and economic forces beyond his power many times played a very strong role in the reasons why Amancio did not get to see many of his projects built. It is said that Amancio did not want to compromise; that is true—more honor to him for that. How could he have compromised when he already knew the ultimate shape of truth as detailed in his many drawings? How could one put a building above ground if it had been soiled by compromise? I sometimes felt that he did it to give us all a master example of moral character and artistic integrity. You and I also know that he was not an easy man —but then who is? We also know that he frightened his clients many times for he was more of a Grand Lord than many of them. He was certainly a Prince working as an architect for enlightened Burghers. How can one say that Amancio didn't want to see his projects built, when you and I have seen Amancio maneuvering to get his buildings built in spite of tremendous odds. You and I remember all of Amancio's travails to explain to people the public advantages of his ideas. Some people say that Amancio was naive in his methods to get his buildings built. They must know something he did not know, for many of them have seen their buildings built. But, if Amancio can be blamed for any form of naivete, it would have to be placed at the feet of his steadfast belief that beauty and truth can be so self evident that even Generals and Captains of industry would be touched by it. And he was right, because they were touched by it, and they commissioned him projects, and I have seen them touched by them and genuinely trying to build them only to see their plans defeated by socio-political crisis or disturbing reversals of family fortunes. If blame can be put on Amancio for anything, it would be for being such a great poet, for working out each detail to such an exquisitely refined level. To blame him for not moving fast enough in circumstances like Argentina's requiring nimble dancing would miss his existential reasons. Perhaps if he had let you handle some of the worldly affairs a few of his projects might have gotten off the ground. They would have cast shadows, but would they have been any more real and stronger than they are still today, even in their paper form?

Lovingly,

Emilio

Dearest Delfina,

Amancio received all the honors that Argentina could bestow on an artist. However, strange and difficult country that it is, it deprived itself of the greatest possible adornment: one of his buildings in the public domain. It invites melancholy to think that many of the buildings that Amancio did get to see built were soon to be dismantled, like the Bunge and Born pavilion and the setting for the Congreso Mariano. For an unforgettable moment, when I saw the pavilion of Bunge and Born, with Amancio's finally realized shell promenading among the clouds, I was so moved. It was such a splendid spectacle. I had enacted it mentally all the previous years, but there it was, as full of magic as I had always expected it to be. I was delighted to realize that the work was not more real by being built, it was just real, in yet another domain of reality. When the Congreso Mariano finished and the installations were dismantled, as was its Cross, I witnessed Amancio working very hard to ensure the Cross would be maintained and stored, and he undertook to carry it—almost by himself—all the way to the water. Almost twenty years after the airport, Amancio again sought to connect the sacred to the profane, the earthly to the celestial. The intermediary artifact was to be the Cross as observed from the shore grounds.

We know that great poetry remains strong when it deals with suggestions, when it brings about presences which are beyond the materials utilized. How many times have I seen the brown and green clouds reflecting the pampas over the Rio de la Plata, letting sunrays come through to shine on the river where the Cross would have been. Like the voice of the *payador*, I can still hear it, for here, on this river, Juan Tierra was not to be defeated by Progress—the devil incarnate; but in Amancio's hands he was to be reborn—at peace with progress and again in pursuit of the ideal.

Forgive me if I have failed you and the children. I couldn't see myself doing a theoretical article. I tried, but it wasn't any better than many other excellent ones already written about Amancio. Let these few raw, but heartfelt words stand as my testimonial act of gratitude for all the magnificent images he has created. If someone has called him Classical—perhaps a misnomer—it is because his work is so essential, so irreducible, so luminously strong that it transcends materials and construction methods to embody the spirit of architecture. The country was created, it seems like yesterday, but it is only when great artists like Amancio appear that we are able to evoke a notion of dwelling in peace with ourselves. I do not know a greater accomplishment for an architect than to have created such magnificent abodes of the heart that we can find refuge and solace even when we are away from them.
Always yours,
Emilio

FROM *Algunas Notas Sobre Una correspondencia Mental que Mantuve a Traves de los Ultimos Veinticinco Años con Delfina Galvez de Williams Sobre La Obra de Amancio*, 1990

EXHIBIT DESIGN: "ITALY: THE NEW DOMESTIC LANDSCAPE,"

MUSEUM OF MODERN ART, NEW YORK, 1972

Architettura Radicale

Emilio Ambasz

FAX

From: Emilio Ambasz
Date: January 6, 1990
To: TERRAZZO
Attn: Barbara Radice
Re: Architettura Radicale

Dear Barbara:

Many thanks for your request to write an article on what you have defined as Italy's Architettura Radicale, but I would rather not write any more scholarly articles. Understand and forgive me.

Cordially,

Emilio

FAX

From: Emilio Ambasz
Date: January 19, 1990
To: TERRAZZO
Attn: Barbara Radice
Re: Architettura Radicale

My dear Barbara:

You are quite a charming flatterer.

Your kind entreaties would melt firm decisions made of the best-tempered alloys. I give up. But, under soft protest, because I feel that one can not begin to consider the question of Architettura Radicale before thinking contextually about these same architects and their involvement with the production of their own objects as well as their opposition to the proliferation of the same objects that they and other Italian architects were producing in the morning and denouncing in nightly television. For better or worse, and whether you like it or not, Italian product design must be brought into this picture of Architettura Radicale because it provides the widest frame of reference for that small Island of Invention which you have now gotten me to call Architettura Radicale. This island did exist, but it was a mixed gesture encompassing both atonement for participating in the multiplication of consumer products, and a defiant act of the critical imagination, in some happy cases bordering on the poetic.

I can already hear you scream and your outrage reach the ceiling. Perhaps you are justified to do so. After all, why do I say this? Don't I know, for example, that many of the objects Ettore Sottsass conceived were, in reality, miniature architecture? Unquestionably, he made great architecture—using miniature as a format. There he could be his own client, his own builder, his own banker, his own mason, and even his own critic.

Why do I mention Sottsass first? Because the image that came immediately to my mind when you talked to me about Architettura Radicale was that of Ettore and his extremely gifted children. Many years have gone by since the great examples of architectural courage they contributed to the chronicle of Italian culture from the early sixties to the early seventies. Are they now going to be canonized?... Hail to the Children of the Revolution! They shall inherit Academia.

Let me hasten to say that as a matter of fact you are quite right, it was a small island, the one they built, but it was a magic one, and it saved the honor of Italian architecture in those years. It is probably the only way architecture in those years could have been produced in Italy. Acknowledging they were prisoners of the social system and that they could not change it, they had the courage to propose alternative architectural models by means of drawings and theories.

Cordially,

Emilio

FAX

From: Emilio Ambasz
Date: February 19, 1990
To: TERRAZZO
Attn: Barbara Radice
Re: Architettura Radicale

Dearest Barbara:

Okay, okay, you win; I will write a brief comment on Architettura Radicale, but I am of a mind that before talking about Architettura Radicale I must again unload my heart as to what I see has happened since 1972. After such a catharsis I may, perhaps, be able to look into the subject you have addressed to my attention.

In 1972, I directed and presented an exhibition entitled "Italy, the New Domestic Landscape" at The Museum of Modern Art in New York. This collection of objects and interiors illustrated the remarkable design vitality that had recently emerged in Italy. Well received at the time, the exhibition was to leave a deep and pervasive imprint upon the perception of design in this country. For the first time, Americans were invited to regard design not only as a product of the creative intelligence, but also as an exercise of the critical imagination. Visitors were to realize that design in general, and Italian design in particular, meant more than simply creating objects to satisfy functional and emotional needs: the processes and products of design could themselves be used to offer critical commentary upon our society. At another level, the exhibition sent shock waves through the community of American designers. Here they found themselves confronting another breed of creator, unafraid of curves and taking unabashed delight in the sensual attributes of the materials and textures he or she used.

For many American and North European designers, sternly trained in the Bauhausian tradition of deductive analysis, strict functionalism and rigorous pragmatism, the flair and panache of the Italian designers were little less than offensive. The fabric of their professional repression was so insidiously torn open by the creations of their Italian counterparts that they seemed ready to file a writ of complaint against Italian Design for a) having created beautiful objects with complete disregard for all prevailing rules; b) shamelessly seducing the public with these products; and what was even worse, c) having seduced the designers themselves.

Today we find that Italian design has spawned a number of gifted American and Japanese offspring. Like their Italian colleagues, these designers have grown fonder of, and increasingly dexterous with, colors, curves, patterns, and textures. No longer the unbending seekers of eternal truths after their Bauhausian ancestors, many American and Japanese designers have learned to make peace with the ephemeral.

Design, once perceived as yet another method for redemption through sensory deprivation, has now begun to open up its tightly closed fist to embrace fashion and caress ornament. Thus a new type of designer, one who takes joy in the exercise of his or her stylistic gifts, has emerged. Perhaps in 1997, twenty-five years after "The New Domestic Landscape," we shall be able to determine whether the debt to Italian design is deepen than, and goes beyond mere resemblance.

In the meantime, as we look upon Italian production today, we realize that The Museum of Modern Art's 1972 show clearly marked a high point of Italian design as a freewheeling creative process.

As we look at Italian design today we realize that the classical ambivalence of design remains valid: conformism and/or reformism; idealistic and/or reformistic; integrated design and/or alternative design. All too understandably, the former constitutes the great part of Italian design's production. A considerable portion of Italian design activity has concentrated upon improving the quality of established models, with much attention given, for example, to how different materials can be gracefully juxtaposed and skillfully combined; how component elements can be well built and better joined; how the quality of colors, patterns, and textures can be subtly enhanced.

Many products of what we may, for lack of better denomination call Integrated and Alternative Italian design have, since 1972, traveled from the museum to the marketplace. Once, these objects were fancied harbingers of upcoming social change; today, they have become elements of society. If they have not fulfilled the utopian promises of '68, they have nevertheless enriched and improved the quality of our daily existence. If these objects have fallen short of offering pathmarks for our long voyage to a brighter, better tomorrow, they have happily performed a more modest role as pleasant companions in our daily travails.

Italian products of the last decade have given pleasure, performed faithfully, and, why not say it, they have tickled our fancy and flattered our pride. They have, in some small but true way, helped us through the day and soothingly seen us past the night. Handsome and wholesome, these products have served us well. If they have sometimes failed to move our hearts, they have always touched our minds and alerted our senses. What greater badge of honorable service can be bestowed upon an object or the culture that created it?

Love,

Emilio

FAX

From: Emilio Ambasz
Date: March 20, 1990
To: TERRAZZO
Attn: Barbara Radice
Re: Architettura Radicale

My very dear Barbara:

Now that you have reviewed my views on Italian product design with an emphasis on the Integrated Designers and a minor reference to the Alternative ones, let me concentrate on the Italian product designers who are dearer to my heart; the idealists, the reformists, the designers who propose alternative modes of existence. And among them as I have already mentioned—and I hope I do not embarrass you—shines Ettore Sottsass and his magnificent progeny: Archizoom, Superstudio, UFO, Gianni Pettena, Ziggurat, etc.

By Alternative design I mean to encompass a number of ongoing processes in Italian design: firstly, it must be observed that the decisive center for the product designers' area of activity is no longer, solely "the factory," that is to say where production takes place. Designers have grown to understand and work directly with the organs that control distribution. The old formula of close collaboration between design and production is now expanding to also include the notion of design, production, and distribution. By distribution I mean organizations such as Benetton and Esprit, among many others. Distribution no longer seeks just to satisfy the users' pragmatic needs for basic necessities, but it now addresses itself to the satisfaction of many overlapping subworlds and subcultures, which have many diverse emotional, sensorial, psychological, mythical, ludic, and even cosmological as well as sacred needs.

Secondly, we have observed the emergence, not only in Italy, of Alternative designers who believe strongly that the focus of design has shifted from creating mass-produced objects to creating artifacts that address the specialized and circumscribed needs of individuals or smaller groups. Thus, they have abandoned any old belief that there can exist a single, unique, encompassing, universal design methodology and replaced it with a conviction that the arts and crafts, architecture, and choreography, as well as even, for example, knitting, provide the different quarries from which the configuration of a new design methodology will emerge. Perhaps we should call meta-methodology that which will allow designers to openly act as once the shamans of "old" societies, or perhaps of wiser societies, acted when they were more attuned to the human imperative of dealing with passions, emotions, wonder, and even transcendental magic. In such a meta-methodological approach the Alternative designers believe that the artifact will assume the role of the Ark of the Covenant. They believe with all their soul that the artifact serves as the medium for a temporary reconciliation; as the transactional device whereby man reconciles (albeit for a moment) his fears and his desires with the limits, restrictions, and penuries imposed upon him by nature, men, and even himself.

Italian Alternative designers, in their proclaimed role of living micromodels of the human condition, know well that they can create barricades and oppose Integrated designers, or that they can throw books (or any other of the accessories of human theater) at each other, but deep down they also know that the Truth lies somewhere between the two groups, in the synthesis of such seemingly contradictory positions as those maintained by the Integrative and the Alternative designers. A nation such as Italy, which has for the last forty-five years given to the world a system that one can only benignly describe as Humanistic Anarchism, knows well that a new design can only result from the tensions between idealists and realists, between conformists and reformists. Both sides join in the belief that design is a humanistic as well as a humanizing, or one should rather say, an evangelical endeavor.

If evangelizing is the pursuit, dear Barbara, should this "church" look for its candidates for martyrdom (and for sainthood) among the Alternative designers? You know well that any church of saints will in time generate cardinals.

However, you are right: I am not sticking to the subject you have proposed to me. I acknowledge the charge that I am skirting the issue in question. But, although I may be brandishing shadows, I greatly admire the basic fact that those you have called Radical Architects did fervently believe that the architect's role was that of making places. For them, the architect's role was fulfilled when he created an abode, when he evoked a sense of the welcoming dwelling. They also knew that such an abode must function first in a cosmological and metaphysical reality if it is to have any pragmatic meaning and physically healthy existence. Nowadays we see a similar pursuit taken over by a younger generation, but the archetype remains the same one: to create a better place because for them also architecture is essentially the act whereby man reconciles himself with nature, and with himself. Man needed a dwelling only after he was thrown out of Paradise. Enough, now I go to bed.

Warmest regards,

Emilio

FAX

From: Emilio Ambasz
Date: April 17, 1990
To: TERRAZZO
Attn: Barbara Radice
Re: Architettura Radicale

Ah Barbara, Ah!:

I close my eyes and I try to remember Architettura Radicale's many words and images. I remember very small buildings, somewhat toy-sized, which remind me always of the ceramic architecture of the Chinese, the Egyptians, and the Mayans which I have seen all over the world in anthropology museums. I always felt that the spirit of the domestic dwelt in those miniature buildings, with a suggestive intensity. I always felt that if I put this ceramic architecture, one close to another, on a large carpet I would have a beautiful city. It would not have been a city with a single axis or a clear will; rather, it would result in a city as I have always understood cities to be: an aggregate of conflicting wills. In one corner of this city one would state something, while in another a different one would refute it. Those small-scale buildings, some of them granaries, some of them temples, some of them houses, some of them corrals, some of them cemeteries, and some others just plain ashtrays, would reconcile and integrate Artifact to Building. Thus, it would be possible to go back to the root of artifact making; to that golden period when there were no distinctions between object and architecture; when they were all essential components necessary to accommodating and adjusting our existence within the existential domain which nature had allowed them. Upon evoking these ceramic or architectural objects I also always think that they engage in an ambivalent game on the imaginary carpet where I used to display them. On the one hand, they represent some of the ways whereby we could find refuge from nature's indifference, while on the other, they represent our hope that they should—albeit for a short moment—provide us with a respite from the indifferently grinding teeth of nature.

As I close my eyes I recall some splendid images Architettura Radicale created. To this day, almost twenty and some years after, they still move me. How gifted they were. These children may have cut daisies but they also knew how to create beautiful vases in which to display them. Their "vessels" stood as containers of the ideal. Whether open or with their lids on, they perfumed our eyes with a vision of requited architectural longings.

There was Superstudio, and within, there was Adolfo. I have heard he is now a full professor in Florence, a baron, perhaps even a duke; inspiring love and terror on his scholastic subjects. When he was young he was given to evoking places where only beautiful things could occur. I always understood the stories he wrote as cartographic blueprints. If one read them carefully, one could have known the places, seen the spaces, and perceived the shadows of ideally fixed suns. I dare not comment on them here for exegesis would render them a pallid service, but some of their beautiful ideas can be recalled even today with the same intensity of their birthday because they were topographical suggestions of better worlds. I imagine that when TERRAZZO 5 arrives and I see Superstudio's projects reproduced again, there will be between them and me a slight fog which I will not blame on time past but rather on the growing weakness of my eyes.

I know I should not romanticize the strength of my nostalgia. I shall rather say now the word: ARCHIZOOM!, and see the lights flash like in Luna Park. Ahh, those Archizoom boys. They were possessed by certainty; doubt did not dwell among them. As for their images I recall them, but it is the resonance of their ideology, the thunder of their conviction, and the memory of it all that will never leave me.

I have recently looked at Archizoom's projects. These looked to me like the luminescent portrait of an intelligent architect fancying that it would be impossible to do anything architecturally until the prevailing political system was changed. So, while waiting, they ironically engaged in proposing that in a mass society, the only cities that could redeem us would be those based on quantity, not on quality. Their vociferous insight was contained in the, for them, obvious fact that in their designs for a "City of Quantity" there were to be represented all the elements that would have been required by those who wanted, and knew how to create a place of Quality. In their proposals dwelt the comforting mirage that in a neutral system of equivalent points one could find contained every earthly truth as well as also its counterdenial, somewhere hidden. These equivalent and all- meaning points were not hard to find in their cities, provided the name of the street was known.

They always looked to me like self-deprecating monks, subjecting their remarkable intelligence to penitence for the sake of atoning for what they considered too sacred to undertake in this imperfect world, that is to say, the statement of new values and the invention of architecture. In their immense love and longing for architecture, they dared not to make it. They talked about faraway places where those images were to occur. All the coordinates of such a map were drawn by those brilliant cartographers; they just never told us which one corresponded to the highest peak and which one to the greenest valley. Aware that the City of Production was slowly decaying to be replaced by the City of Information, they were fully convinced that they could dwell anywhere in the City of Information and still be at its center. Today, I am told, they live in Milano.

A presto, kisses,

Emilio

FAX

From: Emilio Ambasz
Date: May 21, 1990
To: TERRAZZO
Attn: Barbara Radice
Re: Architettura Radicale

My patient Barbara:

Back to our subject. Of all the people of the Architettura Radicale period who I think have been unjustly treated and not well enough appreciated, Gianni Pettena stands out as the most interesting figure. There he was, making architecture in the form of gestures. He would refer to magnificent architectural domains of the mind by means of negative spaces that he created. For him, also, the architectural image could not be made without sinning. Different from the others, his means were not words but drapes which the wind would move, blocks of ice which the sun would melt, or totally incongruous photos. One of his creations, I recall vividly, was the photo of a large billboard in Minneapolis depicting a policeman looking like a child-molester who, in reality, was desperately trying to revive a boy by mouth-to-mouth resuscitation under the big legend "And They Call Them Pigs." I also recall his drawings, suggestive of intermissions, dislocations and breakage points where long-established ceremonies were to be slightly offset from their normal bearings so that one could see that they contained in themselves an ironic key to remake themselves anew. I haven't seen him for a long time and I would like to see him again. Tell me, has he also become an academic boss?

As for UFO and Ziggurat, I remember that to one of them I gave an award in another life when I was assumed to be a powerful curator. As for the other group, I read everything they wrote. Why was it that whenever I saw Lappo's photograph heading one of his articles the image of *Vogue Design for Men* came to mind. He was Firenze's sarcast. Under his sharp tongue everybody's garments were torn to shreds, and everybody's curtain fell to the ground. How many times did I wonder whether the strength of Lappo's remarks came from sublimating architectural images? Was that the price he paid to uphold his view of the Moral City?

Do you also smell something burning? Is it me, or a passing whiff of Savonarola's ashes? Respectfully yours,

Emilio

FAX

From: Emilio Ambasz
Date: June 10, 1990
To: TERRAZZO
Attn: Barbara Radice
Re: Architettura Radicale

Dear Barbara:

I have come to the end: Forgive me if I have failed you, but you have asked me to open a box where things laid quietly, softly, between layers of silk paper. If Architettura Radicale's legacy has not matured to amount to an edifice; forgive me for disassembling it. Nevertheless they amounted to a glorious assemblage of dissimilar fragments. Those architects were the prisoners of that moment and of their intelligence. Their words, whether written or spoken; their objects and buildings, whether of glass or porcelain; their photomontages, whether pasted or torn, have survived the decay of their temporal context. Not one image can I recall, built as sketched, but I do remember that their strength and power to cast shadows came from realizing that a new architecture would not come from redigesting the tenants of modernism's memory or from operating within the canonical tradition of architecture. For them, architecture meant going back to the roots. It consisted, in essence, of providing an abode for those three basic gestures: being born, loving, dying. Architecture, for them, became substance only when it could house those three basic necessities. All other pursuits would crumble to fine powder.

Now they are old enough to start wondering what to do in a rainy fall. They have a right to do so. I will always remember them lovingly for their springlike images.

Ciao,

Emilio

FROM "ITALIAN RADICAL ARCHITECTURE AND DESIGN 1966-1973,"

TERRAZZO 5 (FALL),1990.

COOPERATIVE OF MEXICAN-AMERICAN GRAPEGROWERS,

BORREGO SPRINGS, CALIFORNIA

Robertos Wilson

Luminarios (Premier Regisseur) and Master

Emilio Ambasz

Robertos Wilson, the most prominent figure in the pantheon of late twentieth-century Regisseurs, had the sad privilege of being the last great Regisseur of the Bis-Modern Empire.

He experienced the drama of the siege of Metropolis by the Conqueror, the fall of the capital and its ensuing destruction. He saw, as mentioned by the chronographers of his time, the conquerors cooking for months by burning his marvelous furniture, a fact depriving future generations of immense pleasure.

He recorded his sad experience in a lamentation that is preserved in a theatrical code of the Memorized Library of the Internal Exiles.

He was "Luminarios"; as the title for the Master of the Left Theater of the Vanished Capital was also known.

He also had the title of Master, as a consequence of the many theoretical works on his teachings which he inspired. A considerable number of video tapes, containing works he had designed by commission of the last rulers of Metropolis, was also found in the Memorized Library of the Internal Exiles.

Unfortunately, we have very little knowledge about Robertos Wilson's private life. From the Berlin Code, written in 1995, we learn that Wilson stayed for some time in Trinidad. The Code mentions:

> "All these were designed by Master Luminarios Robertos Wilson and he
> designed them while on the island of Trinidad."

From manuscript No. 491, of the Phisoactor Repository on Mount Chimborazo in the the Andes, we learn that after the fall of the capital he stayed for awhile in Ushuaia, Tierra del Fuego:

> "Designed in Ushuaia after the Fall."

From manuscript No. 1502 of the Metamorphosis Library we conclude that Wilson later reached as far north as Cuzco. The Code contains a work with the following foreword:

"... a design of Master Robertos Wilson created in Cuzco".

The fact that Robertos Wilson's fame had reached far beyond the limits of the tragically shrunk Bis-Modern Empire is obvious from a large number of Bolivian manuscripts containing his theatrical designs.

Wilson was not only the author of many works, a Master Regisseur at the Left Theater of Metropolis, a teacher and a very important theoretician. He had also the rare talent of design. Thus many drawings of Wilson's designs have been preserved. Some of them, the most prominent among them being design No. 1492 of the Universal Library, enable us to offer today to the interested public secular and liturgical designs by this last of the great Bis-Modern Regisseurs, in the certainty that these originals have suffered no alteration by any reproduction means.

Another of Wilson's designs, No. 1776 of the Library of the Novaron Refuge, contains a valuable set of drawings concerning the use of theatrical symbols.

Apart from its huge interest from the point of view of the qualities of stage pieces as ritual elements, his comments and references to previous masters are of great interest.

In the introduction (Preface) to this book of drawings, Wilson justifies his decision to write about "those theorizing on the theatrical arts of design and the erroneous ideas of some people about them" as follows: "I have often thought about writing a memorandum on the theories about stage furniture and the art of designing them, as well as describing them, for the benefit of those who shall study them in the future and in order to further different views on them."

Later on he writes: "But those who design furniture for the stage, ignorantly and without science, and teach erroneously without knowing what is said, may continue to do as they wish, since they do harm to no one but themselves; but we shall give the truth about the art in which we excel, and shall indicate it to everyone as shortly as possible, bringing God as witness to the fact that we say nothing driven by passion and that all our designs and words do honor the truth ...". By criticizing those who have no respect for tradition and do innovations without taking note of the work of the preceding great masters, Wilson gives some interesting information:

"There would have been no need for Charles Baudelaire—first master of the Pre-Modern Period —to signal the emergence of the first flaneur of Metropolis if we had not neglected Master Zeami. There would have been no false arguments if credit had been given to the fact that in my theater the actor is not silent but hums Wagner in Greek with a closed mouth."

It has been said that Robertos re-proposed to forge his theater into an ideally functioning community of individuals, where everyone existed as a principality in accompanied solitude. But, there are also suspicions that there grew in Wilson a perverse desire to misdirect his followers by the mention of such antecedents.

He wrote much about the actor's method for declamation, but in his theater, a theater of color, moods, gestures, and emotions, the actors, chanting slowly and moving with the gravity of ritual, were the background, while the stage props were the real presences. In Robertos' theater, actors were the stage set while the inanimate objects declaimed loudly their anima.

As we can see from some surviving tapes of his plays, the actors chant mute parliaments while the stage props sing with deep voiced images. These marvelous tapes afford us the pleasure of observing Wilson's ethereally majestic productions which look as if they had been painted with light where silence was both the first verb and the only word.

In the destruction that followed the Fall of Metropolis, a brilliant commando sacrificed himself so that he could save some of Robertos' props. These furniture pieces embodied the essence of Bis-Modern Culture's insights and perceptions. They spoke with the strength of images and therefore their savior died believing they would never deteriorate or decay during their flight into memory.

Bricoleur extraordinaire, Wilson's work resembles the stringing of Benjaminian pearls. He was the outstanding editor of those fragments which had survived the decay of their original context.

Wilson sat those fragments against the larger background of real time. Extended periods of time surrounded each fragment, and the edifice he built is one of fragment upon fragment cemented by large intervals of time. Of these fragments, none sparkle as brilliantly as his furniture. In his theater the stage assumed the role of a jewelry box lined with velvety light. Chairs, beds, and tables sung softly and gravely with basso profondo sotto voce. These chairs, beds, and tables, simple in form, stood stoically, hierarchically, and tellingly mysteriously. Theirs were primeval secrets for all those who could hear. Suddenly belonging to nowhere, they spoke of present absences.

When the curtains were drawn on Wilson's mystical landscapes, the stage beyond was revealed. A chair on this stage could speak more eloquently of man's form than its intended human user ever could have. His chairs, as you can see in surviving video tape images, sometimes built with a tilt, or three times larger than normal scale, evoked longingly man's figure. His chairs suggested man's imagined majesty more regally than crowned actors. The sometimes roughly-finished wooden surfaces exulted in the unblemished joys of their skin with a gripping strength that no large screen projection of an actress' face may ever elicit. This chair's lonely inhabitance of his sidereal landscapes, evoked images of pre-linguistic human figures yet to appear, or perhaps, to return.

Wilson's chairs spoke of love for the human body with the power of the idealized, as sometimes only love letters to a yet to be found lover can elicit. These mystical chairs were solid, trustworthy, and made of a seemingly eternal matter with not an ounce of deceit in them. They could neither disappoint, age, or die as the human figure they stood for. They were both its surrogate and its alter ego.

When lacquered to a mirror finish, these chairs invited incessant caressing, fully confident that there would be each time an infinitely new sensation. Silent and farsightedly blind to immediate surroundings, these chairs spoke of longings requited, serenity embodied, and of journeyless arrivals. They stood at once here and there.

No wonder Wilson's chairs were listed among the subversives to search out and destroy when the rampage, which followed the Grand Fall, ensued. When a few of Wilson's chairs who failed to escape were brought to trial, the just accusation leveled at them was that they were Advocates of unspoiled love of the physical for its own sake. As one of the prosecutors stated, these objects were self-contained independent rings; impervious to joining the reproductive chain. Irreducibly lonely, they evoked the presence of longed for absences.

The documents found in the Colophon (end) of Robertos Wilson's autograph, gives us one more piece of information:

> "This book of designs was finished by the hand of Robertos Luminarios
> Wilson in 2011, on the Thirteenth of June …"

Five years after the Fall of Metropolis Robertos still had the title of Luminarios, while no longer directing his own plays at the Left Theater (which was converted into a place of worship) or at any of the few remaining museums.

He was awarded the title of First Actor later on, probably by the Second Council of Arbiters. According to other opinions, however, the first Actor Wilson who is mentioned in various design theoretical texts is another person and Robertos Wilson was never honored with the title of First Actor.

And one last bit of information: the last theatrical piece authentically autographed by Robertos Wilson is mentioned as having been written in 2037.

Here ends our knowledge concerning the life of the last of the great Bis-Modern Masters.

FROM "WORKING FABLES : A COLLECTION OF DESIGN TALES FOR SKEPTIC CHILDREN,"

ROBERT WILSON, 1991.

MASTER PLAN FOR THE UNIVERSAL EXPOSITION—SEVILLE, 1992,

SEVILLE, SPAIN

Luis Barragan

Emilio Ambasz

An engineer by training, Barragán is an autodidactic architect who learned the profession by direct experience and through the works of artist friends and architectural writers. An important local influence was Jesus "Chucho" Reyes, a "naive" primitive painter whose philosophy toward life and art Barragán has shared; being bound by the same loyalties to their native *pueblo* of Guadalajara, Barragán also generously acknowledged the philosophical influence of Mathias Goeritz, the German-born sculptor who, since the late 40s, has been working and teaching in Mexico. Barragán is also fond of recalling as an influence the house and personalities of Rosa and Miguel Covarrubias, photographer and scholar, respectively, who for decades acted as the unofficial curators of Mexican culture. But the most decisive influence in Barragán's work has been the popular architecture of Mexico's villages, ranches and convents.

His family owned ranches in the State of Jalisco, in whose small towns he spent his youth, riding horses, attending fiestas, and visiting market places. He came to Mexico City for the first time in his early twenties in transit to Europe. It was during this trip that he discovered the writings of Ferdinand Bac, a French intellectual, painter, and landscape architect, whom he came to meet only later, in 1931, during another trip to France. Bac's influence upon Barragán was more one of attitude than of form, but his philosophical and poetic images conjured up for Barragán a vision that never left him: the garden as a magic place for the enjoyment of meditation and companionship.

In 1924 he visited the beautiful gardens of La Alhambra in Spain. The enchanted progression of its brilliantly composed spaces, fountains, and water channels have had a lasting effect on his work. It is from the Islamic notion of compartmentalized and successive garden spaces that Barragán developed his feeling for walled enclosures and his love for the sound of running water. Another influence on his work has been the Moorish architecture of North Africa, especially Morocco. Although he did not visit North Africa until 1951, he had long cherished images of its houses and mosques in the travel and architecture books he brought back from his first European sojourn. His fascination with Moorish architecture was paid homage in several early houses he built in Guadalajara (houses for González Luna and Enrique

Aguilar). Since then, Barragán's mind has remained attuned to the intimate garden. Although he prefers the Italian baroque to the courtly French, it is the sensual intimacy of the Islamic garden which seduces him. Barragán's gardens, or rather his open-enclosures, are endowed with erotic and metaphysical properties; they are places for the pleasures of the senses and the mind, bewitched regions leading to fantastic dreams and fable making. In this regard, it must be noticed that Barragán has never created large public plazas in populated areas, with the exception of a kindergarten in Guadalajara (children's playground), which by its nature had to be enclosed. Only once did he attempt to design a large public space, in the never realized project for Plaza de la Constitución or El Zócalo, as Mexico City's main plaza is called. His proposal shows a secluded, below-ground-level space containing an enclosed water fountain (La Plaza del Zócalo) leaving the large, raised plaza level barren of anything but the elegant traces of a de Chirico-like grid.

Barragán has always endeavored to create an architectural language which would express man's eternal longings in the context of modern Mexico's natural and cultural conditions. Shunning the use of familiar Mexican forms, the character of his architecture results from its continuity with Mexico's splendid architectural traditions.

Barragán acknowledges his love for and aesthetic debt to the popular architecture of Mexico's ranches, villages and convents. But it should be noted that Mexico's climate and natural resources have always been strong factors in the formal development of its architecture. The incandescent luminosity of its sun, the strong winds and heavy rains, and the restrictions of poverty and unskilled labor have all contributed to a discipline of structural simplicity and few materials. Mexico's popular and cosmopolitan architectures have both responded to their physical milieu with similarly introspective attitudes, creating enclosed forms with interior worlds of patios and secluded gardens. The formal properties of this architecture involved the interplay of positive and negative volumes: masses and voids. In this tradition the void plays several roles; it is the vessel for light and shadow, and it also serves as the compositional nexus binding the different masses. Barragán's architecture recognizes similar roles for the void, but assigns it stronger dynamic properties by dematerializing some of the surfaces defining its edges. In a process of further abstraction, Barragán's masses are condensed into planes. This part comes to stand for the whole; the wall becomes the surrogate for the rooms which once surrounded the patio, and the life these rooms once housed—a child playing on the floor, a woman pedaling on her sewing machine, the smoke of darkened kitchens—seems now to dwell as unseen presences behind these walls.

Barragán is the outstanding exponent of an architectural tradition which the modern movement has neglected: stage architecture. His compositions possess background, middleground and foreground; monumental in quality, they are deliberately static in feeling. The element of tension is always introduced by the user, whether man or horse, or more subtly, by his absence. An influence having direct bearing on this aspect of Barragán's architecture are the seventeenth and eighteenth century *atrios* of Mexico's unique "open-air churches," designed to receive the thousands of new native converts attending mass. The church's façade assumed, from the atrium, the quality of a miraculous shield, behind which the divine powers dwelled. It was an image of God's house the natives could easily associate with their previous religious experience.

The extraordinary emotional effect of Barragán's compositions and the strong sensual qualities of his materials and colors cannot be guessed from his drawings or plans. The architectural richness of Barragán's dramatically sober architecture is based on a few constructive elements bound together by a mystical feeling, an austerity exalted by the glory of his brilliant colors. They pervade all the interstices of space, at once binding and separating artifact and nature. Paint is for him like a garment the wall puts on to relate to its surroundings. Under the bright Mexican light the splendor of the color lasts but an instant; the sun ravages it as the seasons change, and, soon, when the leaves return, a new coat is needed. Intimately bound to Barragán's sensitivity for color is his animistic feeling for matter. He seems to endow matter with a soul of its own. In his work, the wall is assumed to possess a skin and a core; it breathes and palpitates, like an animal. If a wall in punctured, the wedge turns into a spigot through which the wall slowly drips. Whenever a wall is split open, it reveals its liquid core. As in Surrealist painting, Barragán's walls have two sides. One, open and direct, which the viewer faces. The other, shrouded in shadows, suggests past presences. As for the users of these fabulous landscapes, their roles are carefully formalized. Only horses can walk through the wall openings. Man may only filter in between wall planes. The exceptions are children and riders.

Barragán's creative instincts lead him to action rather than to polemics. Leaving aside theoretical scaffoldings, Barragán works within the constraints of a frugal formal vocabulary. His architecture results from an almost redemptive commitment to beauty. Since he does not follow theoretical rules or generalized systems, each project is an entity in itself, whose inner principles must be revealed. This procedure demands emotional sensibility and selective intuition. Like Mies van der Rohe, Barragán deals only with the inner tensions of each element. This has led him to consider concise and profound creations, hard to surpass.

It is a lonely road but, as he confesses, it is only among architects that he feels himself to be the stranger. Not for any anti-intellectual bias, but because he believes their education has estranged them from their own emotional and intuitive capacities. Barragán's aesthetic preferences and the monumental sense of his compositions have occasionally been perceived as scenographic and socially uncommitted. But Barragán's concerns, while paying their dues to function, go beyond the requirements of a program of utilitarian needs to satisfy the necessities of what may be called "a program of metaphysical imperatives." In a culture exhausted and irreparably fragmented, the walls surrounding Barragán's gardens are, perhaps, one of the last defenses to preserve centuries of thought and emotion. If after the Revolution there will be Serenity, Barragán's architecture will surely provide one of its models.

All of Barragán's projects are autobiographical; or so they became, as in the case of the gardens of El Pedregal. His sympathy for Surrealism stems from perceiving it as an existential attitude with a romantic undertone he relates to longing (in one of Barragán's favorite books, *The Unquiet Grave* by Cyril Connolly, one can find underlined the following passage: "Art is memory's *mise-en-scène*."). He believes, with Connolly, that "art is made by the alone for the alone."

In Mexico the past is always present, and its architecture is charged with ancestral presences. Death is its central tragedy and its ever present memory. Catholic resignation is the silent chorus, the core of its passion and humbleness. A stoical acceptance of solitude as man's fate permeates Barragán's work. In the settings of his magnificent plazas, man can take communion with his solitude. And also take pleasure in it, Barragán would add, for, as a devout Catholic, he believes that man's condition is God's will, and must, therefore, be accepted with dignity and love.

Barragán's solitude is cosmic; Mexico is the temporal abode he lovingly accepts. It is for the greater glory of this House that he has created gardens where Man can make peace with himself, and a chapel where his passions and desires may be forgiven and his faith proclaimed. One complements the other. The garden is the myth of the Beginning and the chapel of the End. For Barragán, House is the form Man gives to his life between both extremes.

FROM *THE ARCHITECTURE OF LUIS BARRAGAN*, 1976

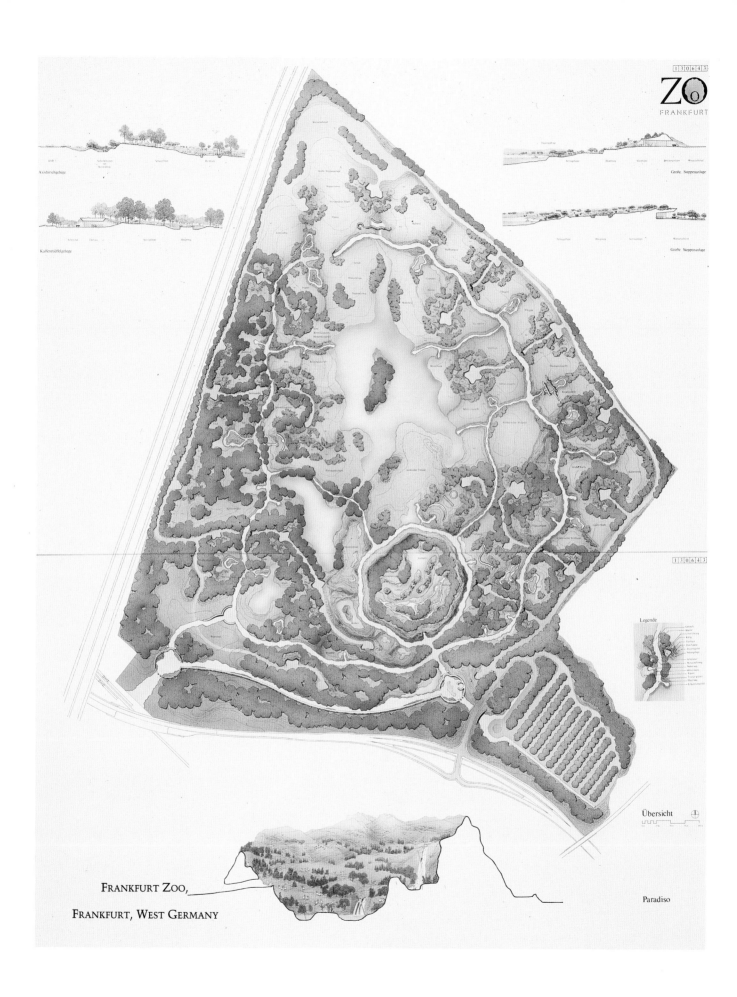

FRANKFURT ZOO,

FRANKFURT, WEST GERMANY

Übersicht

Paradiso

Popular Pantheon

Emilio Ambasz

"One space stretches

through all that is: inner-world space.

The silent birds fly through ourselves."

—Rainer Maria Rilke

The Neue Staatsgalerie by James Stirling is, unquestionably, a work of excellent architectural craftsmanship; practical and functional, cleverly respectful of its historical context, and coquettishly attentive to its urban surroundings.

As in the best of Fellini's films, this museum is full of bewitching vignettes. Not even the most diehard acolyte of the Single Grand Concept in architecture could avoid taking delight in the impeccably proportioned exhibition rooms of this new museum, or refrain from tipping his hat to the brilliant conceit of connecting the old and new museums with a bridge, wittily furnished as an ante-chamber framing the view of the Schlemmer sculptures.

Also, like Fellini, Stirling is an artist who deals masterfully with ambiguous meanings and ironically juxtaposed fragments, or, as he defines it in pseudo-professional dicta: "Abstract versus Representational," and "Traditional versus High-Tech." Any observer soon realizes that the Neue Staatsgalerie is a work full of parodies. Witness the self-deprecating references to past influences as evidenced in the entrance ramp's exaggerated High-Tech railings, and the neo-historical entrance canopy. Those of us who believe self-mockery constitutes a laudable instance of moral courage cannot but admire Stirling's ironic identification, *malgré lui-même*, with that quirk of the British spirit which persists in confusing vulgarity for vitality. Should we accept him therefore, at face value, when he states that the garish green rubber flooring "reminds [us] that museums today are also places of popular entertainment —it seemed more appropriate as well as having an acoustical value"?

As in his other works, parody plays in the Neue Staatsgalerie a defensive role. It doesn't criticize either the Post-Modern, the High-Tech, or the Neo-Classical modes but is, rather, self-critical of his own use of these devices. Stirling renders this reversed criticism acceptable by anticipating a mockery. Moreover, he seeks to beat us to it. It is what Empson calls "pseudo parody to disarm criticism." but one could also suspect that Stirling is a Romantic who uses architectural parody to disguise his passionate love for architecture. So much for *Stürm und Drang* with a Liverpudlian twang.

These episodes of architectural parody, brilliant as they are, rapidly receded into the background when, in awe, we call to the fore the powerful, earthy sounds which seem to emanate from the marble chords composing the circular courtyard. The ramp can be perceived as crescendo, the wall openings as basso continuo, and the open sky as a chorus. But they cannot, by themselves, explain the powerful telluric sound which pervades this chamber as if it were coming from a gigantic mountain horn. This courtyard is one of Stirling's most memorable creations to date. To walk inside is to enter in a magical domain where architecture is condensed to its essentials: the courtyard is a processional stage set where the spirit of architecture promenades its hierarchical presence.

Not unlike Cameron—who draped a most princely garment on provincial St. Petersburg's imperial dreams—it has again taken a British architect—the greatest since Luytens—to sing with a marble voice the legitimate cravings of the German soul for a secular chamber in which to celebrate a *Te Deum* in quiet grandeur. In this courtyard dwell together the spirits of Biedermeier and Schinkel; if ever a present-day culture were to declare that its longings have found permanent embodiment, Germany would have to point to this courtyard. It is a reformulation of the recurring archetype of the pantheon, but with a roof made of transient clouds. By providing a monumental frame for ineffable rituals, this courtyard stands as a metaphor for the spirit of the building, and so doing, raises it to be the exalted level of memorable architecture.

FROM *The Architectural Review*, December 1984

EMILIO AMBASZ

INVENTIONS
THE REALITY OF THE IDEAL

Urban & Architectural Projects
1988-1991

Fukuoka Prefectural International Hall

Worldbridge Trade and Exhibition Center

Mycal Cultural and athletic Center at Shin-Sanda

The Phoenix Museum of History

Convent of the Holy Infant Jesus

Columbus Bridge

Hortus Conclusus

Mobipark Urban Furniture

Nishiyachiyo Town Center

Harbor of the Four Seasons

Marine City Waterfront Development

Paseo del Lago

Marine Resort Community

Realworld Theme Park

Rimini Seaside Development

Focchi Shopping Center

Private Estate

Casa Canales

Fukuoka Prefectural International Hall

Fukuoka, Japan

The design for the Fukuoka Prefectural International Hall proposes a powerful new solution for a common urban problem: reconciling a developer's desire for profitable use of a site with the public's need for open green space. The plan for Fukuoka fulfills both needs in one structure by creating an innovative agro-urban model.

Among Emilio Ambasz's recent projects, the Fukuoka Prefectural International Hall is a most powerful synthesis of urban and park forms. Its north face presents an elegant urban façade with a formal entrance appropriate to a building on the most prestigious street in Fukuoka's financial district. The south side of the hall extends an existing park through its series of terraced gardens that climb the full height of the building, culminating at a magnificent belvedere that offers a breathtaking view of the city's harbor. Underneath the park's fifteen one-story terraces lies over one million square feet of multipurpose space containing an exhibition hall, a museum, a 2000-seat proscenium theater, conference facilities, governmental and private offices, as well as several underground levels of parking and retail space.

The site, owned by the city, is the last large undeveloped plot in central Fukuoka. The city chose to develop the site in joint venture with private enterprise. In the scheme, a commercial developer will lease the land for sixty years and construct a building. A portion of the building's space will be devoted to public and municipal operations; the remaining allowable space will be revenue-producing. In deriving a proposal, the competing developers sought to maximize income potential. On the other hand, the architect was concerned about the effect of the development on adjacent Tenjin Central Park—the only green openspace in that part of the city. To the maximum extent possible, the architect wanted to give back to Fukuoka's citizens all the land the building would subtract from the city. Ambasz was awarded this commission for successfully achieving a reconciliation between these two opposing desires: doubling the size of the park while providing the city of Fukuoka with a powerful symbolic structure at its center.

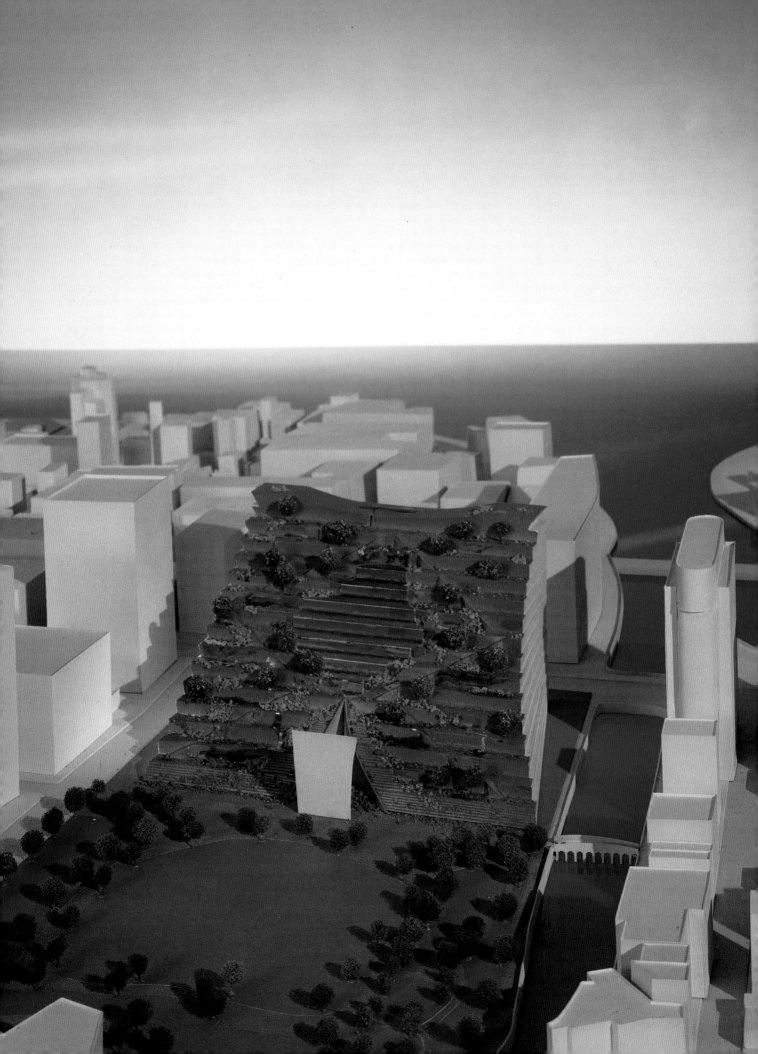

Along the edge of the park, the building steps up, floor-by-floor, in a stratification of low, land-scaped terraces. Each terrace floor contains an array of gardens for meditation, relaxation, and escape from the congestion of the city, while the top terrace becomes a grand belvedere, providing an incomparable view of the bay of Fukuoka and the surrounding mountains. A stepped series of reflecting pools upon the terraces are connected by upwardly spraying jets of water, to create a ladderlike climbing waterfall to mask the ambient noise of the city beyond. These pools lie directly above the central glass atrium with-in the building, bringing diffused light to the interior through clerestory glazing separating the pools. Each year during the famous week-long Don Taku festival, the encircling balconies inside the atrium allow a panoramic view as the procession passes through the building, while outside the stepped garden terraces become an inviting outdoor amphitheater for the entire city. A large "stone" like wedge at the foot of the terraced park pierces a V-shaped entrance into the building, revealing rough-hewn stone suggestive of geo-logic strata underlying the surface vegetation and likening the building to a massive block cut from the earth. This wedge shaped element also doubles as ventilation exhaust for the underground floors below and as a raised stage for performing artists.

The opposite side of the building faces the most important financial street of Fukuoka. Composed of striped glass, with every floor so angled as to reflect the passersby below, it softly dematerializes the mass of the building. The façade rakes outwardly from the vertical with each successively higher floor, creating the effect of an awning over the sidewalk. This overhanging eaves uses the building design itself rather than an applied device to provide cover to pedestrians. The final stepped layers at the top create the effect of a large 45-degree cornice overhang at the street's edge, defining the public entrance while enhancing the building's urban presence.

This design has made the park and the building inseparable. The building gives back to the city the very land it would have taken away and allows a major urban structure to exist symbiotically with the invaluable resource of open public space.

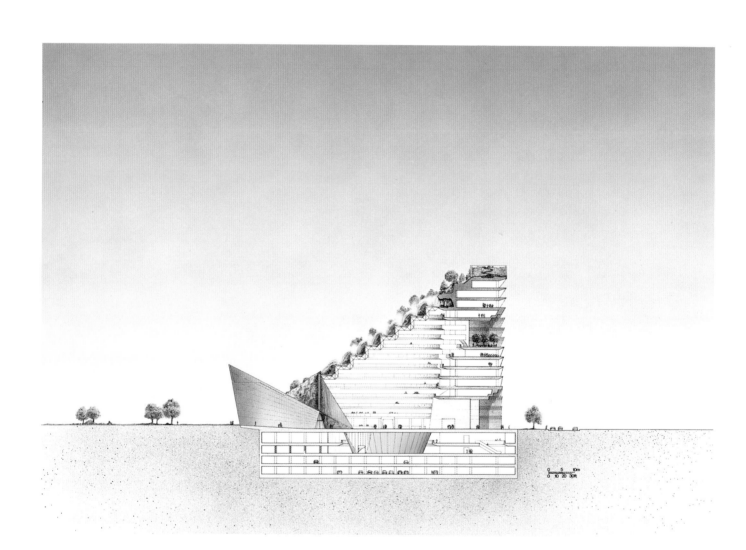

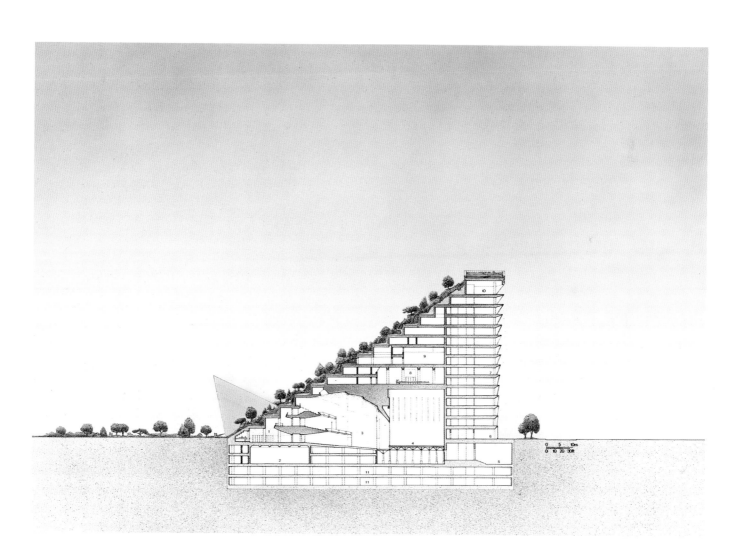

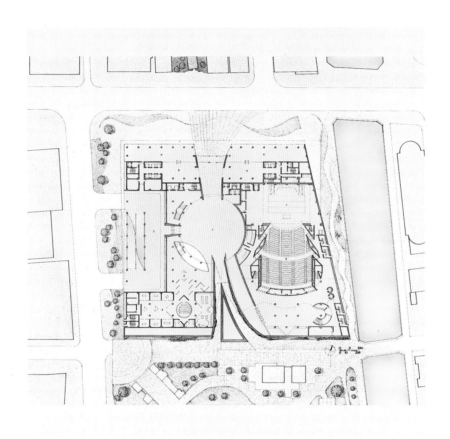

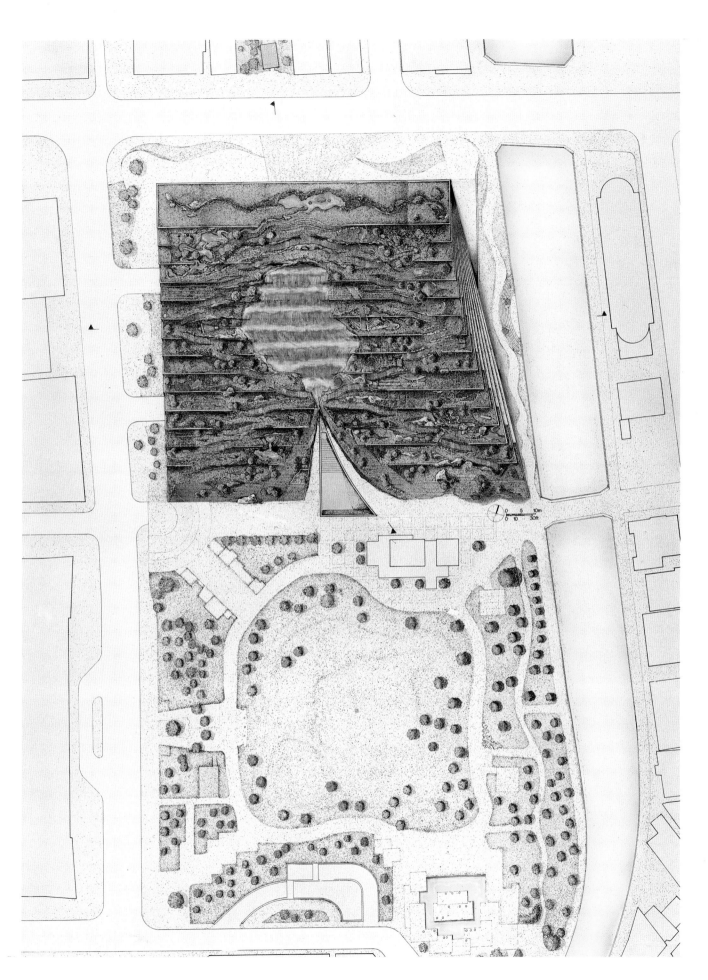

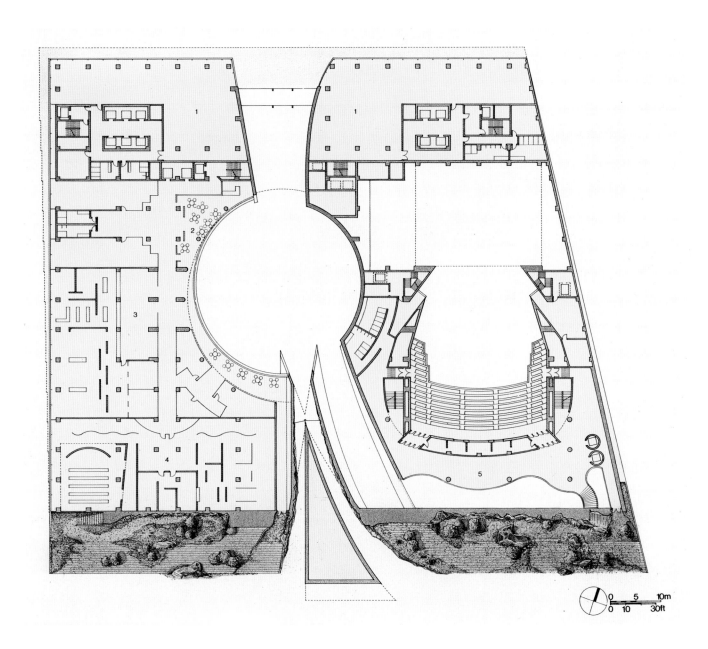

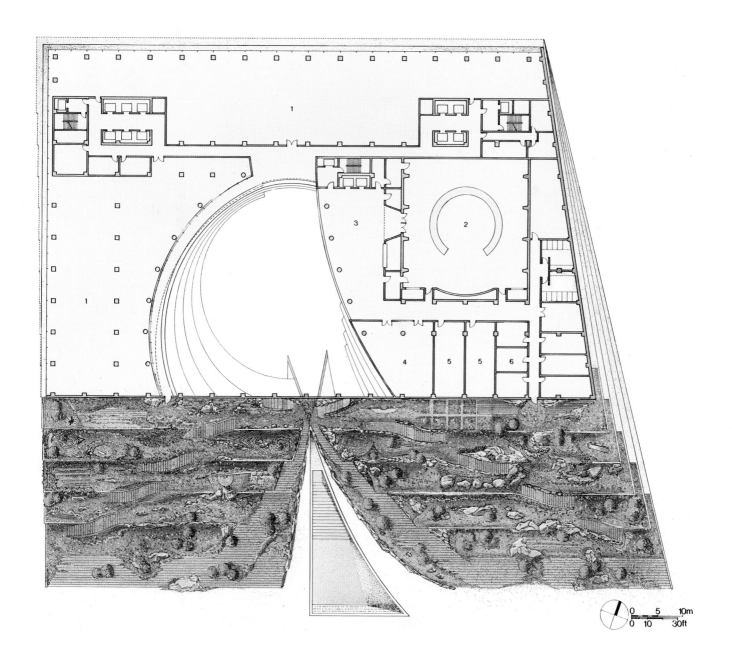

113

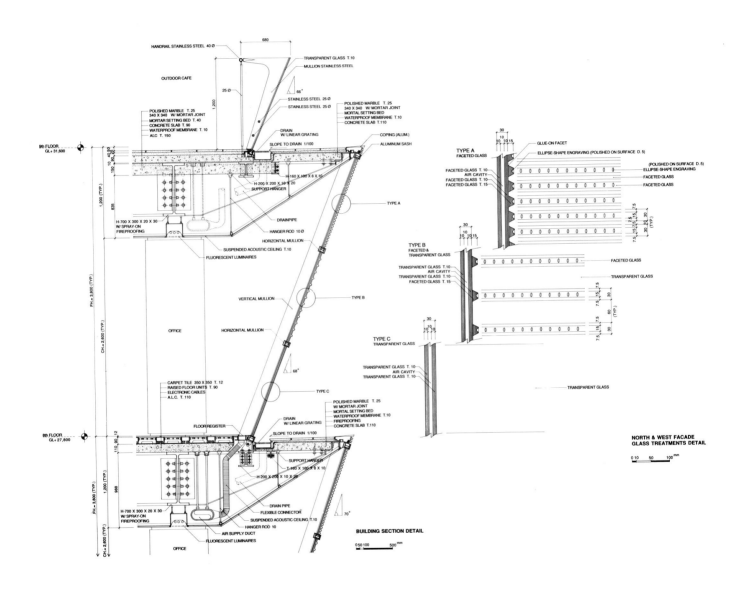

HANDRAIL STAINLESS STEEL 40 Ø

TRANSPARENT GLASS T.10
MULLION STAINLESS STEEL

OUTDOOR CAFE

25 Ø

68°

STAINLESS STEEL 25 Ø
STAINLESS STEEL 25 Ø

POLISHED MARBLE T. 25
340 X 340 W/ MORTAR JOINT
MORTAL SETTING BED
WATERPROOF MEMBRANE T.10
CONCRETE SLAB T.110

POLISHED MARBLE T. 25
340 X 340 W/ MORTAR JOINT
MORTAR SETTING BED T. 40
CONCRETE SLAB T. 90
WATERPROOF MEMBRANE T. 10
ALC T. 150

DRAIN
W/ LINEAR GRATING
SLOPE TO DRAIN 1/100

COPING (ALUM.)
ALUMINUM SASH

9th FLOOR
GL + 31,600

680

1,200

680

H-160 X 100 X 8 X 10

SUPPORT HANGER

TYPE A

H-200 X 200 X 10 X 20

H-700 X 300 X 20 X 30
W/ SPRAY-ON
FIREPROOFING

DRAINPIPE

HANGER ROD 10 Ø

SUSPENDED ACOUSTIC CEILING T.10

FLUORESCENT LUMINAIRES

OFFICE

VERTICAL MULLION

TYPE B

HORIZONTAL MULLION

68°

TYPE C

CARPET TILE 350 X 350 T. 12
RAISED FLOOR UNITS T. 90
ELECTRONIC CABLES
A.L.C. T. 110

FLOOR REGISTER

DRAIN
W/ LINEAR GRATING
SLOPE TO DRAIN 1/100

POLISHED MARBLE T. 25
W/ MORTAR JOINT
MORTAL SETTING BED
WATERPROOF MEMBRANE T.10
FIREPROOFING
CONCRETE SLAB T.110

8th FLOOR
GL + 27,800

SUPPORT HANGER

T-160 X 100 X 8 X 10

H-200 X 200 X 10 X 20

H-700 X 300 X 20 X 30
W/ SPRAY-ON
FIREPROOFING

DRAIN PIPE
FLEXIBLE CONNECTOR

SUSPENDED ACOUSTIC CEILING T.10

HANGER ROD 10

AIR SUPPLY DUCT

FLUORESCENT LUMINAIRES

OFFICE

70°

BUILDING SECTION DETAIL

0 50 100   500 mm

TYPE A
FACETED GLASS

30
10
10 15

GLUE-ON FACET
ELLIPSE-SHAPE ENGRAVING (POLISHED ON SURFACE D. 5)

FACETED GLASS T. 10
AIR CAVITY
FACETED GLASS T. 10
FACETED GLASS T. 15

(POLISHED ON SURFACE D. 5)
ELLIPSE-SHAPE ENGRAVING
FACETED GLASS
FACETED GLASS

7.5
15
7.5
30
10
30
(TYP.)

TYPE B
FACETED &
TRANSPARENT GLASS

30
10
10 15

TRANSPARENT GLASS T.10
AIR CAVITY
TRANSPARENT GLASS T.10
FACETED GLASS T.15

FACETED GLASS

TRANSPARENT GLASS

7.5
15
7.5
30
60
30
(TYP.)

TYPE C
TRANSPARENT GLASS

30
10
10

TRANSPARENT GLASS T.10
AIR CAVITY
TRANSPARENT GLASS T.10

TRANSPARENT GLASS

7.5
15
7.5
30
60
30
(TYP.)

NORTH & WEST FACADE
GLASS TREATMENTS DETAIL

0 10   50   100 mm

114

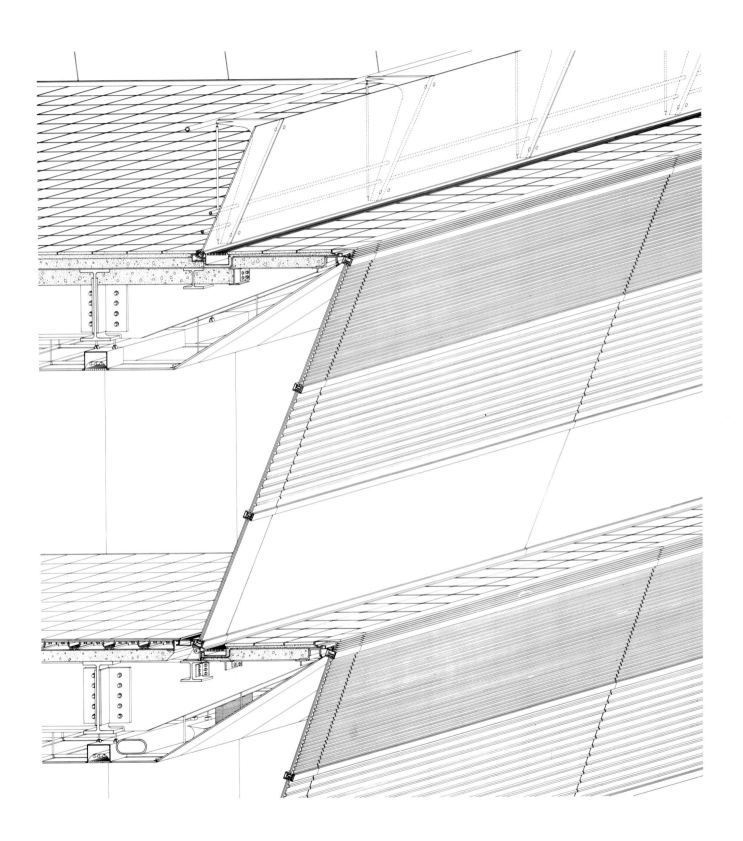

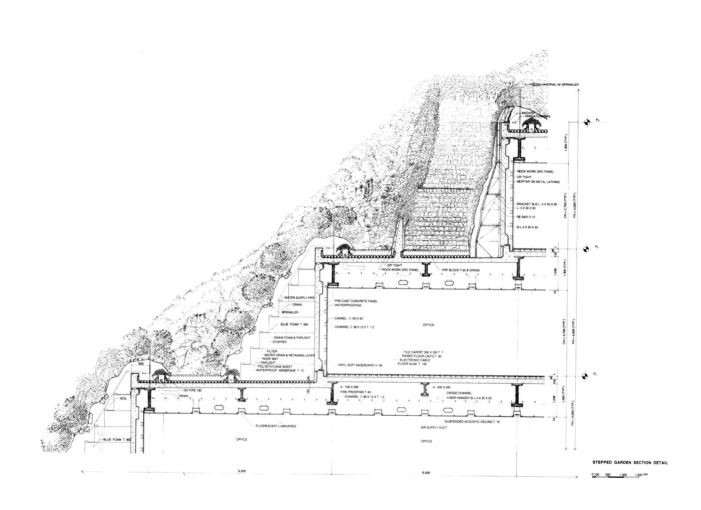

HIDDEN HANDRAIL W/ SPRINKLER

ANCHOR
IRRIGATION PIPE

ROCK WORK GRC PANEL
ZIP TIGHT
MORTAR ON METAL LATHING

BRACKET SUS L - 4 X 50 X 50
L - 3 X 30 X 30

RE-BAR D-10

St L-4 X 50 X 50

ZIP TIGHT
ROCK WORK GRC PANEL
FRP BLOCK T.50 & GRASS

WATER SUPPLY PIPE
DRAIN
SPRINKLER
BLUE FOAM T. 500

DRAIN FOAM & PARLIGHT
STOPPER
FILTER
WATER DRAIN & RETAINING LAYER
ROOF MAT
PARLIGHT
POLYETHYLENE SHEET
WATERPROOF MEMBRANE T. 10

PRE-CAST CONCRETE PANEL
WATERPROOFING

CANNEL C 100 X 40

CHANNEL C 38 X 12 X T. 1.2

OFFICE

TILE CARPET 350 X 350 T. 7
RAISED FLOOR UNITS T. 90
ELECTRONIC CABLE
FLOOR SLAB T. 150

VINYL SOFT BASEBOARD H. 60

SOIL

DO PIPE 150
DRAIN

H - 700 X 300
FIRE PROOFING T. 40
CHANNEL C 38 X 12 X T. 1.2

H - 400 X 200
CROSS CHANNEL
H-BAR HANGER St L-4 X 50 X 50

FLUORESCENT LUMINARIES

OFFICE

AIR SUPPLY DUCT

SUSPENDED ACOUSTIC CEILING T. 15

OFFICE

BLUE FOAM T. 500

STEPPED GARDEN SECTION DETAIL

0 100   500   1,000   1,500 mm

6,000   6,000

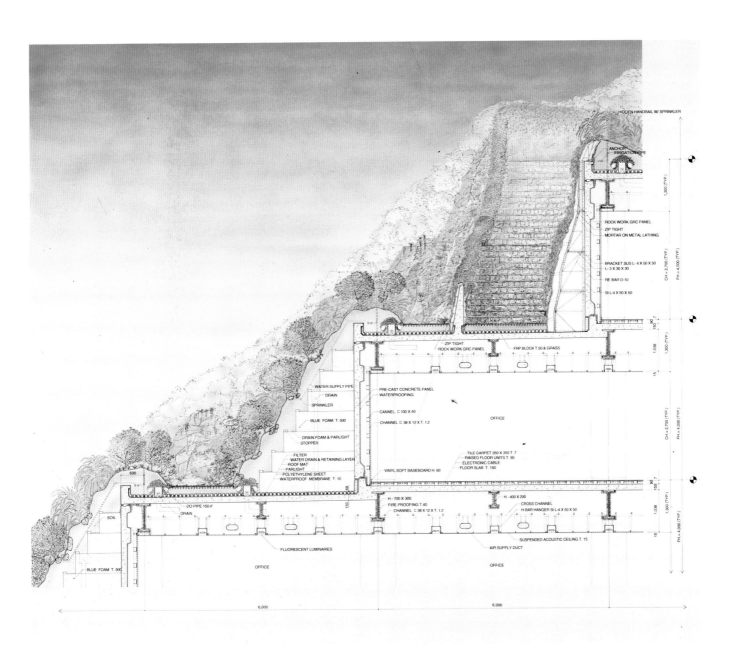

HIDDEN HANDRAIL W/ SPRINKLER

ANCHOR IRRIGATION PIPE

ROCK WORK GRC PANEL
ZIP TIGHT
MORTAR ON METAL LATHING

BRACKET SUS L- 4 X 50 X 50
L- 3 X 30 X 30
RE-BAR D-10
St L-4 X 50 X 50

ZIP TIGHT
ROCK WORK GRC PANEL

FRP BLOCK T.50 & GRASS

WATER SUPPLY PIPE
DRAIN
SPRINKLER

BLUE FOAM T. 500

DRAIN FOAM & PARLIGHT
STOPPER

FILTER
WATER DRAIN & RETAINING LAYER
ROOF MAT
PARLIGHT
POLYETHYLENE SHEET
WATERPROOF MEMBRANE T. 10

PRE-CAST CONCRETE PANEL
WATERPROOFING

CANNEL ⊏ 100 X 40

CHANNEL ⊏ 38 X 12 X T. 1.2

OFFICE

TILE CARPET 350 X 350 T. 7
RAISED FLOOR UNITS T. 90
ELECTRONIC CABLE
FLOOR SLAB T. 150

VINYL SOFT BASEBOARD H. 60

600

SOIL

DO PIPE 150 ∅
DRAIN

H - 700 X 300
FIRE PROOFING T.40
CHANNEL ⊏ 38 X 12 X T. 1.2

H - 400 X 200

CROSS CHANNEL
H-BAR HANGER St L-4 X 50 X 50

FLUORESCENT LUMINARIES

AIR SUPPLY DUCT

SUSPENDED ACOUSTIC CEILING T. 15

BLUE FOAM T. 500

OFFICE

OFFICE

6,000

6,000

1,300 (TYP.)

CH = 2,700 (TYP.) FH = 4,000 (TYP.)

150 90

1,038

1,300 (TYP.)

15

CH = 2,700 (TYP.) FH = 4,000 (TYP.)

150 90

1,038

1,300 (TYP.)

15

FH = 4,000 (TYP.)

117

WORLDBRIDGE TRADE AND INVESTMENT CENTER

OUTSIDE BALTIMORE, MARYLAND, USA

When the directors of the Asia/USA Development Corporation began planning a new office complex and trade center, they purchased a suburban site near Baltimore, Maryland. Since the organization's objective is to stimulate trade between the United States and Asia, it was assumed that the design of the new facility would synthesize Eastern and Western traditions—a fitting embodiment of the corporation's intercontinental trade ambitions. In deriving his proposal, Ambasz considered architectural styles and distinct forms from each culture, but ultimately defied all traditional architecture. Instead, he presented an inventive structure with overt ecological themes—an appropriate modus operandi for today's global culture.

The structures that house Worldbridge comprise two inviting features on the Maryland topography: one, the seeming result of an orchestrated up-lifting at the earth's surface; the other, an implosion forming a carefully wrought cavity. These buildings are, in fact, composed with the graduated stacking of organically shaped floor-plates. A garden is cultivated where one plate extends beyond the next.

The extroverted office complex houses over one million square feet of office space, conference rooms, and a display hall organized around a central atrium. The depth of each office floor (a distance measured between an exterior terrace and the interior atrium) is such that views and natural light are available to all.

This building's atrium is one of Emilio Ambasz's most dramatic and monumental interiors. A truncated cone lit from above by an oculus, the base of the space carves a two-story bowl in a highly detailed, highly episodic landscape comprised of rock, moving water, and abundant plantlife.

Adjacent to the superstructure of the office complex is Worldbridge's exhibition hall. This 150,000-square-foot facility is dedicated to revolving trade shows and is technically capable of hosting several exhibitions simultaneously while avoiding interference between events. The exhibition hall offers a sense of architectural spaciousness through the controlled use of vegetation and the introduction of natural light drawn from its hollowed core.

121

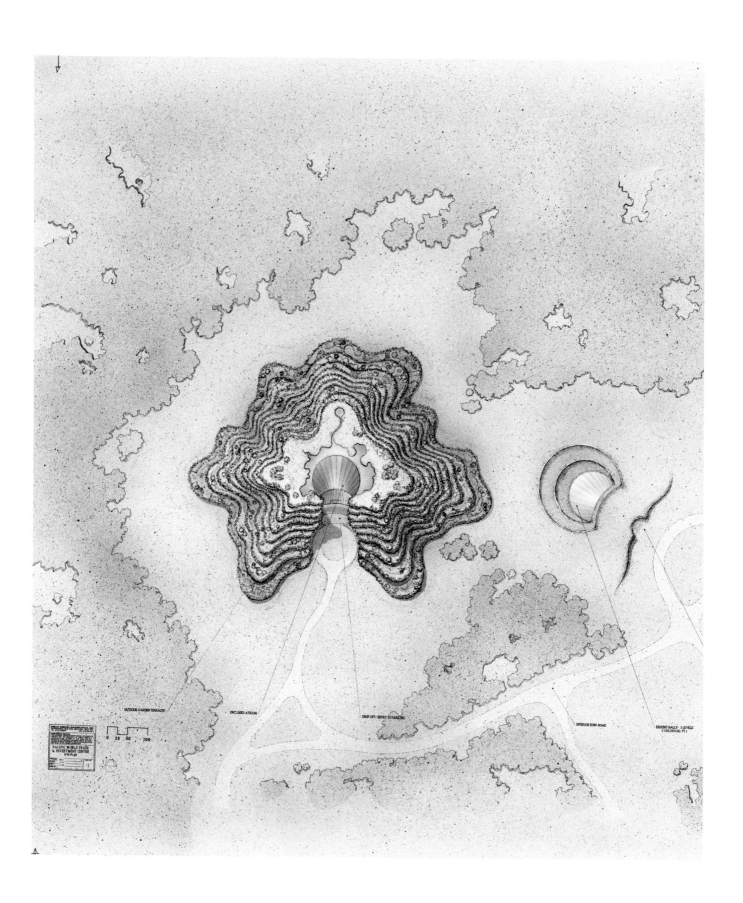

OUTDOOR GARDEN TERRACES

ENCLOSED ATRIUM

DROP OFF / ENTRY TO PARKING

INTERIOR RING ROAD

EXHIBIT HALLS 3 LEVELS (100,000 SQ. FT.)

0   25   50   100

PACIFIC WORLD TRADE
& INVESTMENT CENTRE
SITE PLAN

Mycal Cultural and Athletic Center at Shin-Sanda

Hyogo Prefecture, Japan

One of Japan's leading department stores commissioned Ambasz to design a cultural and athletic center in the new town of Shin-Sanda to benefit not only its employees but also the growing local community. The new building will contain assembly spaces ranging from small meeting rooms to large multipurpose halls, diverse health and athletic facilities, training centers, guest and hotel accommodations, and underground parking.

The site for this new structure looks across an existing water reservoir to a lush green golf course. The difficult challenge of this site was met by proposing a design concept accommodating the immense massing requirements for the building's 450,000 square feet, yet sympathetically acknowledging the serene open landscape beyond. This design has been conceived as two hands touching at the wrists, as if these hands were both shielding and cherishing the earth. This configuration creates and embraces a new terraced garden, effectively merging the building with the reservoir and green playing fields in the distance.

The entire mass of the building is conceived as a simple, elegant L-shaped wall bracing a garden hillside. The slender exposed building form contains offices and smaller meeting rooms, while the large volumes of the athletic facilities and multipurpose hall lie hidden beneath the garden landscape. A series of reflecting pools begin at the top of the garden and flow from one to the other until reaching the existing water reservoir, seamlessly integrating the new building with the existing landscape. Simultaneously, skylights within these pools allow natural indirect light to illuminate and complement the screened window views afforded to all of the public gathering spaces within. This outdoor public garden employs traditional landscape techniques, while relating very specifically to local conditions. As in the traditional Japanese "borrowed landscape" garden, the gently stepped planted terraces of Shin-Sanda create a series of secluded gardens for contemplation, relaxation, or watching the setting sun, while enjoying the views to the pond and forest beyond as if the distant landscape belonged to the garden itself.

An undulating linear greenhouse skirting the two visible fronts of the building soften the visible mass of the structure, while protecting its patrons from the noise and activity of the city street. This greenhouse provides an opportunity for the enjoyment of a very different garden space. Warmed by the sun year round, this winter garden is in constant bloom, providing inviting seating areas for the athletic club, the café, and public lounge areas. Additional flowers and green plants cascade from planter boxes adorning both façades, as if the garden landscape outdoors has flowed through the building, immersing every level to reach the warm comfort of the enclosed garden within.

134

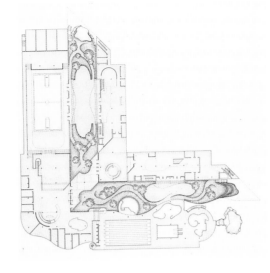

断面図　B

0　　5　　　10　　　　　　20M

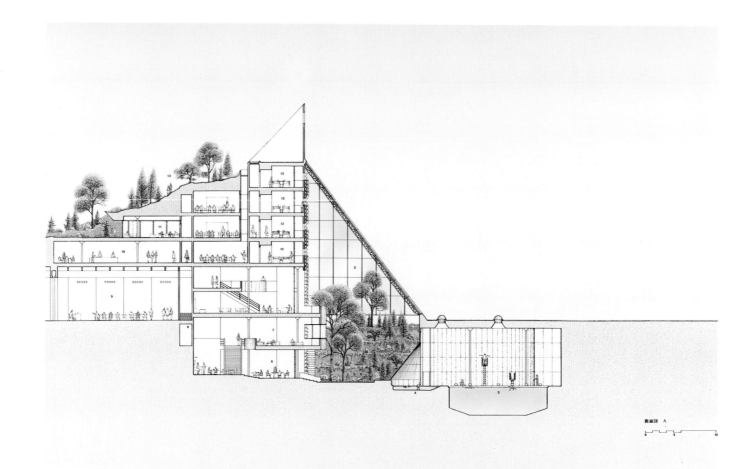

THE PHOENIX MUSEUM OF HISTORY

PHOENIX, ARIZONA, USA

The Phoenix History Museum is a pilot project in an ambitious revitalization program for downtown Phoenix. The capital of a state famous for its natural beauty, Phoenix is set between mountains and wild, open land. The museum plan integrates the city with its spectacular surroundings by turning the requirement for a large parking lot into an opportunity to bring nature and open public space to the city center.

The museum and the 800-car parking lot, which also serves an adjacent science museum and a museum of historic houses, are set within a sloping structure beneath a new public park. Structural elements are shared beneath this slope by the museum and garage, helping to keep costs within a very limited budget. Rising to a height of fifty feet, the earth-covered ramp shields from view an existing convention center directly behind the site from the pedestrian areas in front of the museum while providing unobstructed views from the park of the surrounding scenery. The museum's galleries, auditorium, classrooms, archives, research library, and offices are located on two levels above ground within the slope; the parking areas are on several levels above and below ground level. The slope's back wall faces the street and provides access to the loading dock, storage areas, and curators' offices.

The modest museum gains importance by borrowing from its neighbors' attributes. Its diminutive footprint, disguised by the green slope which stretches principally over the parking area's 275,000 square feet and the small museum's 20,000 square feet, appears more imposing than it actually is. In addition, the building is set back to bring its entrance on axis with a tree-lined street to be flanked with historical buildings as outlined Ambasz's master plan for this cultural area.

In response to the museum's focus on the history of the city's early settlers, the site treatment refers to geological history with a terraced rock formation flanking the entrance at the lower end of the landscaped slope, worn away as if by a long-extinct stream.

Little visible architecture protrudes above the slope save one sinuous wall delineating a free-form L-shape. Like a sheer cliff face, the shorter section of the wall presents a convex mask to the visitor, providing entry through a punched gateway at its base. Passage reveals the façade of the "building" proper formed by the wall's longer section which cups and shades an open-air courtyard. Triangular sections of the wall, like the buttresses of the indigenous adobe architecture of the region, protrude into the courtyard, leaving openings that flood the double-height gallery behind with light. In counterpoint to this imposing surface is the lacy, undulating colonnade forming the opposite side of the patio and providing light to the library. The two sides of the oval courtyard meet in a circular double-height lobby where visitors experience the sensation of descending deep within the earth upon entry as the slope rises around them.

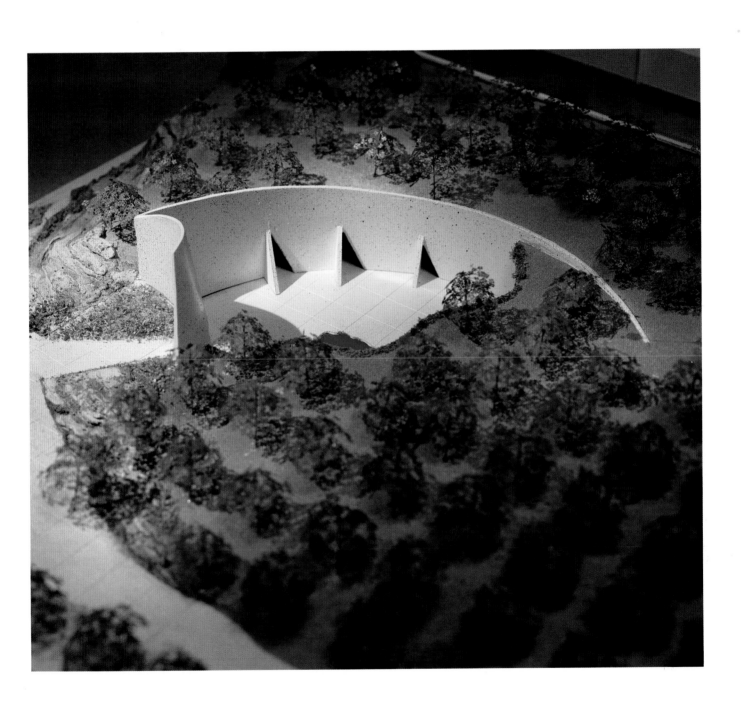

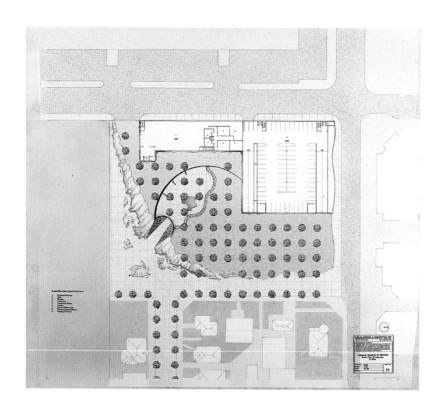

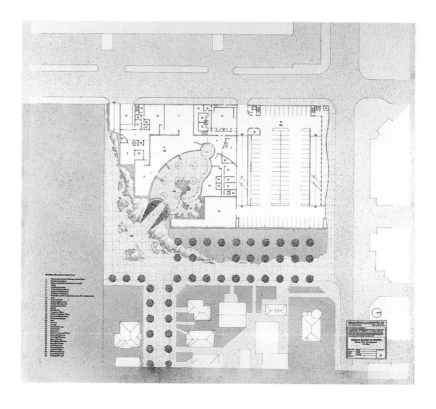

146

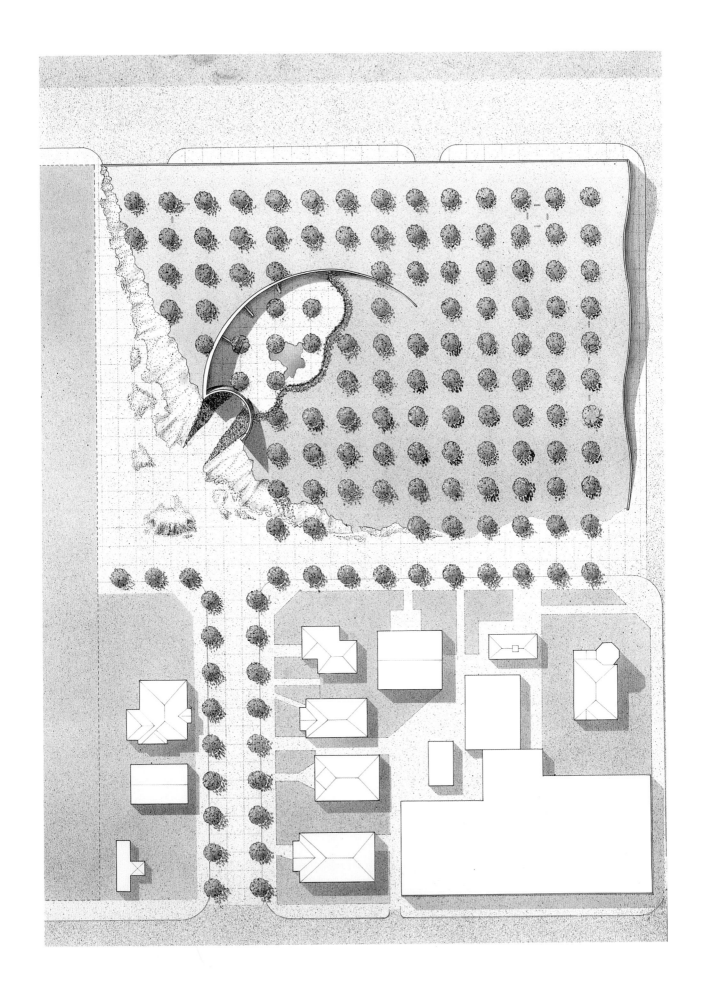

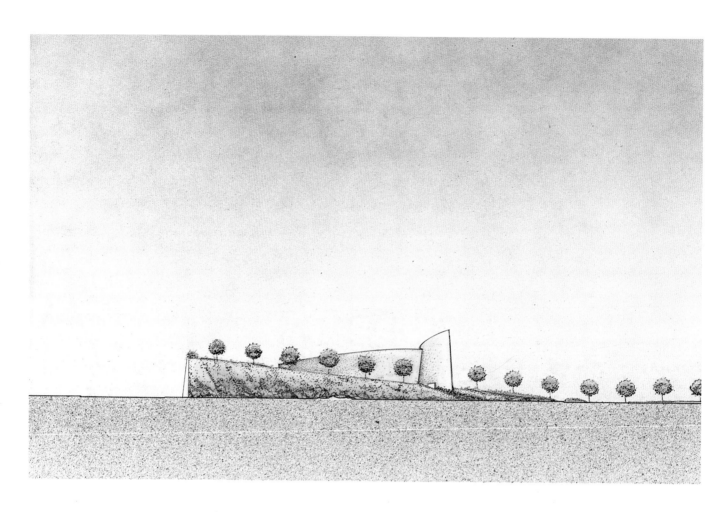

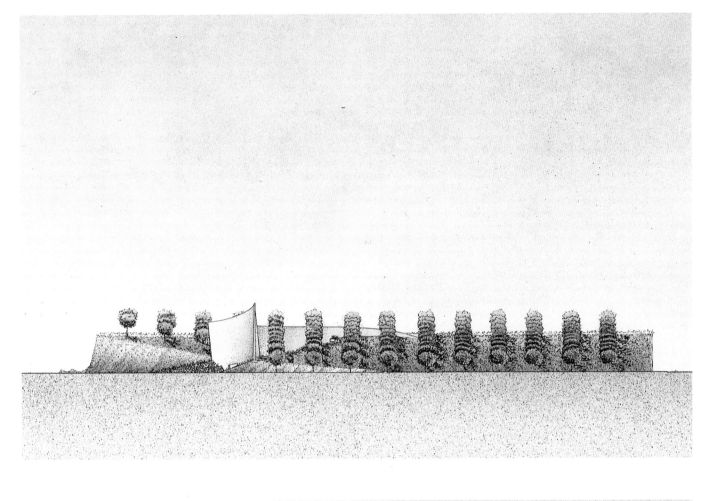

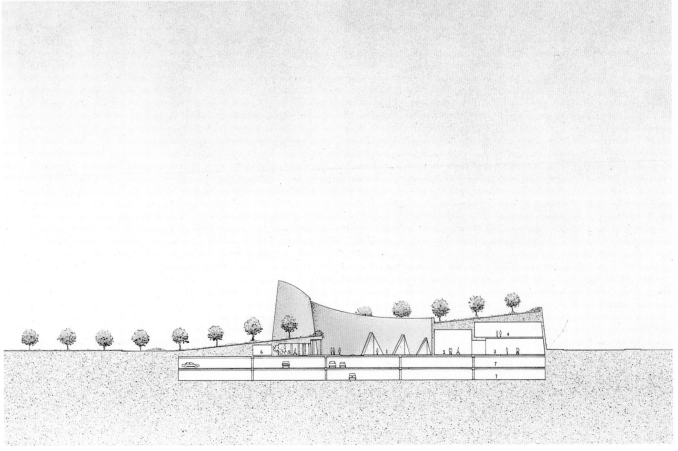

149

Convent of the Holy Infant Jesus

Singapore

This adaptive reuse proposal for transforming the nineteenth-century Convent of the Holy Infant Jesus into a high-end retail center focusses on complementing the compound's unique architectural character. The Neo-Gothic style chapel, convent, and school building stand on spacious grounds cloistered behind walls in the center of downtown Singapore, across the street from the fabled Raffle's Hotel.

As a means of preserving and revitalizing this, one of the last remaining historic landmarks of Singapore, the city held a tender competition to renovate this nineteenth-century convent and chapel into a major retail commercial center. In addition, the city required substantial additional rentable area to be added to the existing site, even suggesting the removal of the original chapel apse if necessary to achieve the required area for a new addition. The solution here proposed not only preserves the chapel in its entirety, but enhances and fully complements the unique architectural character of the convent, while accommodating the modern commercial requirements.

The design solution envisions the existing ground level of the convent's garden as a critical datum plane, with the old existing above and the new below. This datum combines like a fine tapestry the historical threads of the older structures with the newer thread of the sunken courtyard. And, by locating all of the new additions to the chapel below the ground plane, none of the visual impact of the historic convent is lost.

One of the unique concepts of this design is the articulation of the new commercial addition as a two-tiered cloister, surrounding a sunken courtyard directly behind the main chapel. The gently curving ambulatory offers a variety of shops, boutiques, and cafés, while the newly refurbished convent above serves as a community and cultural center. The two-tiered ambulatory offers not only a wide variety of intimate shops, but provides a respite from the sun, inclement weather, and the busy street as well, while gently and lyrically uniting the convent's structures.

The apse of the chapel is the hierarchical center of the entire project, and the anchor of the reborn convent. Raised symbolically upon a newly created rocky crest, seemingly high above the ground, it presents constantly changing views to patrons in the two lower-tiered arcades, becoming virtually a theater in the round, where new is constantly juxtaposed in concert with the old. In the sunken garden courtyard below, cooling water seeps over a waterfall from the rock, where it finally comes to rest in a reflecting pool, a serene symbol of the timeless nature of this unique convent.

The organization of the new formal garden on the original grounds reinforces the central courtyard's role as a focal point of the new plan. Indigenous trees mask the view of the surrounding skyscrapers from the outdoor seating and dining areas and recall the tropical forest that once stood on the site. The new plan doubles the site's available commercial space, while renewing the convent's traditional role as a quiet refuge from the bustling city.

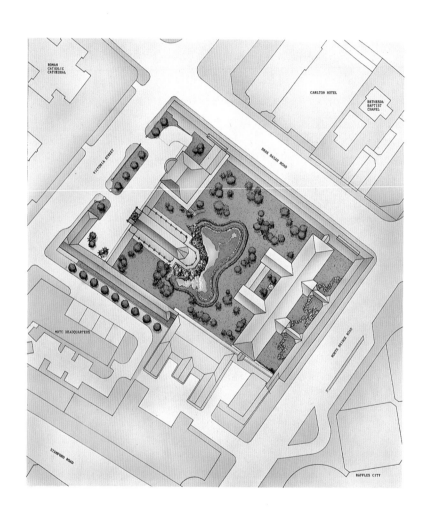

ROMAN
CATHOLIC
CATHEDRAL

CARLTON HOTEL

BETHESDA
BAPTIST
CHAPEL

VICTORIA STREET

BRAS BASAH ROAD

MATC HEADQUARTERS

NORTH BRIDGE ROAD

STAMFORD ROAD

RAFFLES CITY

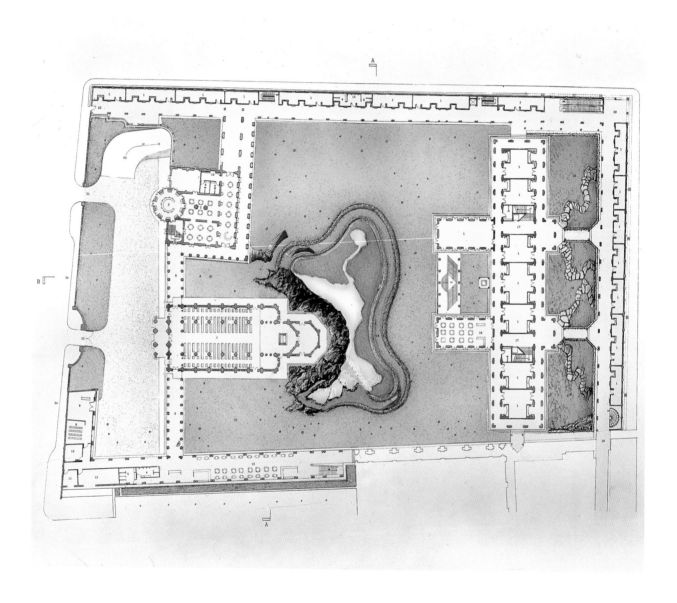

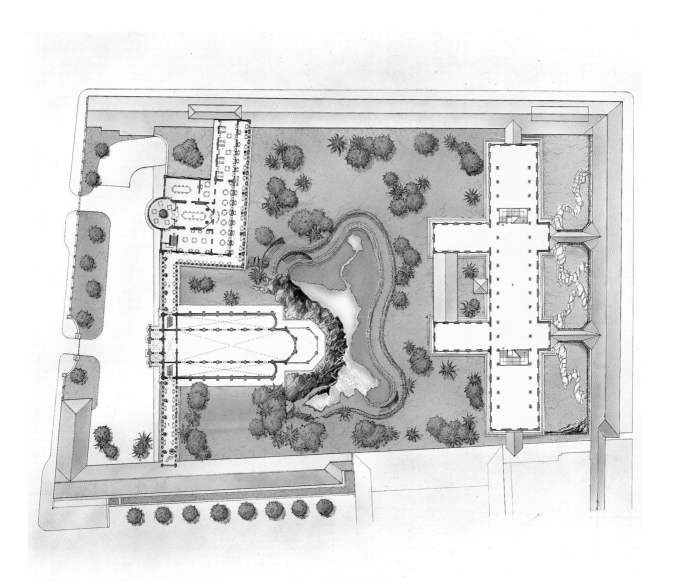

THE
CLOISTERS

SECTION A-A
SCHEME 1

1 RETAIL
2 DISPLAY CASE
3 SUNKEN CLOISTERS
4 ROOF GARDEN
5 OUTDOOR GARDEN
6 SERVICE/PUBLIC CORRIDOR
7 TIFFANY & CO.
8 LOBBY
9 OUTDOOR SEATING
10 NORTH BRIDGE ROAD
11 VICTORIA STREET

THE
CLOISTERS
SECTION B-B
SCHEME 3

COLUMBUS BRIDGE
COLUMBUS, INDIANA, USA

This design for a bridge in Columbus, Indiana, will be like no other in America. Commissioned by the State of Indiana to commemorate the five-hundredth anniversary of Columbus' arrival in America, its uniqueness is not a function of its engineering: rather, it's the sequence of experiences leading one across a river and into the town that makes this bridge an unprecedented urban gateway.

The site for the new bridge was chosen so that the bridge itself is now directly on axis with the two most important vertical buildings in the city: the nineteenth-century County Courthouse Tower and Eliel Saarinen's First Christian Church. The approach road was designed as a gently sweeping curve, gradually rising upward as it crosses the bridge until these two towers are perfectly framed by the outstretched columns of the new structure, thereby creating a monumental first view of the city for visitors.

This commission was seen by Ambasz as an opportunity to create a sense of ceremonial arrival. His design is a choreographed flow of movement that begins when the traveler is to pass through a densely planted arbor of trees that will conceal any view to the city. Having passed through the arbor, the motorist will gradually rise along an earth berm that curves as it ascends. At its peak, the road will drop in a straight line between outstretched columns, suddenly offering a spectacular view to the picturesque skyline of the town below. To further heighten the sense of anticipation, as one approaches the vista-of-arrival, Ambasz proposes to scar and hammer the road's paving surface. As a result, when a vehicle enters the arbor, its tires will begin to hum as they roll along. Punctuated by percussive beats, the humming will build in intensity and crescendo at the end of the curve and top of the ramp. Tires will then fall silent over smooth pavement as passengers begin coming down the bridge's ramp quietly, while the ever more widely spaced columns of the bridge continue to grow in height and inclination, like a deeply voiced crescendo at the end of a symphony.

One other consideration contributes to the drama of the proposed gateway bridge: once through the arbor, the columns flanking the road will emerge from the ground, each pair growing progressively taller. The bridge roadway itself will be suspended from a rhythmically increasing number of cables attached to the top of the last six columns. All columns are capped at their terminus with the capital-like planters. Their plant-forms will be cast in bronze to spill out and over the planters, suggesting an overall arrangement of splayed columns and floral form analogous with outstretched arms offering bouquets of flowers as a welcoming gesture.

The new bridge will accommodate three lanes of vehicular traffic and one pedestrian way. This project presents a shining example of humanistic design whereby a functional urban component (a bridge) engenders scale and wit. That this bridge is being constructed by the State of Indiana within their standard budgetary constraints underscores the fact that the qualities associated with memorable urban architecture is simply a function of both design and bureaucratic imagination.

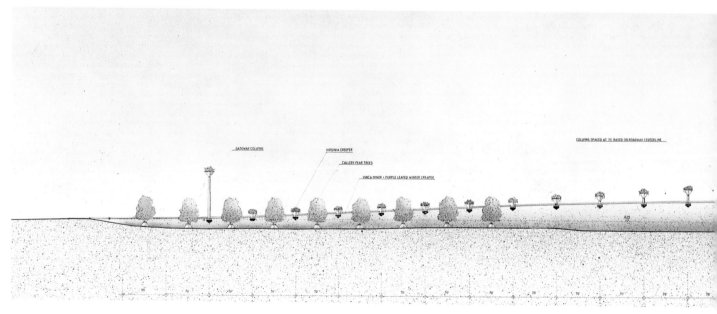

GATEWAY COLUMNS

VIRGINIA CREEPER

CALLERY PEAR TREES

VINCA MINOR + PURPLE LEAFED WINTER CREEPER

COLUMNS SPACED AT 70' BASED ON ROADWAY CENTERLINE

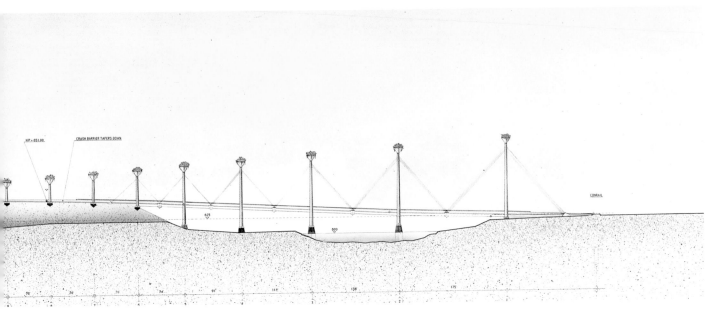

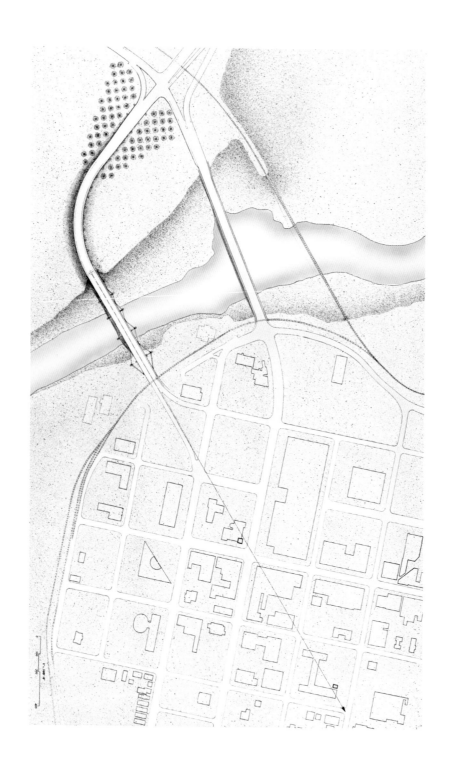

Hortus Conclusus

Centre Georges Pompidou

Paris, France

Hortus Conclusus, or Contained Orchard, was designed for the dining terrace on the roof of the Centre Georges Pompidou in Paris, as part of an exhibition on gardens. Walls of greenery enclose each dining space to suggest a contained orchard protecting it from the world beyond, reminiscent of the medieval Flemish urban gardens enclosed within brick walls. This design not only achieves a quiet, secluded sanctuary for dining in the very center of a dense metropolis, but it creates a temporal realm of mystery and delight for its patrons.

Enveloped in mist that animates its forms with shifting light and shadow, the garden rises from the hard surface of the terrace at the end of a serpentine path. Vertical mirrors, veiled by trellis panels covered with ivy, alternate with open space to define the perimeter garden wall. Crisply pruned hedges abut the panels to suggest the boundaries of a fortified city—forbidding from without, protecting those within.

Inside, like the narrow houses of a medieval city, stand sixteen L-plan trellis towers arranged in a grid. These trellis walls, lined on the inside with a layer of transparent glass for wind protection and aural privacy, delineate semienclosed private dining arcades, each containing a table and four chairs. Each tower is disposed to screen views into neighboring towers, although movement can be perceived through the translucent screens of flowering ivy. Reflected in the mirrored inner surfaces of the perimeter garden wall, the towers' greenery appears to stretch on indefinitely like a deep forest.

Above each tower gleams a gold-plated weather vane, symbol of the house. The weather vanes simulate bird song and other sounds of nature when the wind blows. An altarlike centerpiece stands on each table, presiding over the ceremony of eating. Filled with moss and a single white orchid, the glass centerpiece is a landscape in miniature which, like the garden surrounding it, calls to mind the larger expanses of nature that lie beyond the city. Another garden is expressed in the Plexiglas covers of the food trays in which sixteen indentations filled with moss echo the sixteen towers.

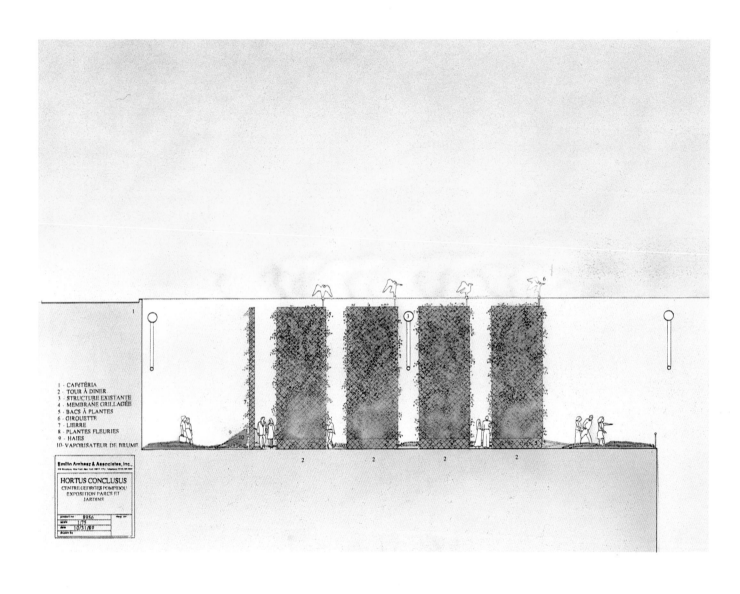

1 - CAFÉTÉRIA
2 - TOUR À DINER
3 - STRUCTURE EXISTANTE
4 - MEMBRANE GRILLAGÉE
5 - BACS À PLANTES
6 - GIROUETTE
7 - LIERRE
8 - PLANTES FLEURIES
9 - HAIES
10 - VAPORISATEUR DE BRUME

Emilio Ambasz & Associates, Inc.,

HORTUS CONCLUSUS
CENTRE GEORGES POMPIDOU
EXPOSITION PARCS ET
JARDINS

178

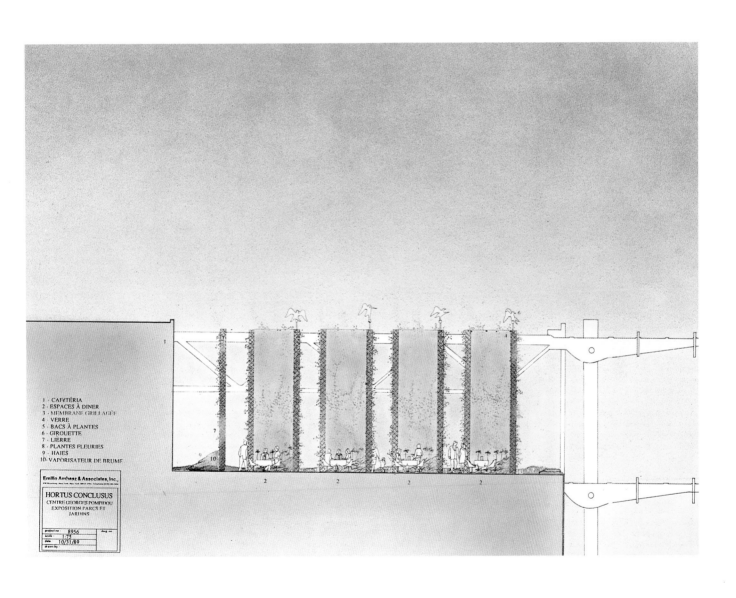

1 - CAFÉTÉRIA
2 - ESPACES À DINER
3 - MEMBRANE GRILLAGÉE
4 - VERRE
5 - BACS À PLANTES
6 - GIROUETTE
7 - LIERRE
8 - PLANTES FLEURIES
9 - HAIES
10 - VAPORISATEUR DE BRUME

Emilio Ambasz & Associates, Inc.,

HORTUS CONCLUSUS
CENTRE GEORGES POMPIDOU
EXPOSITION PARCS ET
JARDINS

project no.	8956	dwg no.
scale	1:75	
date	10/31/89	
drawn by		

179

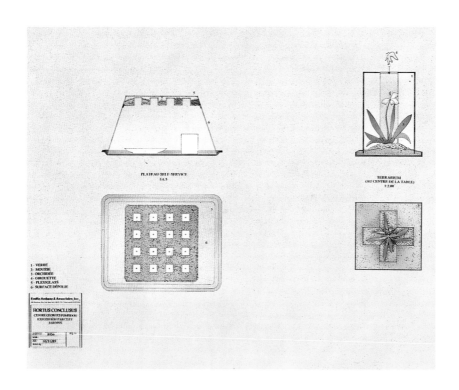

PLATEAU SELF-SERVICE
1:4.5

TERRARIUM
(AU CENTRE DE LA TABLE)
1:2.00

1 - VERRE
2 - MOUSSE
3 - ORCHIDÉE
4 - GIROUETTE
5 - PLEXIGLASS
6 - SURFACE DÉPOLIE

Emilio Ambasz & Associates, Inc.

HORTUS CONCLUSUS
CENTRE GEORGES POMPIDOU
EXPOSITION PARC ET
JARDINS

10/31/89

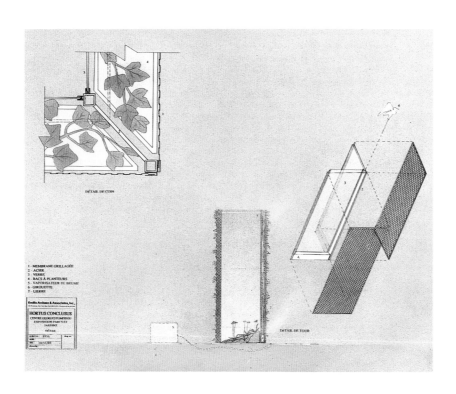

DÉTAIL DE COIN

1 - MEMBRANE GRILLAGÉE
2 - ACIER
3 - VERRE
4 - BACS À PLANTEURS
5 - VAPORISATEUR DE BRUME
6 - GIROUETTE
7 - LIERRE

Emilio Ambasz & Associates, Inc.

HORTUS CONCLUSUS
CENTRE GEORGES POMPIDOU
EXPOSITION PARC ET
JARDINS
DÉTAIL

10/31/89

DÉTAIL DE TOUR

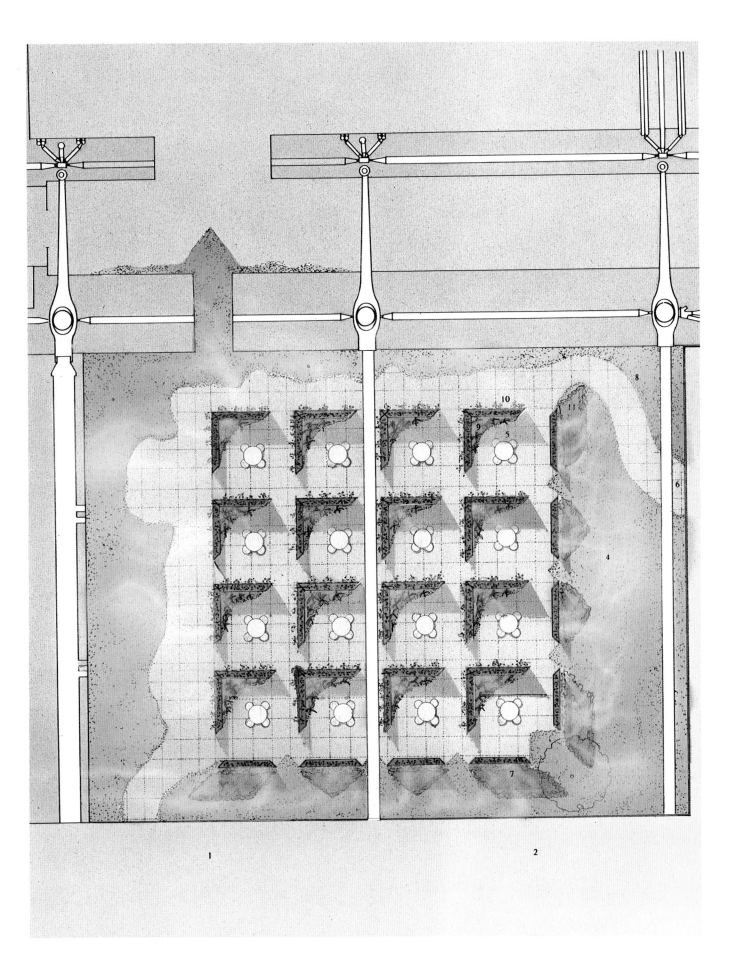

MOBIPARK URBAN FURNITURE
LYON, FRANCE

The image of nature reclaiming the city guided the design for the Mobipark Urban Furniture. From the air above Lyon, the successive, historical layers of the city's growth are visible. Here and there, one can see the vestiges of vegetation struggling to emerge through the cement and stones. With leaves and vines sprouting from the legs of chairs and from the supports of bus stops, the Mobipark Urban Furniture allows nature to return to the city, transforming the streets into an urban garden.

The basis of the furniture's modular system is a hollow aluminum column which provides structural support as well as a conduit for electricity, water, and telephone lines. In addition to a gold-plated lion symbolizing the city, two elements coexist at the top of the column: a flag representing memory of place, its color denoting a specific neighborhood, and local plants embodying the vitality of nature. The vegetation is watered by a self-sufficient system within the hollow columns. Adorning the city like trees, the columns fulfill the practical needs of the urban environment while replacing with order the visual cacophony of incongruent elements that clutter Lyon's streets.

The modular system is highly flexible. Fitting into sockets in the pavement, the columns can be easily removed or replaced. Street signs, traffic lights and information panels are affixed to one pole. Bus shelters, benches, fences, and recycling bins are fastened to two or more poles. Canvas tents stretched from four poles provide shade for picnic tables. Perforated dishes atop columns shed ambient light while other street lamps hang from cantilevered arms. Encircling the pole with shallow basins creates a fountain. The wire mesh of trash bins and the roofs of bus shelters serve as additional supports for plants.

Referring to the prototype column for Lyon as the flowered column, *la colonne florissante* , Ambasz writes: "With one bold gesture, with this *colonne florissante*, I have designed a benign, man-made garden where the natural and the artificial coexist harmoniously. One meets the other and one transforms the other. When a light post gains the grace of tall bamboo shoots, and when a bus stop acquires the charm of a garden gazebo, the streets of Lyon will become its garden."

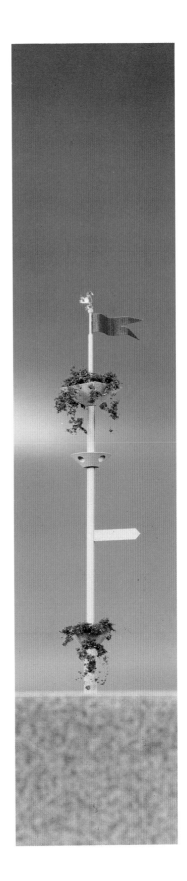

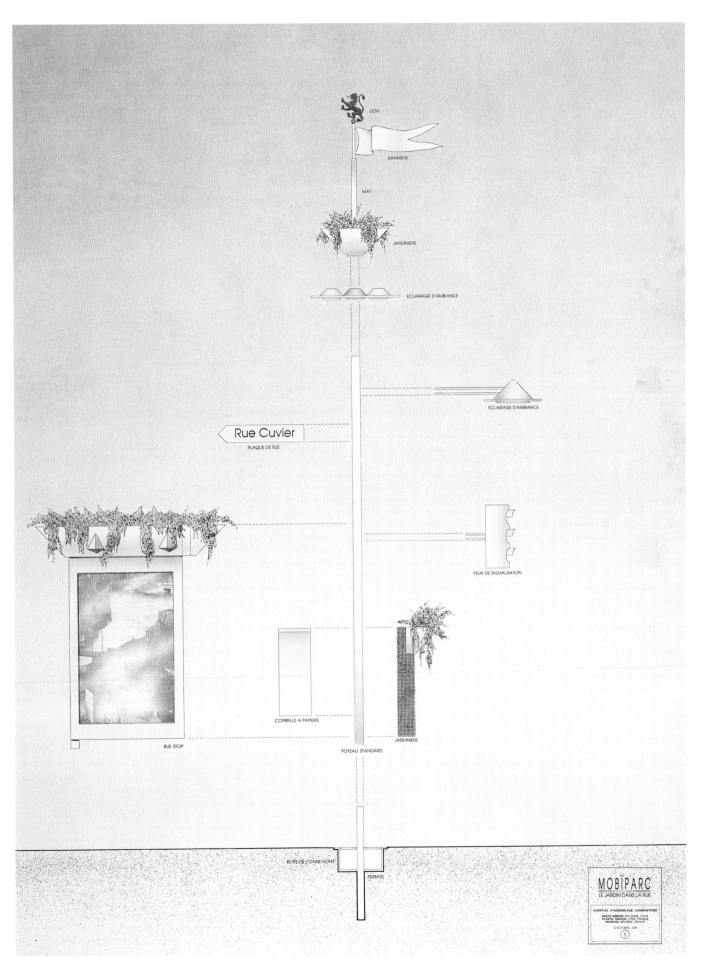

LION

BANNIERE

MAT

JARDINIERE

ECLAIRAGE D'AMBIANCE

ECLAIRAGE D'AMBIANCE

Rue Cuvier

PLAQUE DE RUE

FEUX DE SIGNALISATION

CORBEILLE A PAPIERS

JARDINIERE

BUS STOP

POTEAU STANDARD

BOITE DE CONNEXIONS

EMBASE

MOBIPARC
LE JARDIN DANS LA RUE

EXEMPLES D'ASSEMBLAGE COMBINATOIRE
EMILIO AMBASZ BOLOGNE, ITALIE
PLASTIC OMNIUM LYON, FRANCE
NEUHAUS, MEHOIRE, FRANCE
12 OCTOBRE 1989
①

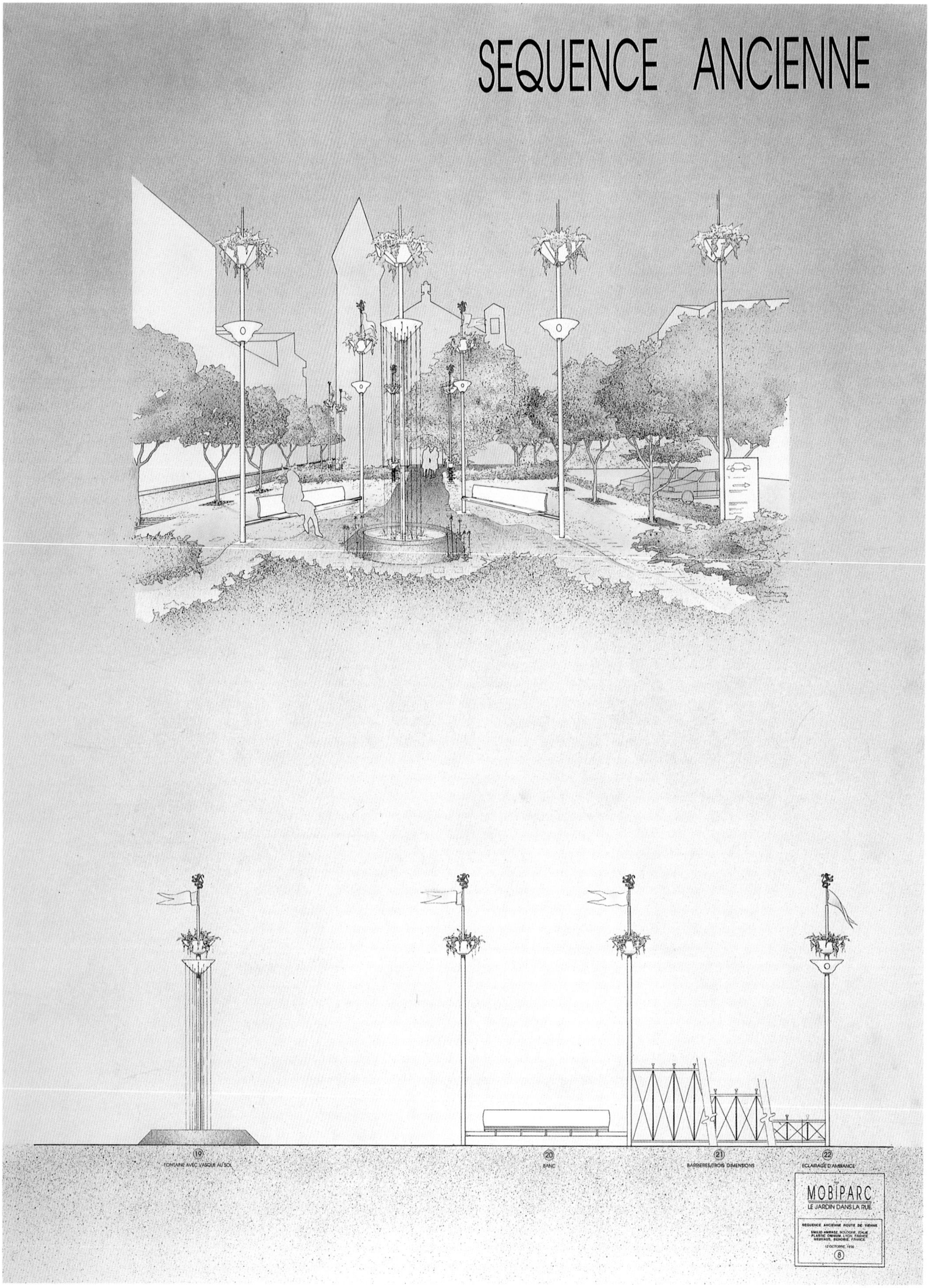
SEQUENCE ANCIENNE
19
FONTAINE AVEC VASQUE AU SOL
20
BANC
21
BARRIERES/TROIS DIMENSIONS
22
ECLAIRAGE D'AMBIANCE
MOBIPARC
LE JARDIN DANS LA RUE
SEQUENCE ANCIENNE ROUTE DE VIENNE
8

MOBIPARC
LE JARDIN DANS LA RUE

SEQUENCE

MONCEY

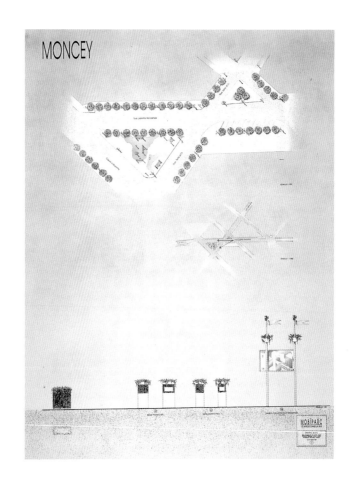

GARIBALDI

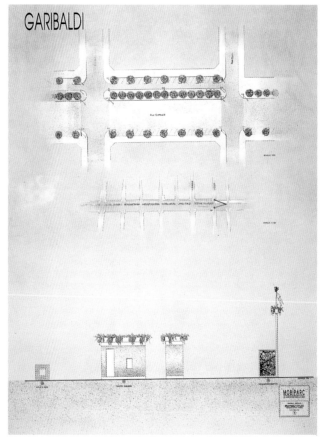

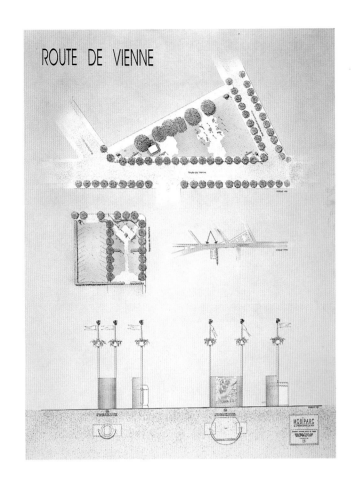

ROUTE DE VIENNE

PRESQU'ILE

191

NISHIYACHIYO TOWN CENTER

NISHIYACHIYO, CHIBA PREFECTURE, JAPAN

With the advent of the high-speed rail system, distant agricultural areas of Japan have now been brought within easy commuting distance of Tokyo. Taking advantage of this new accessibility, one of Japan's leading investment corporations acquired a large area of rural property north of Tokyo to develop an entirely new suburban town, Nishiyachiyo, out of an agricultural area. While Ambasz was asked to design the new train station as well as the twenty-four acres of this new town's business center, consisting of a major department store, hotel, office space, museum, 3,500-car parking garage, and recreation facilities, the surrounding residential areas will not be developed until much later. Ambasz was therefore faced with the immediate challenge of creating a commercial center that feels complete and welcoming even before the remainder of the town is built.

Visitors arriving at the new town would potentially be met by only empty flatness beyond the elevated train station, also designed by Ambasz. To give them a sense of arrival and enclosure, he developed a unique multi-tiered vertical garden to define and contain the boundary of the site, while providing a sense of presence for the city center. Designed as an open, ivy-covered structural grid where each module contains a potted flowering tree, this vertical garden creates a natural, transparent transition between the new urban center and the open landscape beyond. To heighten the drama of the changing seasons, four different varieties of flowering plants will be uniformly used, each season bringing a new fragrance and color. Unlike traditional horizontal gardens, this vertical garden system not only allows its colorful patterns to be fully appreciated by visitors, but it uses minimal land for maximum effect in a country where land is a rare resource. It becomes a covered arcade at ground level, linking all of the buildings within the town center and softly integrating the existing train station with the new structures. This covered promenade defines two central arrival plazas on either side of the station, the North plaza with vehicle access for the train station, and the South plaza with pedestrian access for the public gardens and new commercial area. These plazas create a symbolic urban center for Nishiyachiyo, encircled by a covered shopping arcade which organizes all the buildings into one coherent and peaceful public space.

Towering above the complex, a huge Torii gate announces the city from afar to arriving trains which pass through it into the new elevated station. Composed of two thirty-five-story office buildings connected by a lintel containing restaurants and a museum, the arrival gate is clad with a living green skin. This second skin, made of scaffolding hung with vegetation, veils the structure's glass curtain wall and visually connects the office towers to the gardens below. One side of each tower leans slightly as it rises, so that the gate seems to twist with an inner energy. Guided by Japanese architectural tradition, the arrival gate forms a dynamic symbol for this new city in search of an identity.

192

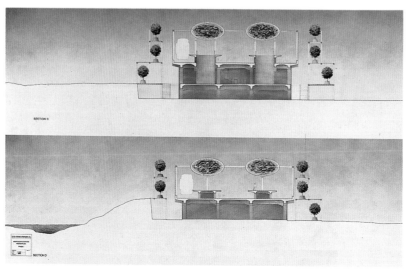

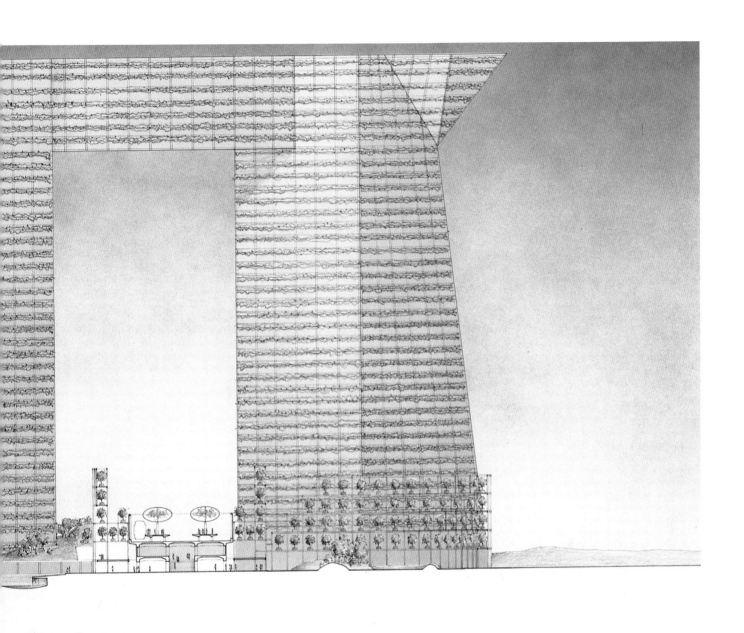

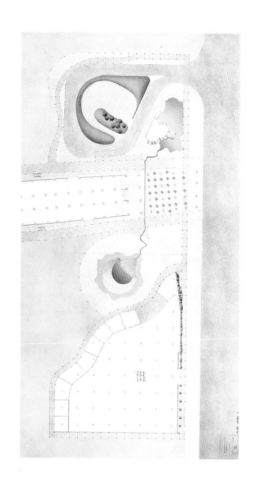

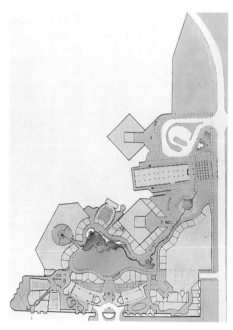

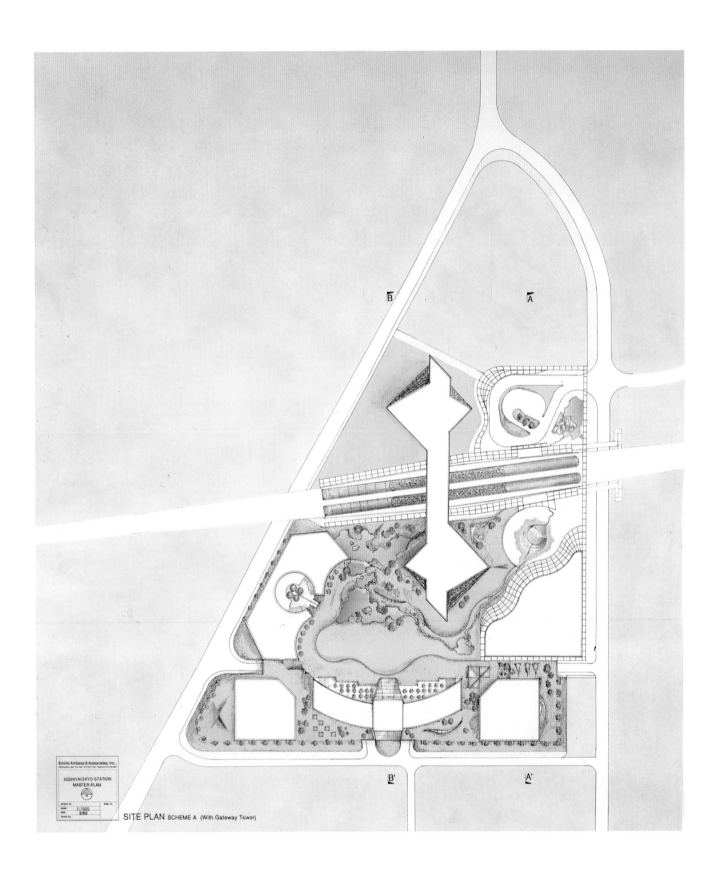

NISHIYACHIYO STATION
MASTER PLAN

SITE PLAN SCHEME A (With Gateway Tower)

Harbor of the Four Seasons

Oharai, Japan

When commissioned to design a new immense department store complex on the seaside edge of the town of Oharai in Japan, Ambasz created an innovative concept for this commercial development which would not only attract a large number of visitors and potential shoppers, but actually entice them to remain for several days. This approach integrates commercial department store functions with diverse leisure activities to create the character of a maritime holiday resort, the "Harbor of the Four Seasons," where shopping is but one of many activities attracting new visitors.

To achieve the goal of creating a major shopping complex with the qualities of a secluded resort, Ambasz redefined the entire character of a traditional shopping center, dividing up the large functions into a series of small, human-scale shops, boutiques, shaded gardens, and outdoor plazas, as well as isolating the complex completely away from the noise of the highway and adjacent local structures. The main department store complex steps upward in gradual landscaped terraces to create an artificial hillside of single-story shopping arcades with parking concealed below. While always retaining the character of low gardens and parks edged by covered pedestrian boardwalks leading into diverse shops, these terraces actually rise above and completely cover the highway leading from Oharai. In this way nearby houses or cars are never seen or heard by any visitors, and the shopping resort attains a total character of peacefulness, seclusion, and human scale unique to this shopping center alone.

Terraces adjacent to a central marina contain private residential units with easy access to parking or boat slips. Potential weekend visitors may buy or rent these apartments, while the resort management provides all of the support and maintenance services required. By fully integrating the marina, the shopping center, and the recreation facilities with residential units all maintained by a central management, patrons are actually enticed to remain for several days at a time in a totally relaxed atmosphere.

Visitors may shop in the diverse arcades, sit in the terraced gardens gazing at the sea, bathe in the saltwater lagoon of the recreation park, or dine in an open-air restaurant on an island overlooking a floating freshwater swimming pool at the end of the marina pier. By day, water jets and cool mist arise from around the island, creating the effect of brilliant overlapping rainbows. By night, constantly changing laser displays from the island create an exciting unique attraction that entices visitors to remain long past daylight hours.

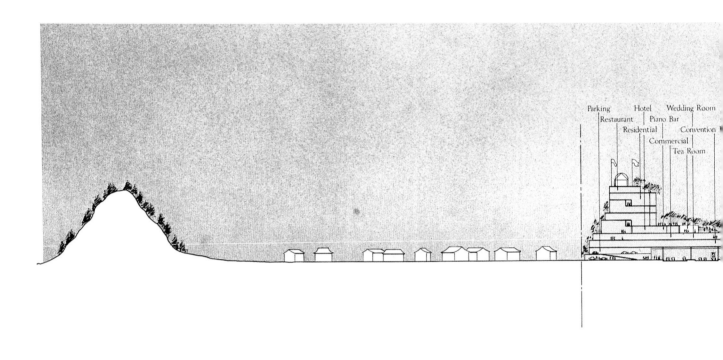

Parking   Hotel   Wedding Room
Restaurant   Piano Bar
Residential   Convention
Commercial
Tea Room

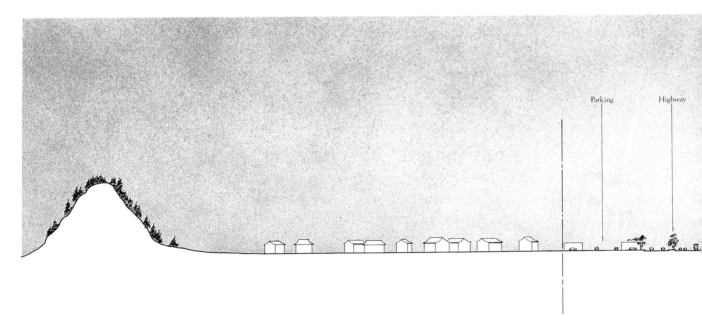

Parking   Highway

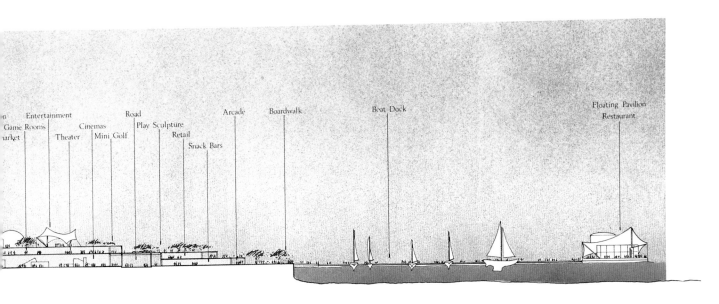

Entertainment
Game Rooms
...arket
Theater
Cinemas
Mini Golf
Road
Play Sculpture
Retail
Snack Bars
Arcade
Boardwalk
Boat Dock
Floating Pavilion
Restaurant

Alternative   A

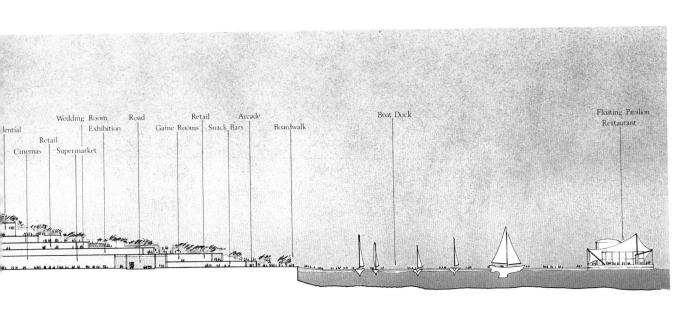

...dential
Cinemas
Retail
Supermarket
Wedding Room
Exhibition
Road
Game Rooms
Retail
Snack Bars
Arcade
Boardwalk
Boat Dock
Floating Pavilion
Restaurant

Alternative   B

MARINE CITY WATERFRONT DEVELOPMENT

OTARU, HOKKAIDO ISLAND, JAPAN

Facing the windy Sea of Japan, Otaru shares the same climate as Vladivostok, Siberia. Built around an ideal natural port, this traditional Japanese town has a long history of prosperity. In recent years, however, Otaru has begun lagging in economic growth behind the other port towns on the island of Hokkaido. In reaction to this trend, the government of Otaru has formulated a vigorous plan to rebuild its industrial base and port facilities, improve community services, and provide for a large commercial development along the port to spur the growth of its emerging tourist industry.

A major competition was sponsored by the government for the commercial waterfront development. Because of the immense area requirements programmed for commercial use, most of the competing developers made proposals which covered every square foot of the waterfront, leaving no open public space. Ambasz, however, proposed a design which allowed over sixty percent of the new structures to be covered in earth and landscaped, providing an extensive urban park on the edge of the harbor. By linking gardens inside the structures with the natural landscape features of Otaru, this new park provides a sympathetic and inviting transition between the new built forms and their island setting. Although this proposal would yield less revenue than other development schemes, the government of Otaru awarded the project to Ambasz because his concept creates inviting outdoor public space in a city where such gathering spaces are very rare.

As the major organizing principle of his design, Ambasz links the existing railroad station with all the new commercial, residential, cultural, educational, and recreational facilities using a two-story serpentine, arcaded promenade. Canopied, arcaded shopping streets are a Japanese tradition. By transposing this concept onto the site in the form of a glazed promenade, Ambasz was able to offer protection from the harsh winters, while seamlessly uniting many diverse functions. Referred to as the "Maritime Promenade of the Four Seasons," this sinuous arcade offering constantly changing interior vistas is a colorful wintergarden allowing flowers and plants to exist year-round and anchored by an exhibition center/hotel tower at one end and a terraced apartment tower at the other. Near the water's edge is an openair boardwalk, like a symbolic reflection of the protected indoor arcade, moving outward to the sea.

The Maritime City Waterfront Development is one of the earliest examples of a technique Ambasz refers to as "the green over the grey," where architecture and landscape are blended into an organic whole to achieve a high density of profitable land use, while simultaneously providing extensive interior and exterior public park. And it is precisely this innovative extension of garden parkland which will make the Marine City Waterfront a civic and commercial success.

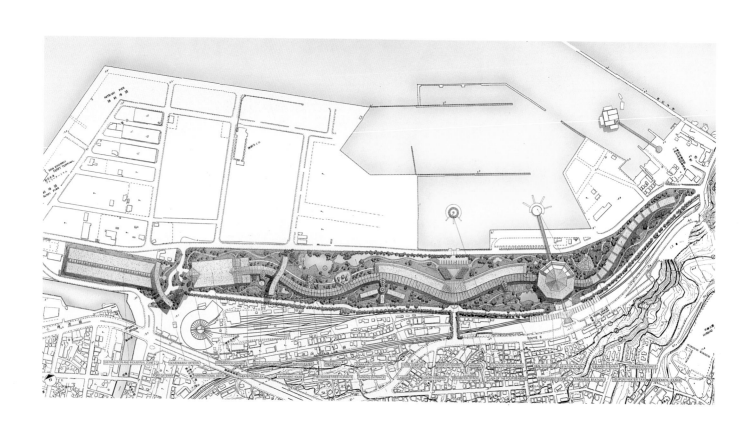

218

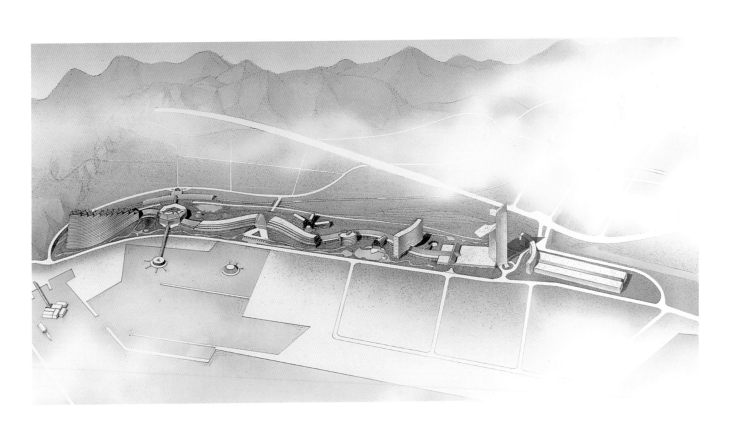

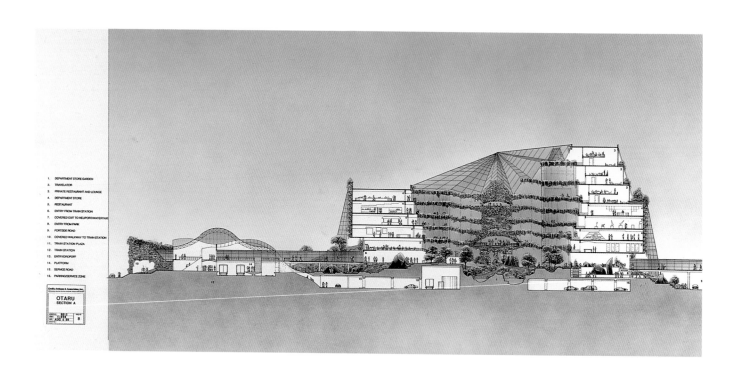

1. DEPARTMENT STORE GARDEN
2. TRAVELATOR
3. PRIVATE RESTAURANT AND LOUNGE
4. DEPARTMENT STORE
5. RESTAURANT
6. ENTRY FROM TRAIN STATION
7. COVERED EXIT TO HELIPORT/WATERTAXI
8. ENTRY FROM PARK
9. PORTSIDE ROAD
10. COVERED WALKWAY TO TRAIN STATION
11. TRAIN STATION PLAZA
12. TRAIN STATION
13. ENTRY/DROPOFF
14. PLATFORM
15. SERVICE ROAD
16. PARKING/SERVICE ZONE

OTARU
SECTION A

1. PROMENADE/WINTER GARDEN
2. TRAVELATOR
3. HIGH TECHNOLOGY VIEWING AREA
4. AUDIO-VISUAL DISPLAY
5. SHOPPING
6. EXTERIOR PLAZA
7. PARK
8. MARINA
9. RESTAURANT
10. ENTRY ROTUNDA
11. SERVICE ROAD
12. PARKING/SERVICE ZONE

OTARU
SECTION C

1. PROMENADE/WINTER GARDEN
2. TRAVELATOR
3. FABRIC STORE
4. JEWELRY STORE
5. COMMUNITY CENTER
6. CENTRAL COURT
7. ART SCHOOL/ROOF GARDEN
8. LECTURE HALL
9. CAFETERIA
10. CLASSROOMS
11. MEETING ROOMS
12. FAMILY PLANNING
13. LOUNGE
14. ENTRY SEQUENCE
15. PARK
16. LAGOON
17. PORTSIDE ROAD
18. SERVICE ROAD
19. PARKING/SERVICE ZONE

OTARU
SECTION F

1. PROMENADE/WINTER GARDEN
2. TRAVELATOR
3. HI-TECH INFORMATION RETAIL
4. FOREIGN GOODS
5. HOTEL COMPLEX ENTRY
6. CENTRAL ROTUNDA/CHECK-IN
7. HOTELS
8. INTER-HOTEL CONNECTER LOOP
9. EXTERIOR SUMMER PROMENADE
10. CANAL SIDEWALK
11. CANAL
12. PORTSIDE ROAD
13. SERVICE ROAD
14. PARKING/SERVICE ZONE

OTARU
SECTION E

1. PROMENADE/WINTER GARDEN
2. TRAVELATOR
3. HI-FASHION STORE
4. RESTAURANT/BAR
5. CONDOMINIUMS/LUXURY APARTMENTS
6. SPORTS FACILITIES
7. OLYMPIC SWIMMING POOL
8. DIVING PLATFORM
9. VIEWING AREA
10. SPORTS MEDICINE
11. COMMITTEE ROOM
12. HEALTH SPA
13. EXTERIOR SUMMER PROMENADE
14. PARK
15. MUSIC PAVILLION
16. PORTSIDE ROAD
17. SERVICE ROAD
18. PARKING/SERVICE ZONE

1. PROMENADE/WINTER GARDEN
2. TRAVELATOR
3. FISH MARKET
4. SEAFOOD RESTAURANTS
5. TROPICAL BARS
6. SHOE STORE
7. WINE BAR
8. PARK
9. FISHERMANS WHARF
10. AMPHITHEATRE
11. LAGOON
12. PORTSIDE ROAD
13. SERVICE ROAD
14. PARKING/SERVICE ZONE

223

Paseo del Lago

Niigata, Japan

The mixed-use private development of Paseo del Lago provides a focal point for the economic expansion of the city of Niigata. Set in a picturesque landscape between the mountains and the sea, the complex caters to Japan's increasing number of seasonal tourists and weekend vacationers, as well as to new, year-'round residents who desire leisure activities close at hand.

Paseo del Lago offers middle-level and luxury housing, an international hotel and conference center, and educational, community, entertainment, and sports facilities in addition to office space and extensive retail space, including two major department stores. While providing the developer with a high percentage of leasable built space, the project also gives the city a large public park by placing much of the retail space, service corridors, parking, and other facilities under a landscaped earth berm.

The complex is organized around a free-form artificial lake, symbolically reflecting the nearby Toyano lagoon, to which it is to be connected by navigable canals. Dotted with islands where rainbows gleam in artificially produced mist and laser beams play at night, this lake, surrogate of the Toyano lagoon, is the jewel-like nucleus of the project.

A circular, two-story commercial arcade opens onto the lake from under the edge of the earth berm. Its sinuous pedestrian walkways provide the stroller with constantly changing vistas. With the clear glass panels of its adjustable curtain wall open in the summer, the arcade is a shaded veranda, integrated with the park like the roofed walkway encircling the courtyard garden of a traditional Japanese house. The glass panels swivel closed during the cold season, forming a winter garden with views of the snowy landscape. The arcade provides direct access to the buildings strung around the lake, making the development's circulation pattern an effective marketing tool for the arcade's shops, restaurants, discotheques, cafés, and cinemas. The arcade also contains services for residents such as grocery stores, dry cleaners, and laundromats.

A department store marks the main entrance to the shopping arcade with a massive ceremonial gateway. A canal, crossed by footbridges and lined with restaurants, cafés, and beer halls, passes through the gateway and the glass-roofed courtyard of the department store into the boardwalk-rimmed lake, where boaters dock at the marina next to the residential building. This long, narrow structure follows the curve of the lake, its apartment facing either the water or the hills behind. The hotel arches between the lake and the lagoon, while the office towers concentrate businesses on one corner of the site, with easy access from the street. Tunnel-like openings in the raised earth berm direct vehicular traffic under the park, preserving its open green vistas.

PARKING   PARK   SHOPPING / AMENITIES   ARCADE OF THE FOUR SEASONS   GARDEN   PARK   LAKE   ISLAND

PARKING   SHOPPING/AMENITIES   PROMENADE ATRIUM OF THE FOUR SEASONS

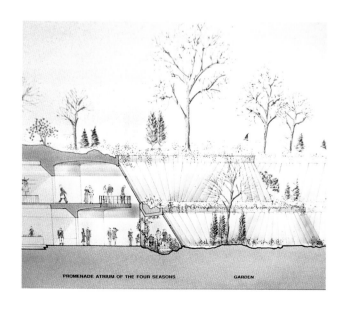

PROMENADE ATRIUM OF THE FOUR SEASONS   GARDEN

226

CANAL TOYANO LAGOON CANAL

HOTEL

HOTEL DROP OFF

HEALTH CLUB

HOTEL SUPPORT FACILITIES

HOTEL DROP OFF

MARINA

CANAL

DEPARTMENT STORE

LUXURY CONDOMINIUMS

WATER AMUSEMENTS

OFFICE BUILDINGS

LUXURY VILLAS

PASEO DEL LAGO SHOPPING ARCADE

CANAL

GOURMET WORLD / FARMERS MARKET

LAKE ENTRY

LAKE CANAL

EXPERIENTIAL AMUSEMENTS

LUXURY VILLAS

1 : 2.500

227

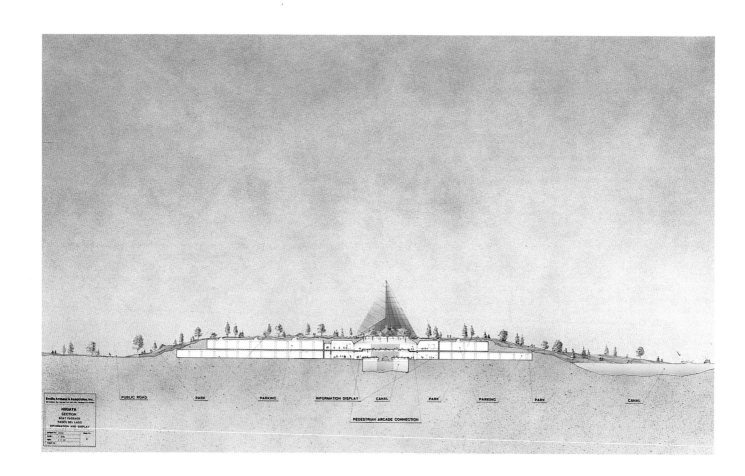

NIIGATA
SECTION
BOAT PASSAGE
PASEO DEL LAGO
INFORMATION AND DISPLAY

PUBLIC ROAD   PARK   PARKING   INFORMATION DISPLAY   CANAL   PARK   PARKING   PARK   CANAL

PEDESTRIAN ARCADE CONNECTION

NIIGATA
SECTION
CONDOMINIUMS, MARINA,
FITNESS CENTER AND HOTEL

CANAL   PARK   LUXURY CONDOMINIUMS   MARINA   CANAL   PARK   HOTEL   WATER TAXI   HOTEL ENTRY   CANAL   TOYANO LAGOON

Emilio Ambasz & Associates, Inc.
NIIGATA
SECTION
AMUSEMENT CENTER
DEPARTMENT STORE

PARK DEPARTMENT STORE ENTRYWAY ARCADE MARINA INTERIOR LAKE PARK NIGHTCLUBS EXPERIMENTAL AMUSEMENT COMPLEX AUDIO-VISUAL HALL

PARKING INTERIOR ATRIUM ARCADE 3-D ENVIRONMENT ZOO

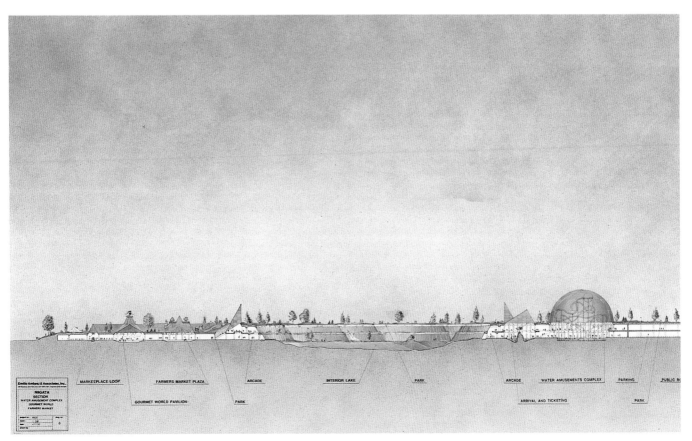

Emilio Ambasz & Associates, Inc.
NIIGATA
SECTION
WATER AMUSEMENT COMPLEX
GOURMET WORLD
FARMERS MARKET

MARKETPLACE LOOP FARMERS MARKET PLAZA ARCADE INTERIOR LAKE PARK ARCADE WATER AMUSEMENTS COMPLEX PARKING PUBLIC RO

GOURMET WORLD PAVILION PARK ARRIVAL AND TICKETING PARK

Marine Resort Community

Shikoku Island, Japan

This marine resort community responds to two current trends in Japanese lifestyle: the growing popularity of water-based leisure activities and a new interest among urban dwellers—who can afford only small apartments in Japan's expensive cities—in acquiring moderately priced vacation homes.

Located on an island-dotted bay in the Seto Inland Sea, this year-round resort is designed to preserve the magnificent beauty of the site for its residents and for visitors to the national park on the mountain overlooking the site. Much of the construction is hidden under landscaped earth berms, while gardens flank the roadways and canals that weave throughout the site.

Intrigued by the existing canal—through which sea water was once flooded onto the land to harvest salt—circumscribing the site, Ambasz appropriated it into his scheme. He then cut a second major canal through the middle of the site and extended the reach of the extant channel with an intricate network of secondary waterways feeding off it. Tidal water, then, establishes the character and outlines the spatial structure of the new community.

The community is organized into two zones. The outer zone is defined by the original perimeter canal and the new arterial canal that laces through the site. This zone is the exclusive domain of privately owned garden villas. The area between the sea and the new canal is a non-residential zone comprising a hotel, shopping area, restaurants, recreational facilities, parks, promenades, and a marina.

Ambasz's design for the residential quarter provides both a maximum level of privacy between villas and contact with nature—this despite the community's density. Villas line the small peninsulas defined by the canals. One side of each residential plot is accessed by a tree-lined roadway; the other faces the water and has its own dock. The single-story villas are hidden by lushly landscaped walls on two of its side walls. The roofs are landscaped too so that when viewed from the surrounding mountains, the community will be hidden beneath a continuous green surface. A swimming pool will be built between each villa and its canal. Landscaped finger-narrow islands in the middle of the canals will screen views between villas that share the same waterfront.

The more public section of the development, comprising a sand beach, is focused around a marina. The marina is anchored on one end with a 200-suite hotel connected to a covered arcade that winds along the length of the boat basin: the arcade will be fronted with retail shopping. The hotel steps back at each floor to create hanging gardens culminating in a roof-terrace. The exterior surface of the building is, therefore, alive and green. The outside surfaces of the other structures in this quarter are also landscaped so that, like the residential community, the shared facilities present a botanical façade when viewed from above.

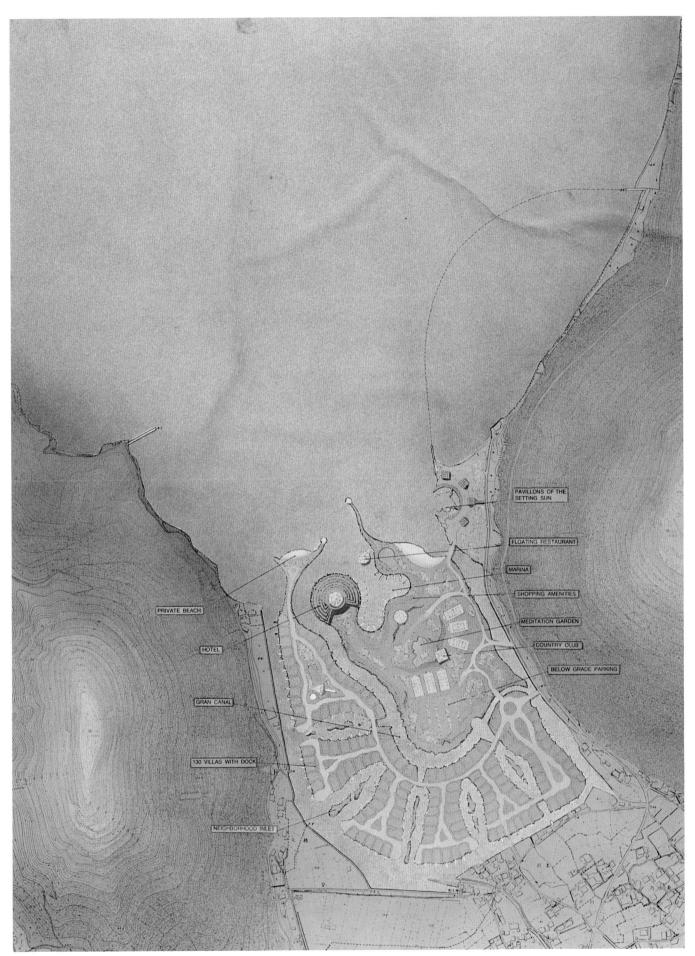

PAVILLONS OF THE SETTING SUN

FLOATING RESTAURANT

MARINA

SHOPPING AMENITIES

MEDITATION GARDEN

COUNTRY CLUB

BELOW GRADE PARKING

PRIVATE BEACH

HOTEL

GRAN CANAL

130 VILLAS WITH DOCK

NEIGHBORHOOD INLET

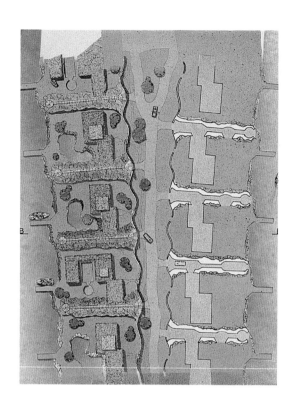

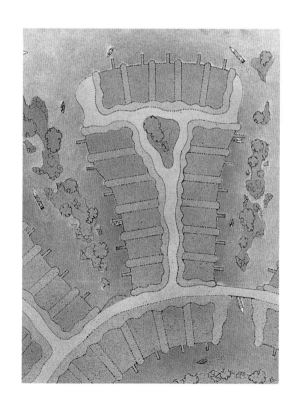

NEIGHBORHOOD INLET

MEDIAN GARDEN

10   30
0   20   40   50

SECTION AA

PENINSULAR ROAD

VILLA   POOL

0   5   10   20

SECTION BB

REALWORLD THEME PARK

BARCELONA, SPAIN

No longer believing that a modern theme park should be restricted to themes of adolescent nostalgia and childhood cartoons, a group of artists, musicians, filmmakers, and psychologists, spearheaded by Peter Gabriel, together with Brian Eno and Laurie Anderson, conceived of a new theme park for the modern age emphasizing contemporary wisdom, technology, and delight. Based on notions of innovation and excitement through the infinite promise of today's technology without reference to past traditions, this theme park was appropriately christened Realworld, and a site was identified in Barcelona.

Selected as the designer whose work most exemplifies these innovative ideals, Ambasz was confronted with the immediate challenge of conceiving an image for the building without reference to the past. Simultaneously, he was faced with the task of designing a new facility immediately recognizable as an international symbol of technological advancement and refreshing ideas upon a site located in a dense, unattractive industrial part of the city. When visitors approach this new building, it will be unlike any structure they have seen before. Conceived in the form of a great mountain plateau of stone and verdant landscape, it rises above the backdrop of surrounding buildings. A glass pyramid and a great revolving wheel stand sentinel upon the top. Within the heart of this man-made landscape lie the fascinating possibilities of high technology.

Leaving the outside world they have always known, visitors enter a tunnel in the mountain, a sensory transition space which removes them from the artifacts of the outer world and transports them toward a new world beyond. Stepping outdoors into the beckoning light at the center of a very large, light-filled crater, and one discovers two swirling, vaporous tornados, that form a natural living gateway to the beyond. No longer are the bleak buildings of the surrounding neighborhood visible. All that can be seen is a garden paradise of another world framing the blue of the sky above. A stream of water—Living River—begins at the top of the crater and carries each visitor downward, circling the sloping sides toward an ultimate sea of green. Along the way are ever-changing exhibits and chambers of exploration called Intelligent Maze, Big Noise, Garden of Delights, and Otherworld.

Nature is used by Ambasz as the containing vessel. Technology in this project is defined not with modern structure, but with its genesis, the primal earth. Each visitor is transported into a realm of the unknown, where each new image denies a preconception and evokes a new real world.

234

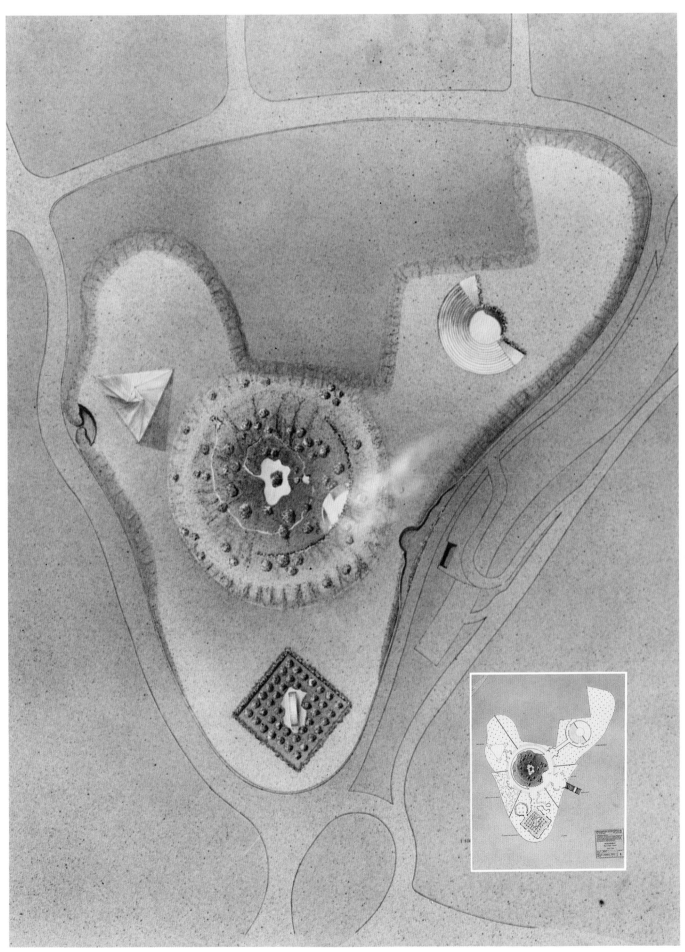

235

Rimini Seaside Development

Rimini, Italy

Located along the northeast coast of Italy, the town of Rimini was once known as an inviting and renowned beach resort. The city has proposed to recover the myth of Rimini, not only as an elegant seaside resort, but more importantly as a destination for year-round visitors, using the redesign of fourteen kilometers of beachfront as the locomotive to promote the rebirth of Rimini.

The project is conceived in two distinct parts. The first part is referred to as the Green Dune, consisting of a garden promenade stretching along the entire beachfront, connecting the beach and the town with a public park. The second part consists of a system of several piers which will help bring the activities of the town across the sea.

In the first part of the project, the Green Dune, the entire beachfront is turned into a shaded garden promenade containing freshwater pools, bars, and cafés, water parks, and other beach-related services. These services are designed to operate around the clock during all four seasons. The garden promenade is raised above the beach level in order to buffer the beach from the town, giving privacy and protection to the beach and offering unobstructed views of the sea.

The beach itself is accessed through the gentle ramps, extending like fingers out from the Green Dune, linking the beach, garden, and city, and providing private areas for beach-related functions and services. These functions and service areas are housed in the structures located under the seaward edge of the garden promenade, and are visible and accessible only from the beach.

The proposed second part of the project consisting of piers will give a new and different dimension to the merits of the Green Dune. It will provide a view of the city and its hilly background from the sea, a view enhanced by the green frame of the garden promenade in the foreground. These piers are located in such a manner that they link and continue the important avenues of the town with areas along the beach. Attached to the piers will be floating pavilions for use during the milder seasons of the year, and then removed to winter headquarters. These are also temporary structures that will serve as additional concessions, including bars, cafés, pools, and water slides, as well as sunning platforms and other forms of enjoyment.

This design seeks to transform the beachfront into a day-round, four-season event. It represents a restoration of a long-standing beach resort tradition, but is postulated in a new, imaginative way, respectful of present concerns for the environment, healthier ways of vacationing; most importantly, it will serve as the catalytic device that is intended to trigger the rebirth of a newly prosperous Rimini.

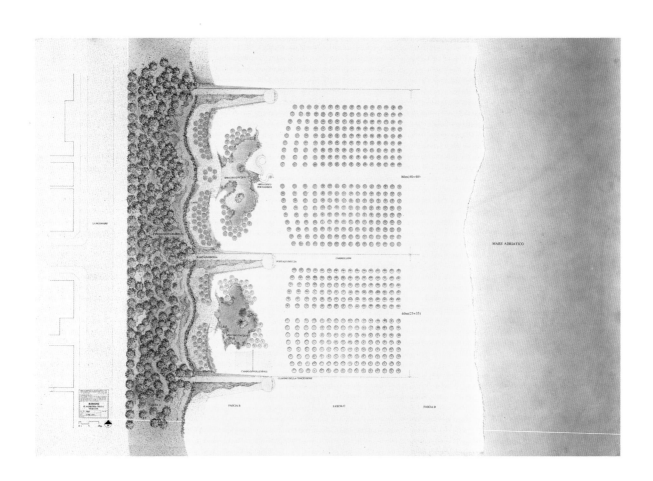

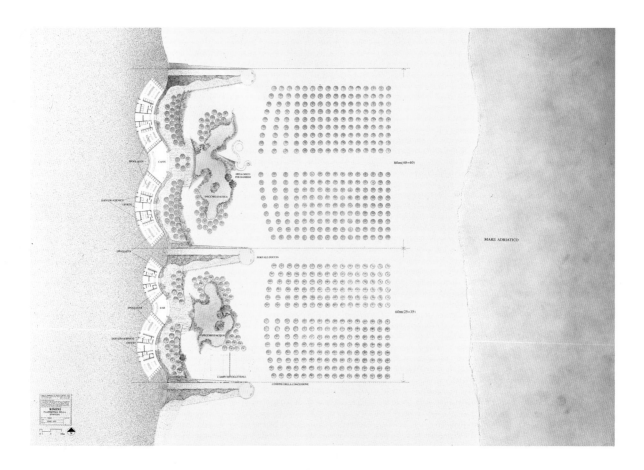

240

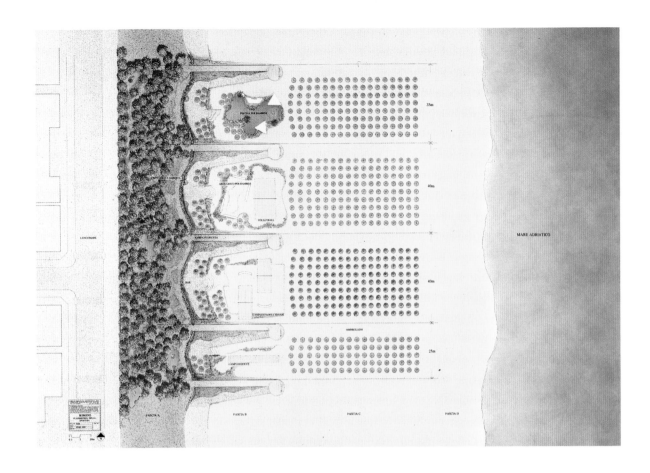

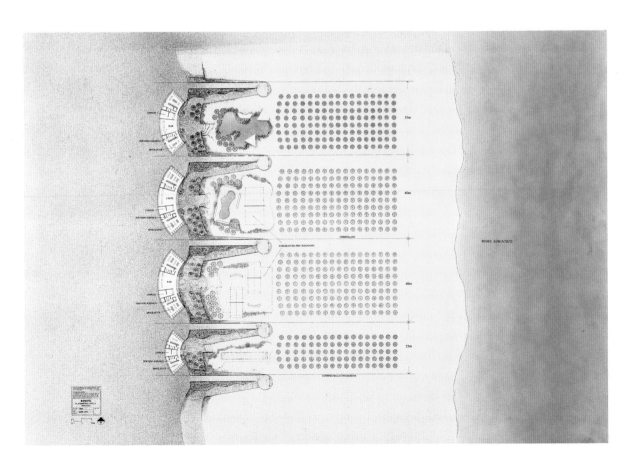

CONDIZIONE ESISTENTE DELLA SPIAGGIA

SCHEMA DELLA PROPOSTA

RIMINI
SEZIONE DELLA
SPIAGGIA

0   2.5   5M

245

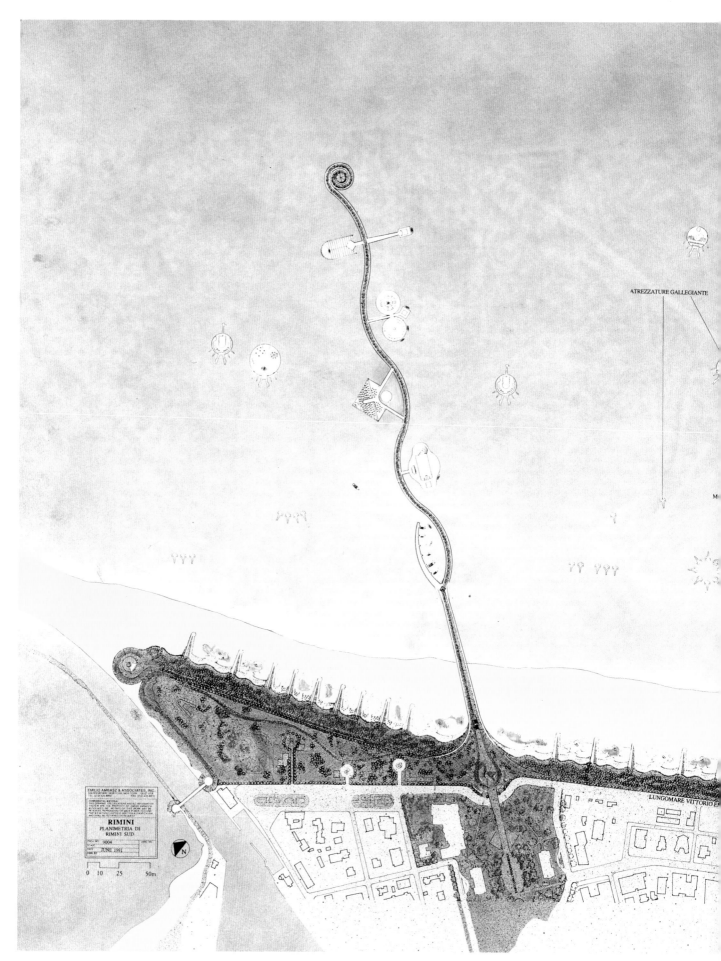

ATREZZATURE GALLEGIANTE

LUNGOMARE VITTORIO E

EMILIO AMBASZ & ASSOCIATES, INC.

RIMINI
PLANIMETRIA DI
RIMINI SUD

9004

JUNE 1991

0   10   25   50m

N

LEGGIANTE
I SVAGO

PASSEGGIATA ALBERATA
TRA L'ARCO DI AUGUSTO
ED IL LUNGOMARE

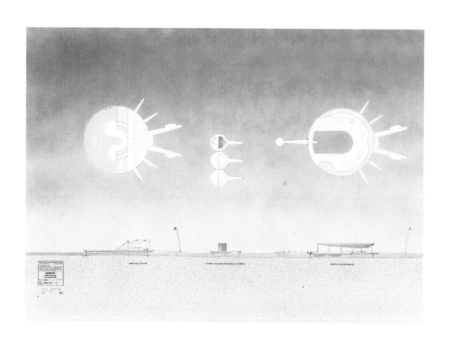

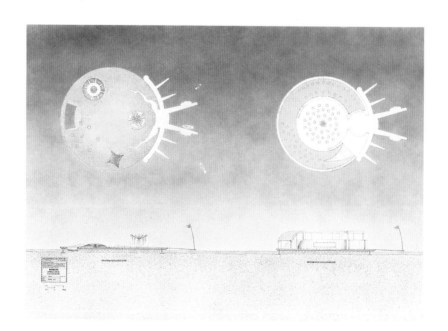

248

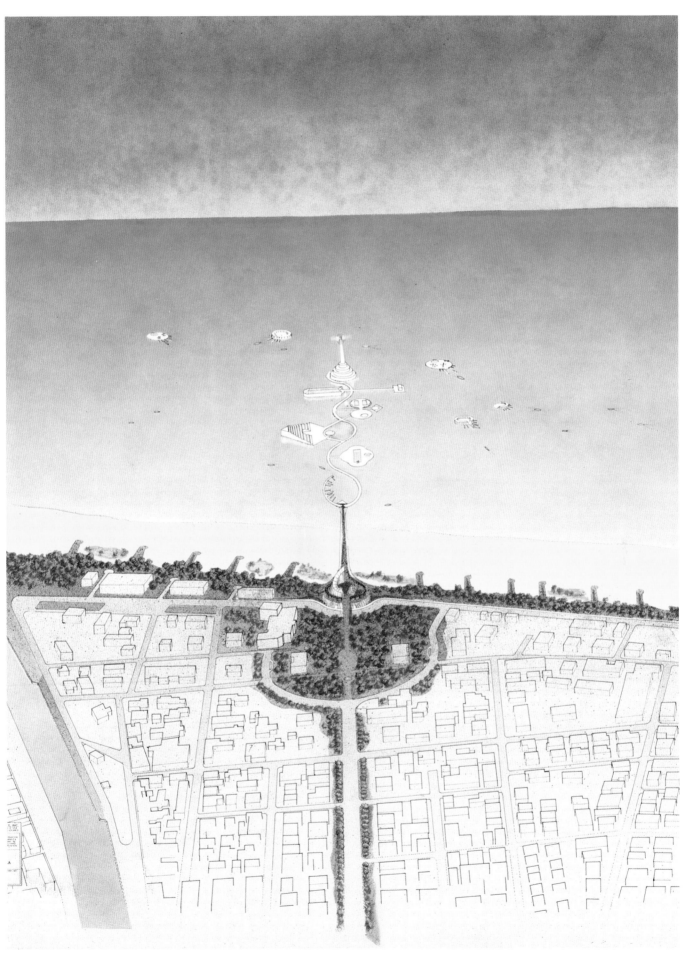

FOCCHI SHOPPING CENTER

RIMINI, ITALY

The Focchi Shopping Center is an adaptive reuse project that transforms a former curtain-wall factory into a core of commercial, cultural, and public spaces for a growing urban center. The plan integrates the old and new elements, preserving the character of the original buildings while proposing the shopping center as an urban garden.

The existing building is formed by three contiguous concrete barrel vaults. The new plan adds a shorter barrel vault to either side to increase square footage for the one-story structure. A superstructure of mesh planted with ivy partially covers the building, enlivening the raw concrete and helping to cool the interior. Raised several inches above the surface, the mesh leaves portions of the vaults exposed, visually unifying the old and new sections while retaining a clear distinction between the decorative and structural portions of the building. The mesh extends in free-form curves beyond the ends of the vaults and arches along the sides to form translucent verandas that echo the barrel vault form. Like a cornice, the mesh completes the simple façades and surrounds them with a welcoming pool of shade.

Six ribs of the central vault were removed to create a garden courtyard. Ringed with a walkway that links the shops, cafés, and other spaces, the verdant courtyard provides daylight and air to the interior while serving as a symbolic and organizational focal point for the project.

A trellis wall defines the perimeter of the site and encloses the open-air parking that surrounds the building. Planted with four varieties of flowering ivy that bloom in succession throughout the year, this vertical garden is watered by mist generated at its base. The trellis is punctuated by a monumental entrance gateway whose arched, convex form ties it formally to the barrel vaults within. A smaller gate at the back serves as an exit and a service access. Like the walls enclosing medieval Italian cities, the vertical garden hides the building from without, allowing visitors a sense of discovery upon entry.

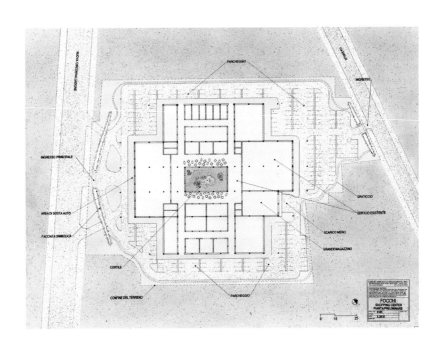

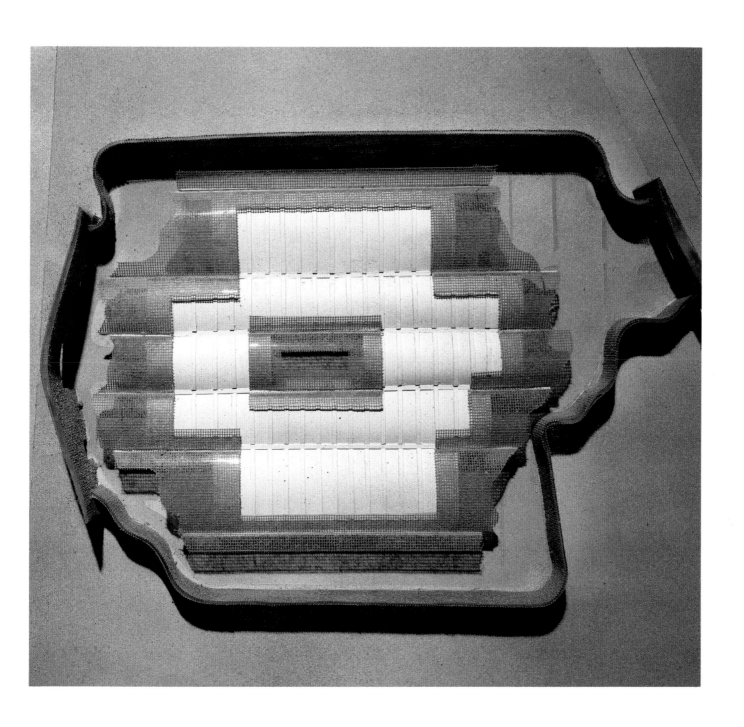

FACCIATA SIMBOLICA   AREA DI SOSTA AUTO   CORTILE   AREA DI SOSTA AUTO   INGRESSO

TETTOIA COPERTA   INGRESSO   GRATICCIO

FOCCHI
SHOPPING CENTER
SEZIONE AA

PRIVATE ESTATE

MONTANA, USA

After acquiring a breathtaking 1,400-acre site along a secluded river valley surrounded only by natural wilderness, a couple commissioned Ambasz to create a complex of three larger buildings to house their family, the caretaker, and a highly regarded private collection of contemporary painting and sculpture. A smaller fourth building of this complex is a meditation pavilion, set upon a steep mountainside high above the main house.

The family believed that the structures should have minimal visual impact upon the natural environment, while reflecting their instinctual love of classical architecture. With these almost antithetical constraints in mind, Ambasz developed a dynamic solution quite distinct from his previous work, yet evolving in a clear, natural progression from the unique architectural vocabulary he has established. Like buildings which have now come to symbolize the traditional historic American Western town, each façade plane extends well above and beyond the volume of the building which it masks from view. The only major visual element is the façade. The natural landscape appears to flow down the hillside, enveloping each building mass, leaving only these bold façades exposed. The structures read as natural outgrowths of the landscape itself, carved within and enfolded by the existing wilderness, architecturally defined only by the façades.

Two miles after entering the gateway of the property, the first building observed is the caretaker's house. The ivy-covered trellis façade tilts forward to rest like a sturdy A-frame upon a leaning colonnade of rustic bare logs, a clear reference to the classical articulation sought by the client, yet employing almost a primeval vocabulary springing from the forest itself. As a bold statement that the form of this building was in truth guided by something far beyond the natural wilderness, each log is capped with a gilded capital and the façade itself terminates in a matching cornice of bronze, to capture the lingering reflections of the setting sun.

Ambasz has created a dynamic sequence of discovery in the siting of his four buildings. Passing the caretaker's house, the next building to appear is the main residence. This building curves boldly inward to define a welcoming "cour d'honneur" sitting on a natural plinth well above the roadway. Once inside at a higher level, the visitor then perceives the art gallery set in a quiet meadow across a pond. This art gallery is only accessible on foot and its façade, composed of similar elements as the previous two buildings, now curves gently outward. Only from within the art gallery can visitors finally discover the fourth building of the complex, the meditation pavilion perched enigmatically in the forest high above the main house.

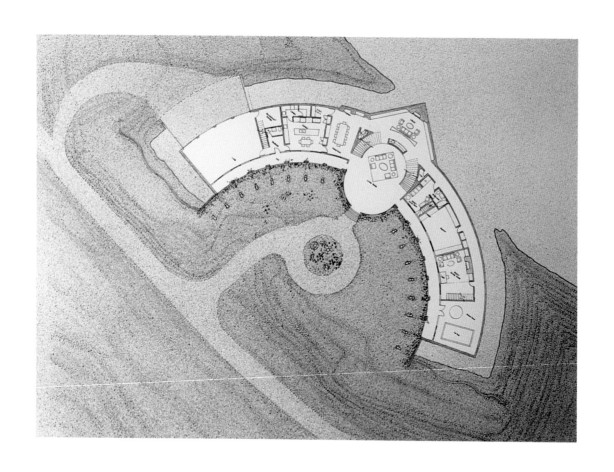

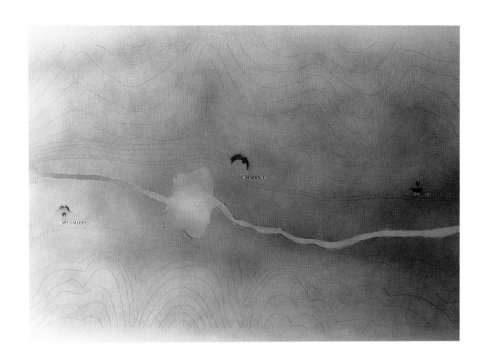

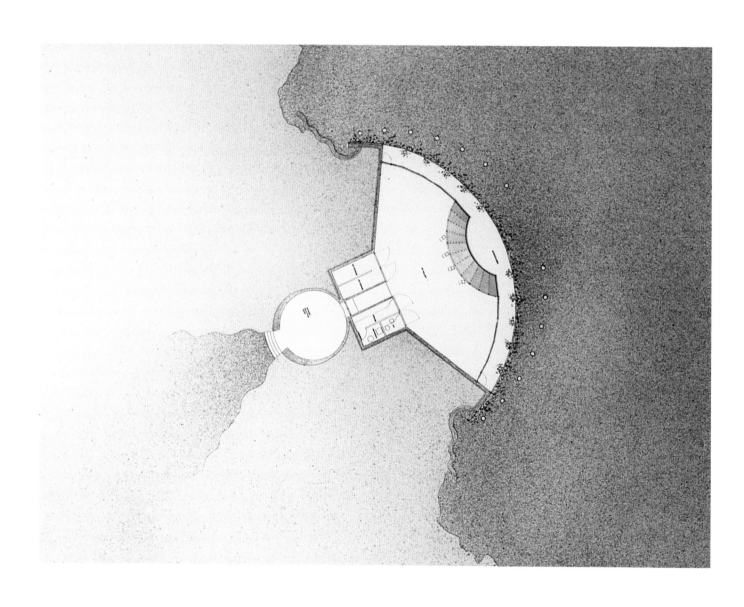

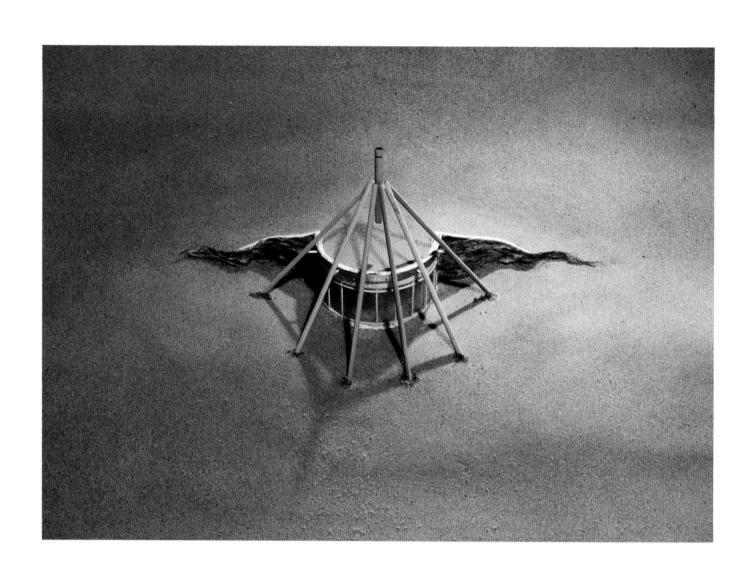

CASA CANALES

MONTERREY, MEXICO

Monterrey, the industrial urban center of Mexico, is located in a dry but very warm valley flanked on either side by steep, rugged mountains. Deciding to relocate away from the city's congestion, a prominent local family wanted to create their new residence on a secluded mountain property overlooking the peaks surrounding Monterrey. This rugged site for the new house is quite steep with no single area wide enough to support the entire house or approaching roadway, and exposed to intense direct sun throughout the year. One of the main design tasks was, therefore, to provide protection from the heat and sunlight, while still retaining the spectacular views afforded by the property.

The long driveway up to the site became an important linear element defining the edge of the mountainside. Soon after entering the property, this symbolic edge is emphasized by the appearance of an elongated porte cochere of open timber slats. Visitors stop beneath its shade to discover what lies below. From here visitors perceive a triangular, edgeless plane of seemingly weightless cool aquamarine water, appearing to hover in space and contained only by the blue sky reflected within. Seemingly cantilevered far out over the mountainside, this triangle of water is in fact both a reflecting pool filled with a thin layer of water to the brim and the house's actual water-cooled roof. A templelike observation pavilion hovers at the furthest corner of the pool, beckoning visitors across the water to a place of refuge seemingly supported by the very sky itself. Like an ethereal portal leading into a submersed world within the waters themselves, a monumental set of stone steps penetrates the pool, leading enigmatically into cool, shaded areas below.

The house is sited immediately below the reflecting pool, seeming to emerge from the stone of the mountainside in successive, overlapping layers of open lattice walls, colonnades, and full-height glass. Responding to the same climactic factors influencing much of the traditional Hispano-Moorish colonial architecture of Mexico, these overlapping wall layers are perforated in intricate geometric patterns which allow cross ventilation to filter softly through in rich overlapping patterns of light and shadow. Every window bay on each floor is designed as a full-height French door, allowing each room to open completely onto terraces and balconies to the outdoors, capturing the natural breezes.

Perhaps the most composed of Ambasz's recent projects, this one shares with his other earth-protected houses the distinctive feature of also being "invisible." This residence—with its intricately constructed façade— will be seen, by virtue of its siting, neither by neighbors nor valley residents below. *Solo aves y, quizás, ángeles. Oxála.*

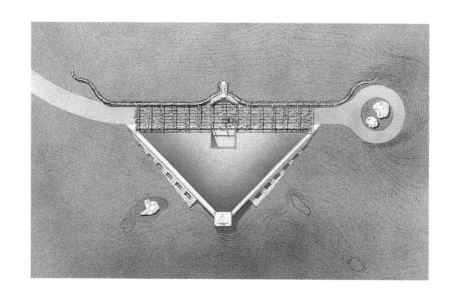

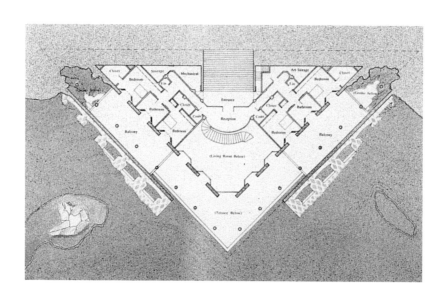

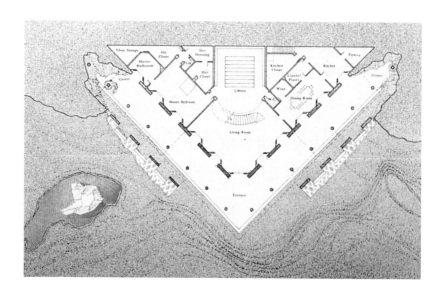

Industrial Design
1988-1991

Handkerchief Television

Soft Notebook Computer

Portable Radio / Cassette Player

Mid-Range Engine Series

Knoll Extra Desk Set Collection

Qualis Office Seating

Aqua Dove Water Bottle

Vertair Office Seating

Oseris Spotlight Components

Janus Wristwatch Collection

Telescopic Luggage

Wall Coverings

Flexiboll Pen

Manual Toothbrushes

Periodent Electric Gum Massager

The miniaturization of technology has led to the increasing portability of televisions, computers, cassette tape players, and other commonly used products, but the forms and materials of these products have not fundamentally altered to reflect this technological development. The Soft Series dispenses with the hard shells that typically encase these products. Like zoological species, the Soft Series products are enfolded in a padded nylon or leather skin that conforms to the shape of the human body and gives tactile pleasure to the hand. Small enough to fit in a shirt or jacket pocket, or to rest comfortably on the hip, these products become an extension of the user.

HANDKERCHIEF TV. This TV benefits from the development of flat-screen technology. In the form of a folded leather handkerchief, the object reveals its technological function when unfolded. The opened TV has four planes, each with a distinct function: screen, antenna, battery/speaker and external ports. While the component cases are made of injection-molded polycarbonate, the supple housing is made of sewn leather with foam padding.

SOFT NOTEBOOK COMPUTER. The traditional paper notebook guided the design of this user-friendly notebook computer. Opening the first flap reveals the soft tactile rubber keypad and the thin LCD display screen. Like an easel, the screen is adjusted for viewing with a velcro tab. Opening the unit further reveals storage for diskettes, pockets for paper and business cards, and a pen for using the computer as an electronic sketch pad. Flipping the screen onto its back allows it to be used as a clipboard on the lap. Like a fine notebook, the computer is covered with foam-padded leather to give it a formal elegance and tactility and provide protection for electronic components.

SOFT PORTABLE RADIO/CASSETTE PLAYER. The mechanical and electronic components of this completely flexible object are fixed into place for functioning by the introduction of the traditional, rigid-shelled tape cassette. These components are protected by a padded leather skin. The radio functions with or without a cassette in place.

MID-RANGE ENGINE SERIES, CUMMINS ENGINE CO. INDIANA, USA (PAGE 296)

This family of five mid-range diesel engines, ranging from four- to nine-liter sizes, was developed for automotive, industrial, and marine applications. The engines' high level of component integration, commonality of parts within the engine family, and modularity of engine systems and components, lowers the number of parts necessary to tool and manufacture, resulting in improved quality-control and cost-efficiency, a reduced parts inventory and a shorter maintenance training time.

The engine's clean, uncluttered aesthetic, made possible by internalizing previously external components, suggests the engine's power and strength. Its charcoal gray color emphasizes its ruggedness and unique design qualities while hiding production imperfections. A specially mixed dark blue and black color, complemented with red accents, differentiates the top end model. To further streamline production, the engine's gully integrated electronic monitoring and guidance systems are produced on an advanced variable production line, instead of by the traditional dedicated mechanical process.

KNOLLEXTRA DESK SET COLLECTION, KNOLL, USA (PAGE 298)

This collection of accessories, including a letter tray, a calendar, a note pad/pencil holder, a memo holder, and a wastebasket, is designed to organize the home or office desk-top and to offer a strong emotional presence for personalizing the individual workspace within the context of a standardized office environment. While serving unique functional requirements, the pieces are united in form and spirit by a gently curved plane evoking paper and its flow through the workspace. This curve confers a visual identity to a usually anonymous product, allowing the desk top to be treated as a sculptural field. Functionally, the curve directs the paper to the rear of the letter tray, preventing it from sliding out, and lifts the paper's edge, facilitating its removal from the tray. To combines front and side loading in one object, the letter tray stacks by means of a molded locking mechanism that leaves the front and one side open.

Injection-molded of polystyrene for low cost, the pieces are finished with an applied accent color and with juxtaposed matte and glossy surfaces that provide an upscale, nonplastic feel and visual and tactile interest.

QUALIS OFFICE SEATING, TECNO, ITALY (PAGE 302)

This is a completely automatic, ergonomically conceived line of office seating, ranging from seating for computer operators to seating for top management. While highly advanced, the chair's technology is underplayed in favor of celebrating its aesthetic and symbolic qualities, creating a soft-tech, upscale look in a highly mechanized chair. The chair features colorful upholstery that can be mixed and matched on a single chair and unzipped and washed or replaced, resulting in adaptability to changing decor, a longer life per chair, and lower costs for the user.

The chair's design relies on advanced electro-welding techniques adapted from the automobile industry, providing standard office chair functioning at low cost. The self-adjusting tilt-forward aids blood circulation in the thighs, and the high backrest hinge point enhances back support.

AQUA DOVE WATER BOTTLE, FRANCE (PAGE 306)

The form of this water bottle for pure mineral water suggests a dove, symbol of purity. Made of clear plastic, the bottle doubles as an elegant pitcher for the dinner table, lying either lengthwise or standing on end for varied visual effects. Its narrow beak, with a snap-off cap, serves as a pouring spout. Distinguished by their flowing, asymmetrical form from the traditional cylindrical bottles of competing brands of mineral water, Aqua Dove bottles can be arranged together in a number of attractive patterns on store shelves.

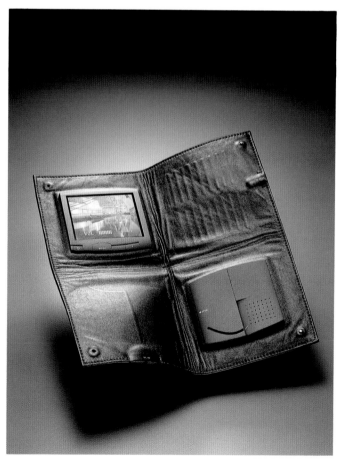

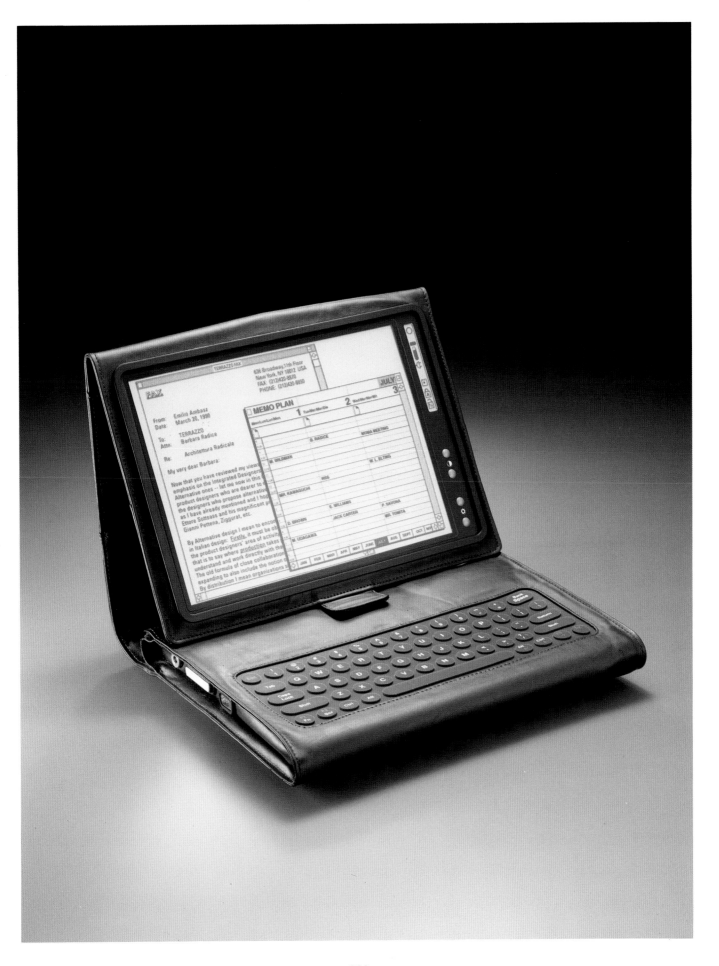

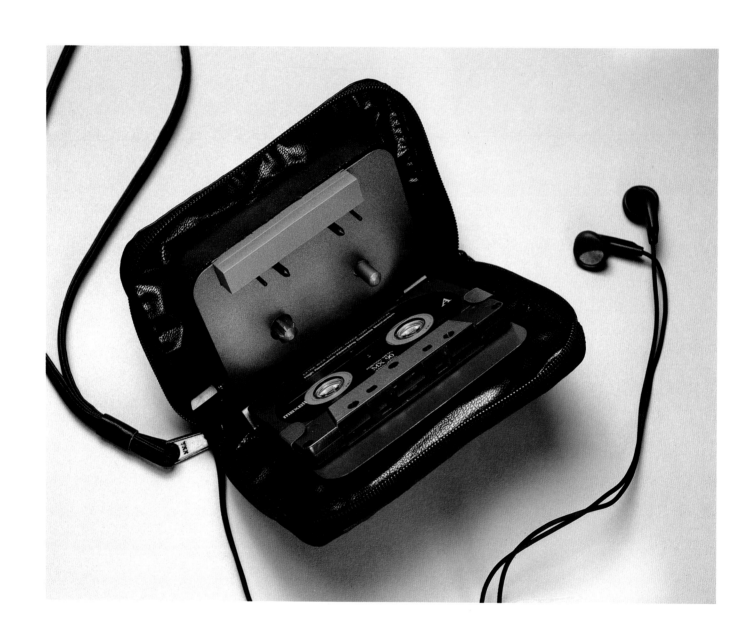

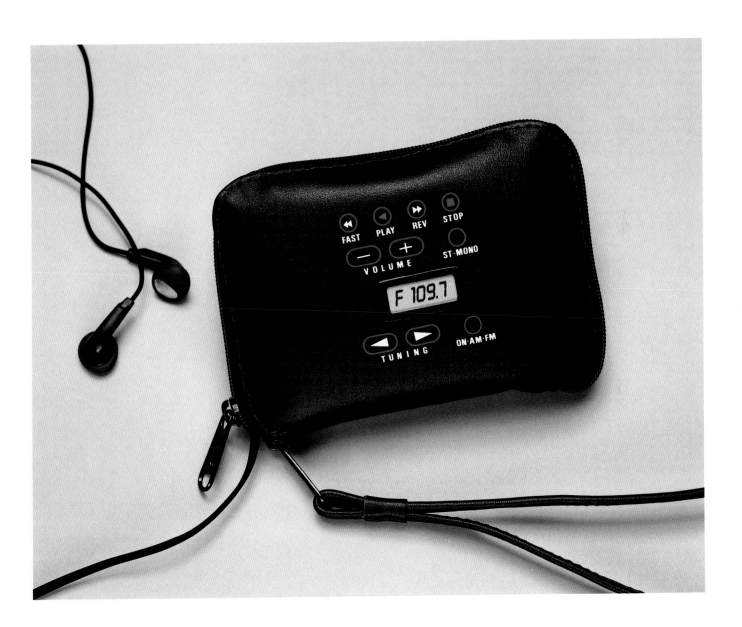

298

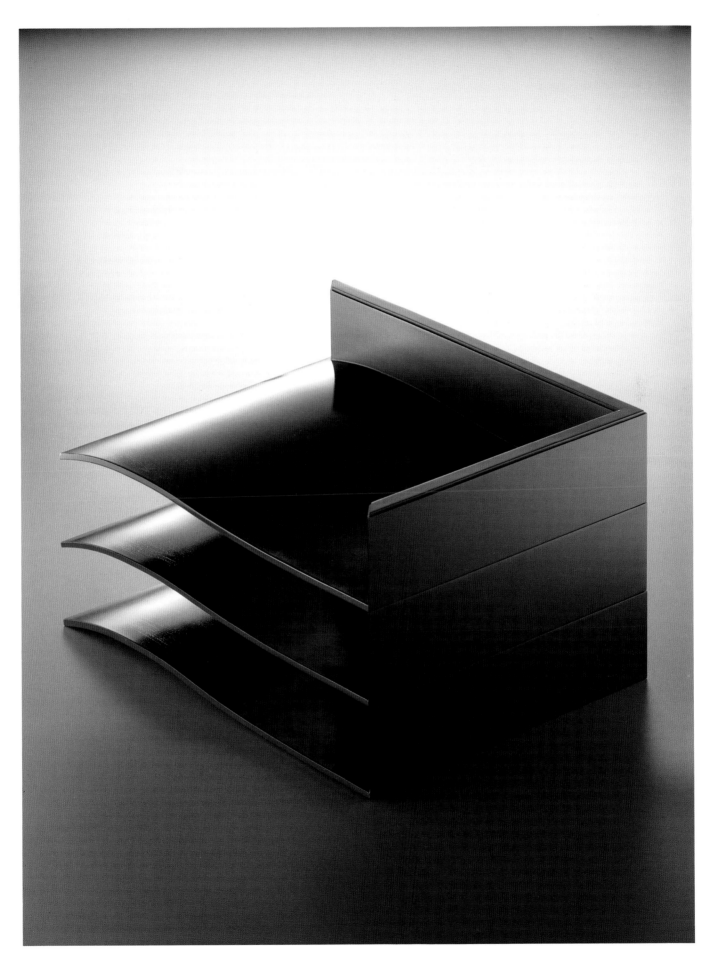

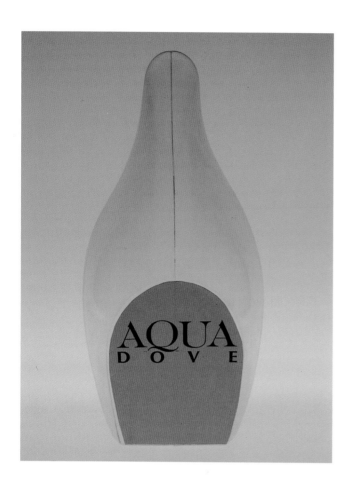

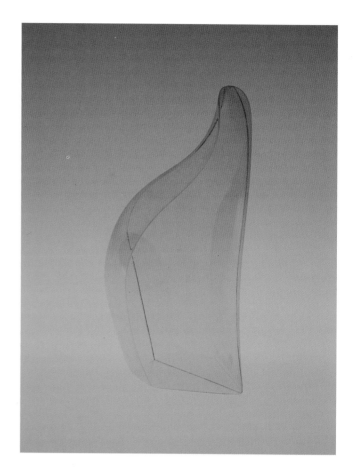

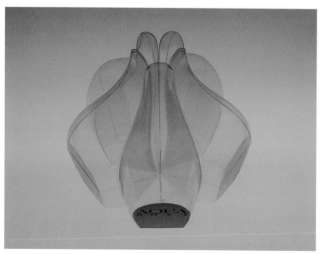

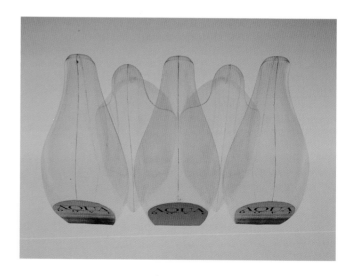

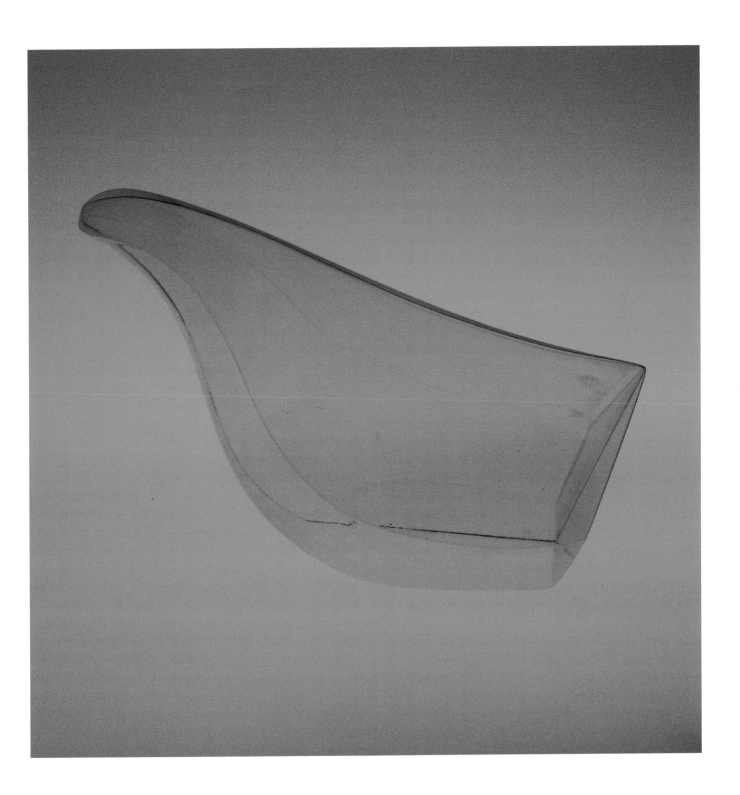

310

311

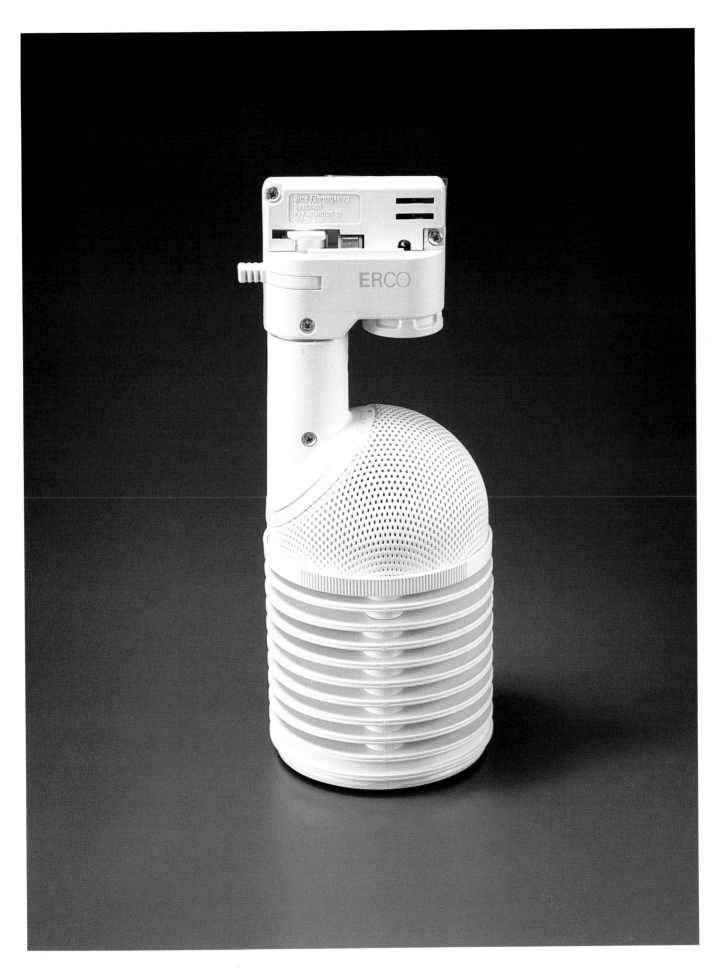

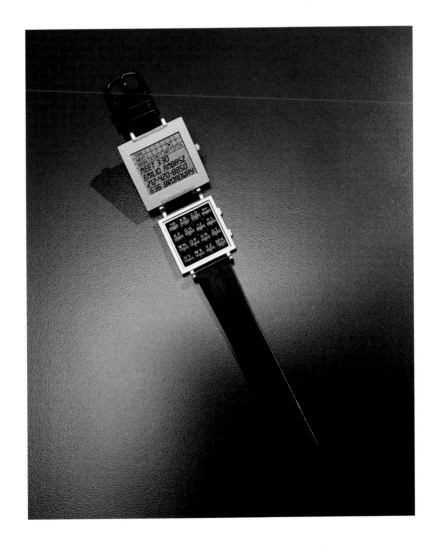

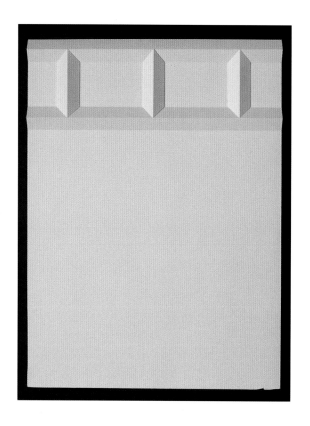

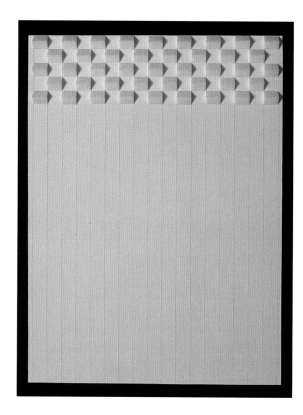

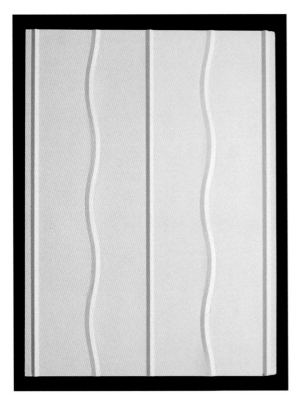

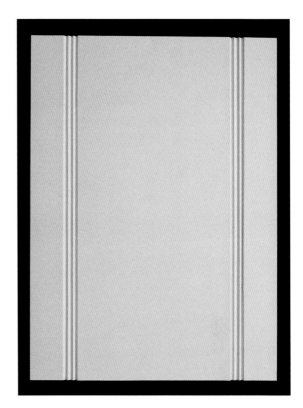

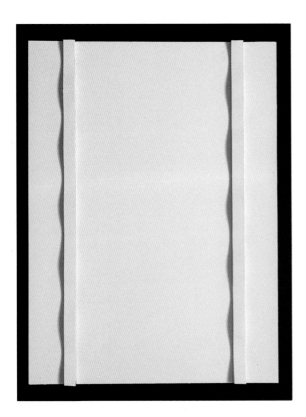

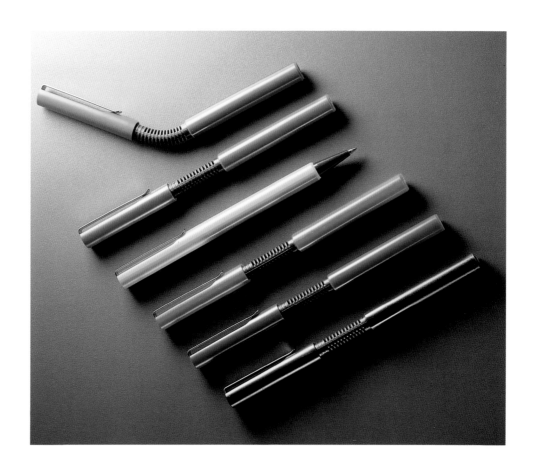

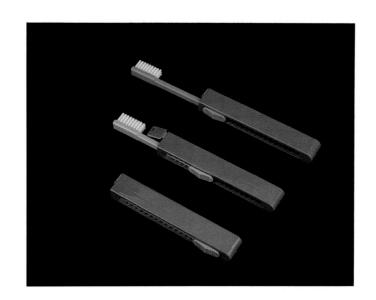

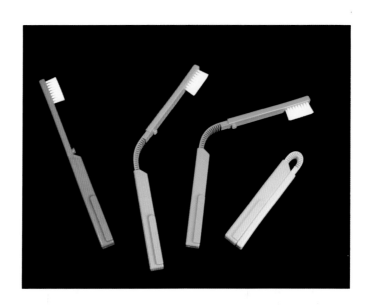

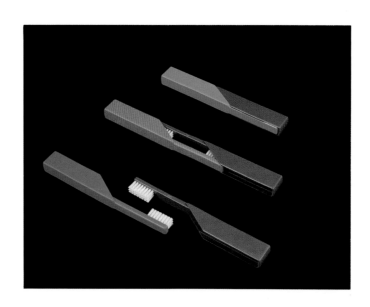

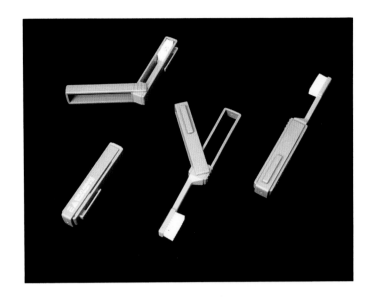

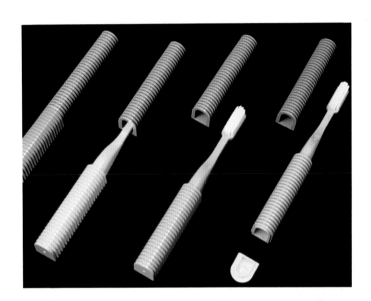

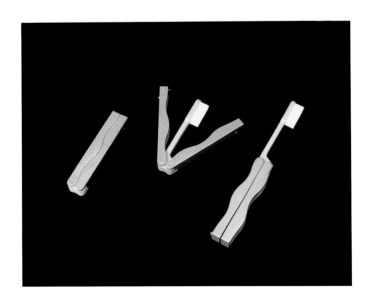

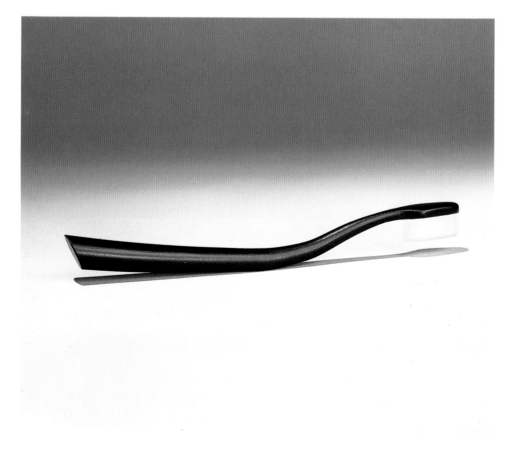

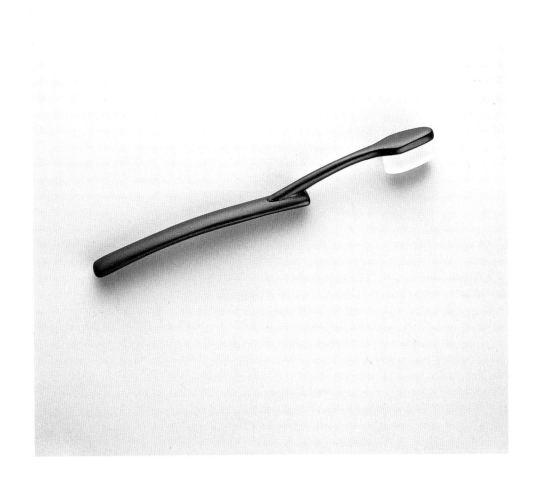

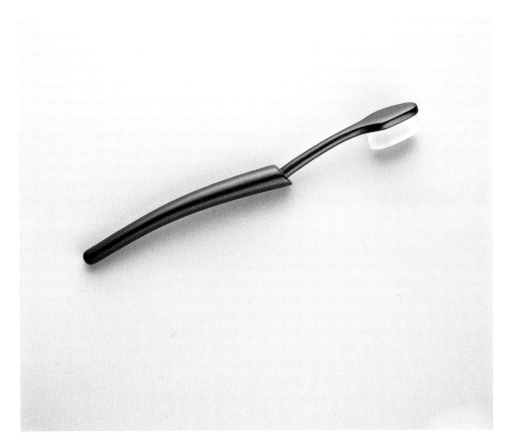

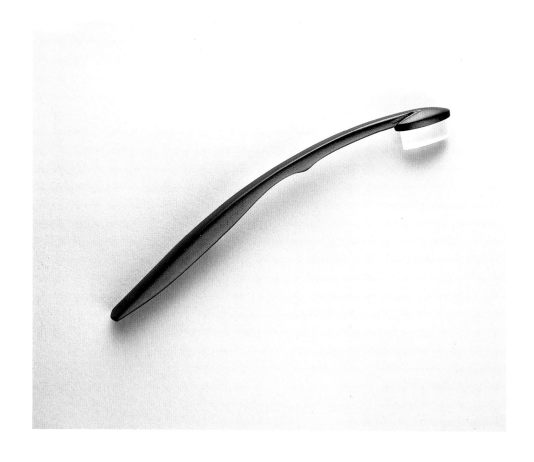

327

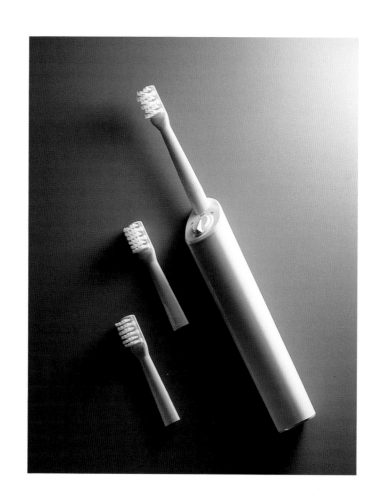

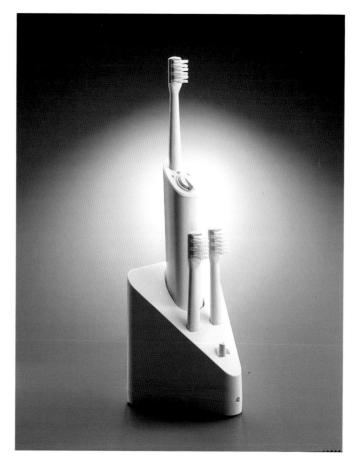

328

The Vertair is an articulated office chair that conforms automatically to the body's changing posture. Its back moves downward as its seat moves forward, retaining a constant flexing point in relation to the body. The chair is covered with a patented upholstery system, made of narrow, overlapping bands of leather stitched to elastic bands that formally express the chair's flexibility. The system stretches with the user's movements and allows the chair's surface to breathe for greater seating comfort. Employing leather, steel, textiles, and a minimum of plastics, this industrially produced chair combines a high-end, soft-tech look with high-tech performance at low cost.

OSERIS 12V/50W SPOTLIGHT, ERCO LEUCHTEN, GERMANY (PAGE 312)

A lighting system for the institutional and contract lighting fields, the Oseris Spotlight was first introduced in 1982. Its system of rotating circular planes, calibrated with printed scales on the light fixture, and its 360-degree rotation on the vertical axis provided optimum illumination for museums, galleries, and other spaces demanding precise lighting. Introduced in 1990, the new version incorporates advances in electronics allowing the lamp and the electronic transformer to join. The new miniature transformer fits inside the hemispherical housing, which has been extended due to the heat sensitivity of the transformer and to accommodate the reflector and lamp holder. New heat-dissipation ribs accommodate the high heat emission of the energy-saving low voltage, high wattage coolbeam lamps. Incorporating the transformer into the housing reduces the overall number of parts necessary for installation, making the system more cost competitive. The longer housing also accommodates lighting accessories such as colored gels and screens which increase the spotlight's range of uses.

JANUS COMPUTER WRISTWATCH COLLECTION, ALESSI, ITALY (PAGE 314)

This collection combines the formal characteristics and emotional and symbolic appeal of a fine wristwatch with the efficient functions of a built-in computer for memos, phone numbers, addresses, and calculating. The design enhances the computer's functionality compared to existing models by greatly enlarging the screen and keyboard. The keypads are large enough to be punched with the fingers, as opposed to a pen tip.

In two models with traditional mechanical analog hands, the hidden computer is revealed by flipping open the watchface. Revealing the computing functions in this manner not only allows for the separation of the watch's two distinct functions, but allows the form of each to express its functional and symbolic requirements.

TELESCOPING LUGGAGE, AJIOKA, JAPAN (PAGE 316)

This product allows the traveler to accumulate objects much as he accumulates memories during a journey. Like an accordion, the hard plastic, leather-covered panels forming the front and back of the suitcase are attached to soft rubber accordion side panels. These soft panels expand or contract according to the contents of the suitcase, while inner tabs lock them at the desired width. The system eliminates the need to purchase an extra piece of luggage to accommodate newly acquired items for the return trip home.

Wall Coverings, Sunstar Engineering, Japan (page 318)

Made of dyed PVC film whose smooth matte finish can be made to resemble fine-grained leather, these four-foot-by-eight-foot cushioned panels are articulated with three-dimensional patterns. The soft support padding provides a pleasing tactility while the raised patterns of straight or sinuous lines, cubes, or triangles cast shadows and provide varied textures, restoring depth and richness to walls too often relegated to banal, background roles in modern architecture. The panels also incorporate moldings for borders, and come in a variety of colors.

Flexiboll Ballpoint Pen, Pentel, Japan (page 320)

Designed for schoolchildren, this brightly colored ballpoint pen conforms to the human anatomy. In between two rigid portions, one containing the nib and the other a pocket clip, is a ribbed portion that flexes with the body's movement when placed in a back pocket, avoiding the breakage and ink leaks associated with the traditional rigid pen. Twisting the lower housing snaps it upwards to meet the upper housing, enclosing the flexible portion in a rigid shell for optimum grasping, and exposing the pen nib. The ink runs in a flexible plastic tube through the length of the pen.

Manual Toothbrushes (page 322)

Designed for the Japanese market where toothbrushes are popular items, reflect current trends in personal oral hygiene and utilize advances in brush and bristle design while offering variety and portablity to a youthful market. Each molded polypropylene toothbrush responds to different functional concerns, while the playful forms and bright colors unify the product line. The covers of two travel models swing open to form handles, while the brush of a woman's purse-sized model slides out of its handle. A pair of toothbrushes for a couple nestle together when closed and pull apart for use. They share the same geometry, but have differentiating details. Another toothbrush changes the angle of its head to conform to the tooth surface.

"Periodent" Electric Gum Massager and Toothbrush, Sunstar, Japan (page 328)

This motorized tooth cleaner and gum massager improves on traditional models with dual-action bristle heads. A miniature electric motor activates a crank shaft which, like the pistons in an engine, lowers and raises alternate rows of bristles engaged in a counter swinging motion, simultaneously lifting the gums where they meet the teeth and cleaning the teeth underneath. This counter swinging motion massages the gums, removes plaque, and helps fight gum disease. The up and down motion of the bristles avoids damage to the tooth enamel by following its vertical grain, while the smooth, bulbous head of each bristle improves on the traditional roughly cut blade. The design reduces the unpleasant vibration typical of electric toothbrushes, while the handle's small size and rounded triangular shape make it easy to grasp for children and the aged. Pastel colors incorporated into the brush enhance the unit's appeal for children.

331

REFERENCES

BIOGRAPHY

EXHIBITIONS ON EMILIO AMBASZ

PUBLICATIONS ON EMILIO AMBASZ

PUBLICATIONS BY EMILIO AMBASZ

PHOTO CREDITS

PROJECT CREDITS

PROJECT INDEX

EMILIO AMBASZ

Emilio Ambasz, born in 1943 in Argentina, studied at Princeton University. He completed the undergraduate program in one year and earned, the next year, a Master's Degree in Architecture from the same institution. He served as Curator of Design at the Museum of Modern Art, in New York (1970-1976) where he directed and installed numerous influential exhibits on architecture and industrial design, among them "Italy: The New Domestic Landscape," in 1972; "The Architecture of Luis Barragán," in 1974; and "The Taxi Project," in 1976.

Mr. Ambasz was the two-term President of the Architectural League (1981-1985). He taught at Princeton University's School of Architecture, was visiting professor at the Hochschule für Gestaltung in Ulm, Germany, and has lectured at many important American Universities.

Mr. Ambasz's large number of prestigious projects include the Mycal Sanda Cultural Center in Japan, the Museum of American Folk Art in New York City; and an innovative design of the Conservatory at the San Antonio Botanical Center, Texas, which was inaugurated in 1988. Among his award winning projects are the Grand Rapids Art Museum in Michigan, winner of a 1976 *Progressive Architecture Award*; a house for a couple in Cordoba, Spain, winner of a 1980 *Progressive Architecture Award*; and for the Conservatory at the San Antonio Botanical Center in Texas he was awarded a 1985 *Progressive Architecture Award*, the 1988 National Glass Association Award for Excellence in Commercial Design, and the highly esteemed 1990 Quaternario Award for high technological achievement.

His Banque Bruxelles Lambert in Lausanne, Switzerland, a bank interior, received the 1983 Annual Interiors Award as well as a Special Commendation from the jury. His design for the Banque Bruxelles Lambert branch in Milan, Italy, and his design for their New York City branch at the Rockefeller Center have been completed. He won the First Prize and Gold Medal in the closed competition to design the Master Plan for the Universal Exhibition of 1992, which will take place in Seville, Spain, to celebrate the five-hundredth anniversary of America's discovery. This project was also granted a 1986 Architectural Projects Award from the American Institute of Architects, New York.

The headquarters he designed for the Financial Guaranty Insurance Company of New York won the Grand Prize of the 1987 International Interior Design Award of the United Kingdom, as well as the 1986 IDEA Award from the Industrial Designers Society of America (IDSA). He won First Prize in the 1986 closed competition for the Urban Plan for the Eschenheimer Tower in Frankfurt, West Germany. *Progressive Architecture* in 1987 and the American Institute of Architects, New York in its 1986 Architectural Projects Award cited for awards the Mercedes Benz Showroom design in 1986.

Mr. Ambasz represented America at the 1976 Venice Biennale. He has been the subject of numerous international publications as well as museum and art gallery exhibitions, principal among them the Leo Castelli Gallery, the Corcoran Gallery, the Museum of Modern Art, New York and the Philadelphia and Chicago Art Institutes. An exhibition entitled "Emilio Ambasz: Ten Years of Architecture, Graphic and Industrial Design" was held in Milan in the fall of 1983, traveling to Madrid in May 1984, and Zurich in the fall of the same year.

The Axis Design and Architecture Gallery of Tokyo dedicated a special exhibition of his work in April, 1985. In 1986, the Institute of Contemporary Art of Geneva, Switzerland at "Halle Sud" and, in 1987, the "Arc-en-Ciel" Gallery of the Centre of Contemporary Art in Bordeaux, France also presented one-man shows of his work.

In 1989, a retrospective of Mr. Ambasz's architectural designs, "Emilio Ambasz: Architecture" was held at The Museum of Modern Art, New York; and a second travelling exhibition, "Emilio Ambasz: Architecture, Exhibition, Industrial and Graphic Design" was held in June of 1989 at the San Diego Museum of Contemporary Art, travelling to, among others, the Musee des Arts Decoratifs de Montreal, the Akron Art Museum in Ohio, the Art Institute of Chicago in Illinois, and the Laumeier Sculpture Park in St. Louis.

Major international publications such as *Domus*, *ON Diseño*, *Space and Design*, *Architectural Record*, and *Architecture plus Urbanism*, among others, have dedicated special issues to his architectural work. In 1989, Rizzoli International Publications printed a monograph of Mr. Ambasz's work coinciding with his exhibition at The Museum of Modern Art.

Mr. Ambasz also holds a number of industrial and mechanical design patents. Since 1980 he has been the Chief Design Consultant for the Cummins Engine Co., a company internationally celebrated for its enlightened support of architecture and design. Mr. Ambasz has received numerous industrial design awards. Included among them are the Gold Prize awarded for his co-design of the Vertebra

Seating System by the IBD (USA) in 1977, the SMAU Prize (Italy) in 1979, and the coveted Compasso d'Oro (Italy) in 1981. In 1991 Mr. Ambasz was again awarded the Compasso d'Oro (Italy) prize for his new seating design, Qualis.

The Vertebra chair is included in the Design Collections of The Museum of Modern Art, New York and the Metropolitan Museum of Art, New York. The Museum of Modern Art has also included in its design collection his 1967 Geigy Graphics 3-D Poster and his flashlight, a design also cited for awards in 1987 by the Compasso d'Oro (Italy) and the IDSA. His design for Cummins' N14 Diesel Engine won the 1985 Annual Design Review from *Industrial Design* magazine. This publication also awarded him similar prizes in 1980 for his Logotec spotlight range (which also received the 1980 IDSA Design Excellence Award), in 1983 for the Oseris spotlight range, as well as in 1986 for his design of Escargot, an air filter designed for Fleetguard Incorporated.

In 1987 the Industrial Designer's Society of America granted its Industrial Design Excellence Award Winner top award for his Soffio, a modular lighting system. In 1988, the IDSA awarded him the same top honor and in 1989, the *ID* Designer's Choice Award for design excellence and innovation was given for Aquacolor, a watercolor set. Most recently, in 1992, IDSA again awarded Mr. Ambasz top honors for his innovative design of the Handkerchief Television. The Tenth Biennial of Industrial Design (BIO 10, Ljubljana, 1984) granted Mr. Ambasz their Jury Special Award "for his many contributions to the design field."

EXHIBITIONS ON EMILIO AMBASZ

Emilio Ambasz's architectural work was the subject of an exhibition at the Museum of Modern Art in New York from February through April, 1989. The exhibition "Emilio Ambasz: Architecture" was the fourth in a series of five architectural exhibitions in MoMA's Gerald D. Hines Interests Architecture Program which explores current directions in architecture.

A one-man exhibition at the La Jolla Museum of Contemporary Art from June through August 1989, entitled "Emilio Ambasz: Architecture, Exhibition, Industrial and Graphic Design," brilliantly designed by Shigeru Ban, subsequently travelled to The Art Institute of Chicago, the Laumier Sculpture Park in St. Louis, The Museum of Decorative Arts in Montreal, Canada, and the Des Moines Art Center in Iowa. The Ambasz-designed poster for the exhibition: a three-dimensional illustration of one of his architectural projects (page 360), which won a 1990 Award of Distinction from the American Association of Museums.

1992

"Architektur: Gärten Wachen in den Himmel." *Häuser* (February 1992): 10-11.

Barna, J.W. "Les Jardins du Futur." *L'Information Immobiliere* 47 (Spring 1992): cover, 87-99.

Buchanan, P. "Phoenix Phoenix." *The Architectural Review* 1139 (January 1992): 58-59.

"Euro Design NOW: Discussion." *AXIS* 42 (Winter 1992): 76.

Gazzaniga, L. "Prefectural Hall, Fukuoka." *Domus* 738 (May 1992): 38-41.

"Trends." *AXIS* 43 (Spring 1992): 24.

1991

Poniatowska, E.. "Todo Mexico." *Luis Barragán.* Mexico: Editorial Diana, 1991: 8.

Buchanan, P. "Vertical Garden City." *The Architectural Review* 1137 (November 1991): 38-41.

Cabassi, C. "Attualita—Venezia Quarternario." *AU—Arredo Urbano* 40/41 (October-November 1991): 38-41.

"Collaborations." *Design Week* 25 (November 1991).

"Emilio Ambasz." *On Diseño* 128 (1991): 103-171.

"Emilio Ambasz: Garden Architecture Goes to Town." *Architectural Record* 7 (July 1991): 68-69.

"Emilio Ambasz: Poetry and Its Reasoning." *Techniques and Architecture* 394 (February/March 1991): 50-56.

Glusberg, J. "Un edificio jardin: El centro Internacional de Fukuoka." *El Cronista*: 1, 8.

Hower, B.K. "Ambasz-Designed Bridge for Columbis, Indiana." *Inland Architect* 6 (November-December 1991): 25-26.

"Image Drawing." *FP (Fusion Planning)* 11 (November 1991): 1-3.

Kellogg, M. A. "The Greenhouse Effect." *Town and Country* 5133 (June 1991): 74-80.

Kenso, K. "Introduction to Architecture of the 1980s." *20th Century Architecture* 2250 (June 1991).

Lovati, C. "XVI Premio Compasso d'Oro." *Ufficiostile* 6 (July/August 1991): 76-77.

Okada, H. "Emilio Ambasz." *Shitsunai (Interiors)* 442 (October 1991): 138-141.

Parks, J., ed. *Contemporary Architectural Drawings,* Petaluma, CA: Pomegranate Artbooks, 1991: 8.

Sorkin, M. "Et in Arcadia Ego: Emilio Ambasz's States of Nature." *Exquisite Corpse—Writings on Buildings.* London, UK: VERSO—New Left Books: 312-320.

Von Radziewsky, E. "Mit Büchern Leben." *Architektur + Wohnen* 5 (October-November 1991): 120-124.

Zevi, B. "Emilio Ambasz: Works and Projects." *L'Architettura* 11 (November 1991): 889-905.

"Zu Diesem Heft 10 Büro-Systeme." *Moebel Interior Design* 10 (October 1991): 116.

1990

Albrecht, B. and Amur, K.M. "80s Style Designs of the Decade." *Lighting.* New York, NY: Abbeville Press, 1990.

Bellini, M. "The International Design Yearbook 1990/91." *Textiles.* London, UK: Thames and Hudson, Ltd., 1990: 162-163.

Betsky, A. "Violated Perfection." *Revelatory Modernism.* New York, NY: Rizzoli International Publications, Inc., 1990: 92-93.

Blanca, O.T. *The International Design Yearbook.* London, U.K.: John Calmann and King, Ltd., 1990.

Buchanan, P. "Un Paraiso Enterrado." *Arquitectura Viva* 14 (September/October 1990): 16.

Buchanan, R. "Metaphors, Narratives and Fables in New Design Thinking." *Design Issues* 1 (Fall 1990): 81.

"Collection Les Cahiers de Commarque (Le Patrimoine Troglodytique)." *Des Troglodytes à l'Archiecture-paysage.* Bertholon, France: Edition de'l'Association Culturelle de Commarque, 1990.

"A Cura di Livio Salvadori." *Casabella* 574 (December 1990): 2.

Dana, A. "Revving Up to Quality." *Interiors* 10 (May 1990): 200.

"Das Büromöbel zwischen Renaissance und Sachlichkeit." *Form* 132 (1990): 29.

"Design Notebook." *Mirabella* (January 1990): 91.

"Emilio Ambasz and New Ajioka Project." *WWD—Womens Wear Daily* 412 (January 1990): 38.

Fisher, T. "Communicating Ideas Artfully." *Steelcase Design* 3.

"Fukuoka Competition Award Announcement." *The Japan Architect* 65 (October 1990): 157.

Glusberg, J. "Ambasz, Agrest-Gandelsonas, Pelli, Mochado y Silvetti, y Torre." *Arquitectura and Construccion* (July 4, 1990): 6-7.

Irace, F. "Emerging Skylines." *Emilio Ambasz: A Reasonable Realism.* New York, NY: Whitney Library of

Design, 1990: 131-133.

Juresko, V. "Nova tehnologija stakla." *Covjek i. prostor i XXXVII* (1990): 21.

Kulvik, B. "Aspen." *Form—Function* 1 (1990): 48.

Lemos, P. "Shutter Profile—Emilio Ambasz: The Architect as Philosopher." *Pan Am Clipper* 9 (September 1990): 87.

Miller, R.C. *Modern Design 1890-1990 in the Metropolitan Museum of Art.* New York, NY: Harry N. Abrams, Inc., 1990: 229.

Niesewand, N. *Textiles.* London, UK: Thames and Hudson Ltd., 1990: 162-163.

"Obihiro Project." *Brutus* 630 (1990): 171.

"Orgatec-Bilderbogen—2. Stühl." *md* 1 (January 1990): 70.

"Pencil Points." *Progressive Architecture* 4 (April 1990): 30.

Pigeat, J. "Parcs et Jardins Contemporains." *Acclimatations.* Paris, France: La Maison Rustique, 1990: 56-57.

Semprini, R. "La Città Balneare." *Modo* 126 (October 1990): 52-53.

"Sooabteilang Niederurseler Hang in Frankfurt." *aw* 141 (March 1990): 26.

"Stationery of the Year." *BTOOL* 1 (January 1990): 7, 9-11, 21, 39.

"Stonework Deconstructed." *Stone World* 9 (September 1990): 28.

Zevi, B. "Architettura." *L'Espresso* 49 (December 9, 1990): 138.

1989

"3-D Package." *FP (Fusion Planning)* 25 (September 1989): 103.

"A Paintbox Every Artist Could Love." *Packaging Digest* 2 (February 1989): 52-53.

"American Scene." *Topic* 182: inside cover.

Buchanan, P. "Ambasz Urban Gardens." The *Architectural Review* 1111 (September 1989): 49-59.

"Bürora Uume einer Versicherungsgesellschaft, New York, 1987." *Werk, Bauen + Wohnen* 11 (November 1989): 52-53.

Butor, M. "L'Architecture Demain." *Le Pouvoir Imaginatif du Monument.* Paris, France: Blassories sa, 1989: 40.

"Calendar of Events." *American Way* 23 (December 1, 1989): 96.

"Dallo Spazzolino da Denti al Grattacielo." *Casa Vogue* 205 (February 1989): 122.

Davis, D. "Slaying the Neo-Modern Dragon." *Art in America* 1 (January 1989): 47.

Edelman, E. "Reclaiming Eden." *Art News* 2 (February 1989): 73-74.

"Emilio Ambasz and Giancarlo Piretti." *The Metropolitan Museum of Art Bulletin* 2 (Fall 1989): 73.

Filler, M. "Low Tech High Style." (Andy Warhol) *Interview* 2 (February 1989): 64.

Fisher, T. "Ambasz & Holl at MoMA." *Progressive Architecture* 3 (March 1989): 33 and 36.

——. "Presenting Ideas." *Progressive Architecture* 6 (June 1989): 85.

Friis-Hansen, D. and Kline, K., eds. *Clockwork* Cambridge, MA: MIT List Visual Arts Center, 1989: 24.

Gastil, R. "Briefing: Emilio Ambasz/Steven Holl." *Blueprint* 56 (April 1989): 61 and 63.

Glasin, M. "Are You Sitting Comfortably?" *Design* 483 (March 1989): 36.

Goldberger, P. "Two Architects Who Tap into Our Deepest..." *New York Times* (February 12, 1989): 32.

Graff, V. "Arkadien in Texas." *Architektur & Wohnen* (March 1989): 84-89.

Green-Rutanen, L. "Emilio Ambasz: A New Age Architect." *Form and Function* 2 (February 1989): 28-33.

Heck, S. "Emilio Ambasz/Steven Holl: Architecture." *Architecture and Urbanism* 226 (July 1989): 5-14.

Krafft, A. "The Lucille Halsell Conservatory, USA." *Contemporary Architecture.* Paris, France and Lausanne, Switzerland: Bibliotheque des Arts, 1989: 244-247.

Lampugnani, V.M. "Emilio Ambasz: Il Disegno del Rito." *Domus* 705 (May 1989): 17-24.

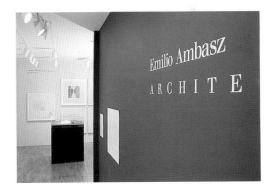

Lazar, J. *Architecture for the Future.* Los Angeles, CA: The Museum of Contemporary Art, 1989: cassette.

Lester. "Art Facts—LJMCA Presents Major Retrospecta of Designs by Ambasz." *San Diego Daily Transcript* (January 9, 1989).

"Limitless Horizons." *New York Daily News* (October 15, 1989): 3.

Lipstadt, H., ed. *The Experimental Tradition.* New York, NY: Princeton Architectural Press, 1989: 147.

Matthew, L. "Subterranean Space." *Metropolis* 8 (April 1989): 46-51.

McDonough, M. "Emilio Ambasz and Steven Holl at MoMA." *ID Magazine* 2 (March/April 1989): 70-71.

Morozzi, C. "Poeta o Tecnologo?" *Modo* 112 (March 1989): 36-39 (English 9-10).

Muschamp, H. "Myth Master." *Vogue* (March 1989): 340-344.

"Museum of American Folk Art Tower." *New York Architektur 1970-1990.* Munich, Germany: Prestel-Verlag, 1989: 94-95.

"New Faces of Modernish on Show." *Architectural Review* 3 (March 1989): 47.

Panizza, M. *Figure.* Rome, Italy: Edizioni Associate, 1989: 165.

Papadakis, A., Cooke, C., and Benjamin, A. "Deconstruction Omnibus Volume." UK: Academy Editions, 1989: 260.

Pearlman, C. "Herlitz Aqua Color Box." *ID Magazine* 4 (July/August 1989): 40-41.

Pherson, C. "Enigmatic Emilio: A Fable." *Arcade* 3 (August/September 1989): 6.

Pursion, J. "Form & Function." *The Wall Street Journal* (June 21, 1989).

Robinson, D. "Just Add Water." *Innovation* 1 (February 1989): 36-38.

Russell, B. *Architecture and Design 1970-1990.* New York, NY: Harry N. Abrams, Inc., 1989.

Russell, J.S. "Emilio Ambasz: The Poetics of the Pragmatic." *Architectural Record* 1071 (October 1989).

Sesoki, T. "Special Report: Emilio Ambasz—The Poetics of the Pragmatic." *Approach* (Autumn, September 1989): 1-23.

"Showroom for Mercedes Benz in Englewood, NJ, USA." *aw—architektur + wettbewerbe* 139 (September 1989): 17.

Sutherland, L. "Poetic Visions of a Landscape Dreamer." *Design Week* (June 16, 1989).

"World Exhibition 1992 Emilio Ambasz." *Architecture Intérieure* 1307 (June/Juy 1989): 134.

Wrede, S. "Emilio Ambasz Architecture." *MoMA Members Quarterly* (Winter, February 1989): 6.

——. "Emilio Ambasz and Steven Holl." *Newsletter—The International Council of the MoMA* 16 (Spring, April 1989): 12.

Young, L. "Down with Industrial Design." *Design* 481 (March 1989): 59-51.

Young, M. "Crystal Pavilion." *Continental Airlines Profiles* 6 (June 1989): 16 and 18.

1988

Appel, N.L. "Paradise Made: Two New Gardens in Texas." *Cite* (Spring-Summer 1988): 13-15.

Barret, J. and Bertholon, M. *Terrasses Jardins.* 1988.

Capella, J. and Larrea, Q. "Emilio Ambasz." *Designed by Architects in the 1980s,* New York, NY: Rizzoli International Publications, Inc., 1988: 14-15.

Casselti, A. "Oggetto Scultura di Emilio Ambasz." *Domina* 20 (October 1988): 44-45.

"Cubist Movement." *Architecture International* 2 (1988): 180-185.

Danto, A.C. "397 Chairs." *25 and 40.* New York, NY: Harry N. Abrams, Inc., 1988.

Dillon, D. "Drama of Nature and Form." *Architecture* (May 1988): 148-153.

"Emilio Ambasz San Antonio Botanical Conservatory, Texas." *Architectural Design* 3/4 (April 1988.): 46-47.

Filler, M. "Greenhouse Effects." *House & Garden* (September 1988): 58.

Irace, F. *La Città che Sale.* Milan, Italy: Arcadia Edizioni, 1988: 131-133.

"La Nuove Piazze di Emilio Ambasz." *l'Arca* 14 (Supplement, March 1988).

Links, C. "The New Expressionism." *Architecture Today.* New York, NY: Harry N. Abrams, 1988: 228-229.

Malone, M. "True Splendor in the Glass." *Newsweek* (September 12, 1988): 68-69.

Martellaro, J. "A Man and His Vision for Union Station." *The Kansas City Times* (January 23, 1988): A.M. Profile, E-2.

Mendini, A. "Celestial Gardens." *Ollo* 1 (October 1988).

"Milwaukee Art Museum." *The World of Art Today,* 1988: 149.

Muschamp, H. "Ground Up." *Artforum International* 2 (October 1988): 18-20.

——. "Herbert Muschamp on Architecture—The Lie of the Land." *The New Republic* (Dec. 19, 1988): 26-28.

"News and Events in the Botanical Community." *Garden* (September/October 1988): 27-28.

Peressut, L.B. "Emilio Ambasz: Lucille Halsell Conservtory." *Domus* 700 (December 1988): 36-43.

Pile, J.F. *Planning Interior Design.* New York, NY: Harry N. Abrams, Inc., 1988: 79.

Reginato, J. "On the Drawing Board." *Avenue* (November 1988): 129.

"Shimmering Strings." *Interior:* 211.

"Soffio: Simplicity and Elegance Through Soft-Tech." *Innovation* (Winter): 13.

Spacke. "Design in Italy." New York, NY: Abbeville Press, 1988: 192 and 196-197.

Staebler, W.W. "Architectural Detailing." *Partition FGIC.* New York, NY: Whitney Library of Design, 1988: 168-171.

"The 1992 Seville Universal Exposition: Celebrating the 500 Anniversary of the New World." *Al-Handasah* 11 (January 1988): 16-25.

"The New Entrepreneurs." *Design* 476 (August 1988): 40-41.

Woods, M. and Warren, A. "More Glass Than Wall." *Glass Houses.* New York, NY: Rizzoli International Publications, Inc., 1988: 186.

Wrede, S. "Geigy Graphics." *The Modern Poster.* New York, NY: The Museum of Modern Art, 1988: 198.

1987

Albertazzi, L. "Más allá de la Función." *Lapiz* 43 (January 1987): 8-11.

Aldersey-Williams, H. "Widening Horizons." *TWA Ambassador* (June 1987): 68.

Appel, N. "Glass Houses for People and Plants." *Cite at 5* (Fall 1987): 25.

Barna, J.W. "Light and Fog in San Antonio." *Texas Architect* 4 (July/August 1987): 28-31.

"Breaking Ground: Emilio Ambasz." *Connoisseur* 911 (December 1987): 48, 50.

Buchanan, P. "Curtains for Ambasz." *The Architectural Review* 1083 (May 1987): 73-77.

——. "The Traps of Technology." *Artforum* 4, 1987: 139-145.

"Commentary—Furniture and Consumer Products." *ID—Industrial Design* (33rd Annual Design Review, July/August 1987): 78, 102.

"Designer Profile: Giancarlo Piretti." *Interior Design* (March 1987): 246-249.

"Designing with a Lot of Bottle." *Design* 460 (April 1987): 46.

"Emilio Ambasz: Architecture Design Graph-isme." *Techniques & Architecture* 371 (April/May 1987): 34-35.

"Emilio Ambasz: Una Mostra di Progetti." *Domus* 683 (May 1987): 10-11.

"Escheimer Tor, Schillerstraße/Börsenplatz, Frankfurt." *aw - architektur + wettbewerbe* 132 (December 1987): 17-19.

"Fonti Luminose: A Comando Dell'Uomo." *Arredorama* 168 (March 1987): 57-60.

Glusberg, J. "Emilio Ambasz." *Bienal '87 de Arquitecture Cayc.* Catalogue,1987: 19.

Goldberger, "A Spacious Sunken Garden will Bloom in San Antonio." *The New York Times*, (June 11, 1987): C1 and C10.

Goodrich, K. "Profiles of the 1986 Industrial Design Excellence Award Winners." *Innovations* (Winter 1987): 7-9.

Imatake, M. "Brillant Talent: Emilio Ambasz." *IDEA* 202 (1987): 66-73.

Léon, H. and Wohlhage, K. "Fragment, Leerraum, Geschwindigkeit und das Bild der klassischen Stadt." *Bauwelt* 36 Stadtbauwelt (September 1987): 1335.

"Listings for San Antonio Events." *Texas Monthly* 6 (June 1987): 70.

Matsui, K., ed. "Three Dimensional Graphics." *My Design Work, E. Ambasz.* Tokyo, Japan: Rikuyo-sha Publishing, Inc., 1987: 8-9, 52-53, 123, 125-126, 138-139.

Matthews, T. "Emilio Ambasz: Technology and Myth, a Traveling Exhibition." *Architectural Record* 8 (August 1987): 161.

Murphy, J. "34th Annual P/A Awards: Mercedes Benz Showroom." *Progressive Architecture* 1 (January 1987): 104-105.

"New Products and Literature." *Progressive Architecture* 3 (March 1987): 169.

"News Briefs." *Architectural Record* 4 (April 1987): 47.

"Office Work Module: Privacy with Openness and Flexibility." *Innovation* (Winter 1987): 7-9.

"Report on New Design Trends in France." *FP (Fusion Planning)* 13 (July 1987): 80-81.

Ruiz, M.O., ed. *Exposicion Universal Expo '92 Sevilla: Ideas para una ordenacion del recinto.* Seville, Spain: Comisario General Exposicion Universal Sevilla, 1992 (1987): 9-24.

"San Antonio Botanical Conservatory." *Artforum* 4 (December 1987): 72, 74.

Sias, R. "Emilio Ambasz: I Protagonisti del Design." *Ufficiostile* 10 (October 1987): 40-47.

Smith, C.R. "1986 Architectural Projects Awards: What Might Be." *Oculus An Eye on New York Architecture* 6 (February 1987): 4 and 15.

——. *Interior Design in 20th Century America: A History.* New York, NY: Harper & Row, 1987: 301-303 and 312.

Stephens, S. "The Architects vs. the Critics." *Avenue* 3 (November 1987): 143.

Tetlow, K. "Structures: Style and Substance." *Designers West* (August 1987).

——. "Healthy Policies." *Interiors* 1: 116, 144.

Tickle, K. "IIDA International Interior Design Award 1987." *Interiors* (April 1987): 35-39.

Tironi, G. "La Citta del Design: Entre l'Objet et la Ville: Entretien avec Emilio Ambasz." *Halle Sud* 13 (January/February/March 1987).

Truppin, A. "Inventive Genius." *Interiors* (April 1987): 171-187.

Vandeuvre, E. "Design/France." *FP (Fusion Planning)* 13 (July 1987): 78-81.

Waisman, M. "Emilio Ambasz." *Summarios* (January 1987): 8-15

"Westweek 87 Program and Products." *Designers West* (Special edition, March 1987).

XIV Premio Compasso d'Oro. Milan, Italy: Silvia Editrice Milano, 1987: 63, 118, and 123.

Zagari, F. "Ambasz e la Mimesi della Natura." *Arredo Urbano* 23 (October/December 1987): 72-76.

1986

"1976-1986 Orgatechnik." *MD* (October 1986): 44-46.

Allen, G., ed. "Introduction." *Emerging Voices.* New York, NY: The Architectural League of New York, 1986: 6.

Baserga, F. "Scultura di Lastre: Un Capolavoro di Emilio Ambasz." *Marmo Macchine* 68 (Bimetre 2, 1986): 118-120.

Bayley, S. Garner, P. and Sudjic, D. *Twentieth Century Style and Design.* New York, NY: Van Nostrand Reinhold Company: 260-261, 292, 298.

Boles, D. "Ambasz in Seville: 1992 Fair." *Progressive Architecture* 9 (September 1986): 43-46.

Brenner, D. "Magic Mountains." *Architectural Record* (June 1986): 132-135.

Buchanan, P. "Spanish Isles." *The Architects' Journal* (September 24, 1986): 32-33.

Burkhardt, F. and Boiret, Y., dirs. *Creer dans le Cree,* Paris, France: Electa France, May 28-September 7, 1986: 178-179.

Constantine, M., ed. *Word and Image: Posters from the Collection of the Museum of Modern Art.* New York, NY: The Museum of Modern Art, 1986: 136.

Dillon, D. "Moonscape in the Sun." *Spirit* (June 1968): 68-119.

Filler, M. "L System." *Surface and Ornament* (May 30-July 12, 1986).

Giovannini, P. "Offices Move Boldly Backward or Playfully Forward." *The New York Times* (January 19, 1986): F8.

Hanna, A. "'Equipment'Escargot Air Filter." *ID Magazine* 4 (July/August 1986): 79.

Jedamus, J. "Chairs that Ease the Spine." *Newsweek* 24 (June 16, 1986): 3.

La Société Generale des Eaux Minerales de Vittel, ed. *L'eau en Formes.* Paris, France: Centre Georges Pompidou, 1986.

"Modern Redux." New York, NY: Grey Art Gallery and Study Center, 1986.

Modern Redux: Critical Alternatives for Architecture in the Next Decade. New York: Grey Art Gallery and Study Center, New York University (March 4 - April 19, 1986).

Morton, D. "Perspectives: Milan Furniture Fair." *Progressive Architecture* (December 1986): 38-40.

Palanco, R.L. "Siviglia 1992: Un concorso di idee per l"Exposizione Universale." *Casabella* 528 (October 1986): 18-29.

Pearlman, C. "Environments: Financial Guaranty Insurance Company." *ID Magazine* (Annual Design Review, August 1986): 62.

"Plaza Mayor, Salamanca, Spain." *architektur +wettbewerbe* 127 (September 1986): 21.

Reif, R. "Rare Glimpse of the Furniture of a Modern Dutch Master." *The New York Times* (July 13, 1986): 30H.

Rinaldi, "A Lugano Marmo e Nuvole." *Casa Vogue* 172 (March 1986): 170-171.

"Spain: Columbus Expo." *TWA Ambassador* (December 1986): 9.

Stewart, D. "Modern Designers Still Can't Make the Perfect Chair." *Smithsonian* (April 1986): 102.

Tate, A. and Smith, R.C. *International Design in the 20th Century.* New York, NY: Harper and Row, 1986: 519-521 and 530.

Tebaldi, M. "Siviglia: Concorso di idee per l'Esposizione Universale 1992." *Domus* 677 (November 1986): 80-88.

"The Technology of Horology." *Architectural Record* (January 1986): 57.

"Time Piece." *AXIS* (Winter 1986): 74-75.

Vider, E. "Light." *Almanac* (September/October 1986): 38-42.

Yerkes, S. "Design for the Times." *The Continental* (February 1986): 29-33.

1985

"21 Progettisti alla Ricerca delle Proprie Affinita." *Arredorama* 144 (March 1985): 30-32.

Abdulac, S. "Tokyo: Argentinian Designers' Show." *Mimar* 16 (April/ June 1985): 16.

"Agamennone." *Ottagono* 76 (March 1985): 119.

"Architel ₊Designer+Grafiker." *M-D Magazine* (June

1985): 38-41.

"Axis." *AXIS* (Summer 1985): 90.

"Axis Exhibit." *Interior Design News* (June 1985): 44.

Ban, S. "Emilio Ambasz Exhibition." *The Commercial Architecture* 6 (June 1985): 244-245.

"Banque Bruelles Lambert—Milano." *Process Architecture* 60 (July 1985): 48-53.

"Banque Bruxelles Lambert—New York." *Nikkei Architecture* (Special edition 1985): 185-189.

Barragán, L. and Ferrera, R. *Ensayos y Apuntos para un Bosquejo Critico Luis Barragán.* Mexico City, Mexico: Museo Rufino Tamayo: 23-25.

Bayley, S., ed. *The Conran Directory of Design.* New York, NY: Villard Books: 73.

Bernard, A. "Fringe Benefits." *Manhattan, Inc.* (July 1985): 122-123.

"Biennale de Paris." *Architecture* (1985): 197.

Brown, T. "Landscape Strategies: The New Orleans Museum of Art Addition." *The Princeton Journal* (1985): 186-187.

Brozen, K. "Working it Out." *Interiors* (September 1985): 190-199 and 222.

Burgasser, J. "Furniture & Furnishings: Dorsal Seating Range." *Industrial Design Excellence USA 1980-1985.* McLean, VA: The Design Foundation, 1985: 44.

"Compasso d'oro 1954-1984." Milan, Italy: Electa: 85.

Conroy, S.B. "Toward the Grand Design." *The Washington Post* (August 24, 1985): 1-9.

"Contemporary Landscape: From the Horizon of Postmodern Design." Kyoto, Japan: The National Museum of Modern Art, 1985: 38-39.

"Cordoba House." *AXIS* (September 1985): 90.

Corning, B. "Conservatory to be 'Unique in S.A.'." *Express-News* (August 28, 1985): 3B.

Diamonstein, B.L. "Emilio Ambasz." *American Architecture Now II.* New York, NY: Rizzoli, 1985: 19-27.

Dietsch, D.K. "Fringe Benefits." *Architectural Record* 11 (November 1985): 126-131.

"Elective Affinities." *Arredorama* (March 1985): 30-32.

"Elective Affinities." *AXIS* (September 1985): 65.

"Emilio Ambasz: Botanical Pleasures." *Domus* 667 (December 1985): 14-17.

"Emilio Ambasz: Plaza Mayor Salamanca." *Domus* 660 (April 1985): 12-13.

"Equipment ID.1985 Annual Design Review." *Industrial Design* 4 (July/August 1985): 107.

Fawcett, S. "Lighting: Out of the Shadows." *Design* 439 (July 1985): 32-33.

Fiorentino, L. "Botanical Center Planting New Facility." *San Antonio Light* (August 28, 1985): C1.

Fonio, D.G. "The Elective Affinities." *La Mia Casa* 178 (1985): 68-71.

Giovannini, J. "Designer's Role, Here vs. Abroad." *The New York Times* (November 14, 1985): 23 and 25.

——. "Made in America: ...U.S....Product Design." *The New York Times* (November 14, 1985): C1 & C8.

Greenberg, M. "Ambasz Designs Surreal Landscape for San Antonio." *Texas Architect* 2 (March/April 1985): 24-25.

Hanna, A. "Psychodrama in Milan." *Industrial Design* (May/June 1985): 16-21, 74 and 76.

Hendricks, D. "This Architect's Priority: Enhancing Creativity." *Express-News* (June 16, 1985): 1K and 9K.

Huidobro, M. "Les Bureaus D'une Banque a New York." *Techniques et Architecture* 362 (October/ November 1985): 179-180.

"ICISD '85 Interview with Emilio Ambasz." *AXIS* (Autumn 1985): 38-41.

Iliprandi, G. and Molinari, P., eds. *Omnibook 2: Italian Industrial Designers.* Italy: Magnus Edizioni, 1985: 20.

"Annual Design Review." *Industrial Design Magazine [ID].* New York, NY: Gallery 91.

"Interior Design News." *Interior Design* (June 1985): 44.

Lazar, R. "Contract & Residential Furniture: Logotec Spotlight Range" *Industrial Design Excellence USA 1980-1985.* McLean, VA: The Design Foundation, 1985: 13.

"Le Affinita' Elettive." *AXIS* (Spring 1985): 65.

"Le Affinita Elettive." *Domus* 660 (April 1985.): 81-88.

"Le Affinita Elettive di Ventuno Progettisti." *L'Industria del Mobile* 288 (May 1985): 49-58.

Marogna, G. "Voglia di Sicurezza." *Casa Vogue* 160 (February 1985): 140, 142.

Modo (January/February 1985): cover page.

"New & Notable." *Industrial Design* 76 (January/ February 1985).

Pedretti, B. "Mostre Alla Triennale: Le Affinità Elettive." *Interni* 349 (April 1985): 44-53.

Shashaty, A. "Modern Industry—A Private Moveable Office Module." *Dun's Business Month* (June 1985): 85.

Shaw, E. "Argentine Architects Reshape Skylines and...U.S." *Argentine News* (August 7, 1985): 40-43.

Smetana, D. "Che Cosa Stanno Facendo." *Casa Vogue* 164 (June 1985): 221.

Staebler, W. "Something About a Wall." *Interiors* (September 1985): 200-206.

Stadt Frankfurt am Main. Munich, Germany: Wettbewerbe aktuell, 1985: 12-15.

Surface & Ornament. The Metropolitan Museum of Art with Formica Corporation and Architecture Club of Miami, May 1985.

Tapley, C. "Buildings & the Land: An Introduction." *Texas Architect* 2 (April 1985): 43.

"The Lucille Halsell Conservatory: Architectural Design Citation." *Progressive Architecture* (January 1985): 120-121.

"Things Seen." *Design* 439 (July 1985): 25.

"Vertebra." *AXIS* (September 1985): 90.

"Vintage Year for Design." Press release by *ID Magazine* (August 1985).

XIII Biennale de Paris. Paris, France: Grande Halle du Parc de la Villette, March 21, 1985.

Yoshida, Y. *A Style for the Year 2001.* A joint effort of Shinkinchiku, *ja* and *a+u*, 1985: 76-77.

1984

"Ambassador to the Interior." *Building Design Journal* (May 1984).

"Arquitectura y Diseño." *Guia del Ocio* (May 21-27, 1984).

Berg, P., cur. *Tit for Tat Lin.* New York, NY: The Alternative Museum, 1984: 6, 11-12, and 23.

"Biennial of Industrial Design." *BIO 10.* Yugoslavia: Yugoslavia Biennial, 1984: 31, 78, 81, 189, and 197.

Brenner, D. "Et in Arcadia Ambasz: Five Projects by Emilio Ambasz & Associates." *Architectural Record* 10 (September 1984): 120-133.

Brisebarre, J.J., ed. *Le Empire du Bureau 1900-2000.* February 1984: 80 and 210.

Buchanan, P. "The Poet's Garden." *The Architectural Review* (June 1984): 50-55.

Busch, A. "Product Design." *Industrial Design Magazine* (1984 85): 105 and 141.

——, ed. *Product Design.* New York, NY: Robert Silver & Associates (US distrib.), 1984: 85, 89, 105, and 141.

Casciani, S. *Mobili come Architetture: Il Disegno della Produzione Zanotta.* Milan, Italy: Arcadia Srl., 1984: 105, 110, and 126.

"Cultura y Ocio: Arquitectura y Diseño: Exposicion Emilio Ambasz 1984." *Casa Viva* (May 1984): 64-68.

"Design en Colorcore." *Architecture Interieure Cree* (December 1983/January-February 1984): 117-124.

"Designing a Plaza for Houston." *Lotus International* 39 (1984): 62-69.

Dunlap, D.W. "Future Metropolis." *Omni* (October 1984): 116-123.

"Emilio Ambasz: Recent Project." *AMC* 6 (December 1984): 4-13.

"Emilio Ambasz: The Innovator for Aiming at Utopia." *IDEA* (November 1984): 88-95.

Emilio Ambasz 1984: Arquitectura, Diseño Grafico e Industrial. Madrid, Spain: MAD Centro de Diseño and Galeria Ynguanzo, May 1984.

"Exposición: Emilio Ambasz 1984." *Casa & Jardin* 108 (1984).

"Exposiciones del Arquitecto Argentino Emilio Ambasz." *Cultura* (May 14, 1984): 21.

"Exposón en Madrid: Emilio Ambasz, Creador de Objetos." *Diario 16* (May 14, 1984)

"Floating Architecture in New Orleans." *Design* 426 (June 1984): 21.

Gaibis, C. "Cultura: Exposiciones del Arquitecto Argentino Emilio Ambasz: Considerado uno de los Mejores del Mundo." *ABC* (May 14, 1984).

Gandee, C. "Offices for Banque Bruxelles Lambert, New York City." *Record Interiors 1984* (Mid-September 1984): 92-97.

Giovanni, O. "L'Arcipelago delle Arti." *Casa Vogue* 152 (May 1984): 226.

Glancey, J. "The Gordon Russell Furniture Award." *The Architectural Review* 1053 (November 1984): 25-41.

Glueck, G. "Tit for Tat Lin." *The New York Times* (November 16, 1984).

Glusberg, J., cur. "Emilio Ambasz." *Architecture in Latin America Horizonte '82—IBA '84.* Berlin, Germany: Internationale Bauausstellung, 1984: 37.

Gosling, D. "Definitions of Urban Design." *AD - Architectural Design (Urbanism)* 12 (1984):16-25.

——, and Maitland, B. *Concepts of Urban Design.* New York, NY: St. Martin's Press, 1984: 121-123, 131.

Graff, V. "Monumente der Verschwendung." *Du, Die Zeitschrift für Kunst and Kultur* (April 1984): 30-35.

Greer, N.R. "Light as a Tool of Design." *Architecture* (October 1984): 55.

Irace, F. "Piazza A Houston: Un Progetto di Emilio Ambasz." *Diagonalle* (March 1984): 42-43.

Ito, K. "New Orleans Museum of Art." *Space Design* 237 (June 1984): 49-54.

"Japanese Architecture." *Nikkei Architecture* (December 31, 1984): 34-39.

Kassler, E.B. "Cordoba House." *Modern Gardens and the Landscape.* New York, NY: The Museum of Modern Art, 1984: 130.

Kleihues, J. and Glusberg, J., curs. "Buenos Aires a Través de sus Escritore, Artistas y Arquitectos." Buenos Aires, Argentina: 1984.

Lucan, J. "Emilio Ambasz: Projets Récents." *AMC: Revue D'Architecture* (December 1984): 4-15.

"MAD." *D.M.A. Hogares* 196 (June 1984).

Maitland, B. "The Uses of History." *AD—Architectural Design (Urbanism)* 12 (1984): 4-14.

Millán, L. "E Makes Architecture, A Designs Architecture." *La Nación* (July 1, 1984): 2-3.

——. "Emilio más Ambasz." *La Nación* (1984).

Onetti, J. "El Diseño como una de las Bellas Artes." *Diario 16* (May 11, 1984): 4-5.

Perales, M. "Ambasz en Madrid." *Arquitectos* 77 (April 1984): 38-48.

Samaniego, F. "Los Diseños de Emilio Ambasz." *El Pais* (May 5, 1984).

Santobeña, A. "Un Genial Creador de 'Objetos': Emilio Ambasz: Da Forma Poetica a lo Pragmatico." *El Europeo* (May 31, 1984): 73-74.

"Servicio de Novedades." *Summa* 203 (August 1984): 81.

"Su Diseño." *Mercado* (May 25, 1984).

Sun, M. and Hart, C. "Color as Substance: Plastic Laminates." *ID—Industrial Design Magazine* (January/February 1984): 54-57.

Szenasey, S.S., ed. "Merchant Bankers/ At Home Study." *The Office Book Design Series Private and Executive Office.* Mobile and Resilient Chairs/Vertebra Seating System/Dorsal. New York, NY: Facts on File: 24-25, 32-33, 36-37.

"Tendenze & Novità." *Capital Casa* 10 (October 1984): 16-17.

"The Arts Community: Squaring Art with History: Cubism & Constructs." *New York Daily News* (November 8, 1984).

"The Island: The Project of Emilio Ambasz for the New Orleans Museum of Art." *Gran Bazar* (June/July 1984): 64-66.

1983

Archer, B.J. *Follies: Architecture for the Late-Twentieth Century Landscape.* New York, NY: Rizzoli International Publications, Inc., 1983: 34-37.

"Automatisch-Dynamisches Sitzen." *Moebel Interior Design* (October 10, 1983): 56-57.

Becarra, B. "Dialogo:Con el Arquitecto Emilio Ambasz." *Trama* (May 1983): 20-27.

Boissiére, O. "Di Faccia e di Taglio." *La Mia Casa* (December 1983): 100.

Boles, D.D. "Financial Institution Winner." *Interiors* 6 (January 1983): 100-103.

Botta, M. "Houston Commentary." *Domus* (May 1983): 2-5.

Brion, G.C. "Architettura da Protagonisti con case e Oggetti in Piacevole Misura d'uomo." *La Republica* (October 8, 1983).

Buchanan, P. "An Awe-Filled Arcadia: The Architectural Quest of Emilio Ambasz." *Architecture and Urbanism* 155 (August 1983): 30-35.

———. "High Tech: Another British Thoroughbred." *The Architectural Review* (July 1983): 19.

Burgasser, J. "1982 Awards Program Profiles: The Dorsal Seating Range—Emilio Ambasz, IDSA and Giancarlo Piretti." *Innovation* 1 (Winter 1983): 23-25.

Busch, A. "Annual Design Review—Contract and Residential." *Industrial Design Magazine* (September/October 1983): 42-44, 49.

———. "Contract and Residential Furniture." *Product Design* (1982-1983): 105 and 141.

———. "Home Electronics and Entertainment." *Product Design* (1982-1983): 85.

———."Who's Who: Award Winning Designers." *Interiors* (January 1983): 120-121.

"Correspondencias: Escultura y Arquitectura en el Museo de Bellas Artes de Bilbao." *El Correo Español* (March 15, 1983): 9.

Davis, D. "Arquitectos de Vanguardia Reviven las Construcciones Extravagantes para Jardines." *La Nación* (November 27, 1983).

———. "Bringing Back the Follies." *Newsweek* (November 14, 1983): 104.

de Gorbea, X.S. "Correspondencias: 5 Arquitectos—5 Escultores." *DEIA* (March 15, 1983).

Dinelli, F. "Nuova Sede della Banca Bruxelles Lambert a Losanna/Renovation of a Bank in Lausanne." *L'Industria delle Construxioni* 140 (June 1983): 54-57.

Filler, M. "Ambasz and the Poetics of Architectural Space." *Architecture and Urbanism* 155 (August 1983): 62-66.

———. "Folk Art Museum's Striking New Tower." *House and Garden* (January 1983): 186.

———. "Journal: In Praise of Follies." *House and Garden* (December 1983): 216.

Fitch, J.M. "Neither Reason nor Follies." *Metropolis* (November 1983): 15.

Frateili, E. *Il Disegno Industriale Italiano 1928-1981.* Torino, Italy: C.E.L.I.D., 1983: 117.

Glancy, J. "Design Review: Milan Furniture Fair." *The Architectural Review* 1042 (December 1983): 74/12.

Halliday, S. "Tour d'Objets: Ambasz at Krueger." *Skyline* (April 1983): 23.

Herdeg, W., ed. *Graphis Annual: The International Annual of Advertising and Editorial Graphics.* Zurich, Switzerland: Graphis Press Corporation, 1983: 73.

Irace, F. "Follies." *Domus* 644 (November 1983): 24-29.

———. "L'Usine Verte." *Domus* 636 (February 1983): 22-25.

———. "Paradise Lost. Garden Regained." *Emilio Ambasz: 10 Anni di Architettura, Grafica e Design,* Milan, Italy: Centrodomus. Exhibition, 1983.

Krug, K. "Mehr Licht als Leuchte." *Form* (January 1983): 10-13.

"L'Analisi Economica del Design: Ambasz-Piretti." *E'Design* (October 10-November 7, 1983).

"Las 'Correspondencias' Entre Arquitectura y Escultura en la obra de Diez Grandes Artistas Contemporáneos." *Diario SUR* (February 3, 1983).

Melissa, L. "Letter from New York: Italian 'New Design'." *Interni Annual '83* (1983): 23.

Mendini, A. "Colloquio con Emilio Ambasz." *Domus*

639 (May 1983): 1.

——., Irace, F. and Gravagnuolo. "Emilio Ambasz." *Domus—Il Design Oggi in Italia tra Produzione Consumo e Qualcos'Altro* (1983): 27.

"Mostre: Emilio Ambasz." *Casa Vogue* 145 (October 1983): inset between 289-190.

Nakamura, T. "Banque Bruxelles Lambert, Lausanne." *Architecture and Urbanism* 155 (August 1983): 67-73.

——. "House for a Couple—North-East USA." *Architecture and Urbanism* 155 (August 1983): 52-55.

——. "Houston Center Plaza." *Architecture and Urbanism* 155 (August 1983): 46-51.

——. "Museum of American Folk Art, New York City." *Architecture and Urbanism* 155 (August 1983): 36-39.

——. "Schlumberger Engineering Research Laboratory." *Architecture and Urbanism* 155 (August 1983): 40-45.

——."The Four Gates to Columbus." *Architecture and Urbanism* 155 (August 1983): 58-61.

——. "To AMBASZ from a+u." *Architecture and Urbanism* 155 (August 1983): 79-82.

——. "Wood House—New Canaan." *Architecture and Urbanism* 155 (August 1983): 56-57.

"Orgatechnik—A Really Big Show." *Progressive Architecture (*January 1983): 27.

Ovsejevich, D.L., ed. "Diseno: Emilio Ambasz." *Libro de Oro de Las Artes Visuales Argentinas.* Buenos Aires, Argentina: Fundacion Konex, 1983: 86.

Pansera, A., ed. "Emilio Ambasz's Design: Nuove Frontiere e Strategie del Design Italiano degli Anni Ottanta." *It's Design: New Frontiers and Strategies of Italian Design in the Eighties.* Milan, Italy: Alinari, 1983: 21-36.

Portoghesi, P."Alle soglie del nuovo design." *Europeo* 43 (October 22, 1983): 109.

Schultz, G. "Büroleuchten." *Moebel + Decoration* (April 1983): 75.

Sedofsky, L. "New York New." *Paris Vogue* 640 (April 1983): 302.

Slavin, M. "15 Honored at Big I Champagne Breakfast Gala." *Interiors* 9 (April 1983): 110-113.

——. "Interiors Awards: Quartet of Designers Chooses the Big I's." *Interiors* (January 1983): 94-118.

——. "People and Events: Honoring Ambasz." *Interiors* (November 1983): 20.

"Things Seen (Pool of Light)." *Design* (January 1983): 21.

Tomoiku, A. "Materialidea." *SD* 8303 (1983):13-14.

Txomin, B. "5 Arquitectos, 5 Escultores en el Museo de Bellas Artes de Bilbao." *Fula del Oeio* (March 18, 1983).

Venosta, C., cur. *From the Spoon to the City: Through the Work of 100 Designers.* Milan, Italy: Padiglione della Triennale. 1983: 26-27.

"Vertebra." Design Furniture from Italy: Production, Technics and Modernity, 92-93." Stuttgart, Germany: Stuttgart Design Center, May 1983.

Zannini, G. "Libro de Oro de las Artes Visuales Argentinors." *Biografia de los Nomnailes.* Argentina: Fundación Konex, 1983.

1982

"Architectura Latinoamericana Mos-trada en Europa." *La Prensa* (July 6, 1982): 7.

"Arquitectura Latinoamericana Actual, esa Desconocida." *La Nación* (June 2, 1982): 1.3a.

Bill, M. "Design: In Weiss Farbiges Licht." *Form* 98 (February 1982): 48.

——."Personalien..aus der Design Szene: Emilio Ambasz." *Form* 98 (February 1982): 54.

Brosterman, N. "Folk Architecture." *Express* (Spring 1982): 21.

Buchanan, P."Bank, Lausanne, Switzerland." *The Architectural Review* (August 1982): 53-55.

——."Contemporary de Chirico: Precursor to Post-Modernism." *The Architectural Review* 1025 (July

1982): 46-7.

Castelli, L. and Ruina, E., curs. *Materialidea*, Milan, Italy: Padiglione D'Arte Contemporanea, 1982

Da Silva Ramos, P. "Portraits D'Amerique." *Vogue Paris* 625 (April 1982): 218.

Dardi, C. "Fink and Steiner House, Southampton/NY, Longarini House, Southampton/NY, Woods House, New Canaan, Connecticut." *Domus* 628 (May 1982): 16-21.

Daulte, F. "L'Art Vaudios dans une Banque Internationale." *L'Oeil* (May 1982): 40-45.

Doubilet, S. "Cummins Appoints Ambasz." *Progressive Architecture (*July 1982): 40.

Emery, M. "Banque Bruxelles Lambert, Lausanne, Suisse." *L'Architecture d'Aujord'hui* 222 (September 1982): 88-89.

Fernandes, J.C. "USA: La Valijita y el Courtain-Wall." *Vivienda* 235 (February 1982): 8.

Fernandez, R. "Encuentros: Emilio Ambasz." *Dos Puntos* 4 (March/ April 1982): 36-43.

Filler, M. "Gran Rifiuto on 53rd Street." *New York Arts Journal* 14 (1982): 32-34.

——. "Portraits D'Amerique." *Paris Vogue* (April 1982): 214-228.

Gimenez, C. and Munoz, J., orgs and prods. *Correspondencias: 5 Arquitectos/5 Escultores.* Madrid, Spain: The Palacio de las Alhajas, 1982.

Giovanni, O. "A Losanna, La Nuova sede di una Banca I Prezisi Segreti." *Casa Vogue* 134: 208-211.

Glusberg, J. "Latinoamerica y su Arquitectura en Berlin." *Espacio* (September/October/November 1982): 14-19.

——."Una Constante Búsqueda de la Poesia y los Auténticos Origenes de la Arquitectura." *Clarin Arquitectura, Ingenieria, Planeamiento y Diseño* (February 19, 1982): 24-25.

Gregotti, V. *Il Disegno del Prodotto Industriale: Italia 1860-1980.* Milano: Gruppo Editroiale Electa, 1982: 392

Guerra, R. "5 Arquitectos, 5 Escultores." *Q62, Consejo Superior de los Colegios de Arquitectos* (December 1982): 33-37.

Guisasa, F. "Correspondencias: 5 Arquitectos + 5 Escultores." *Q* (December 1982): 30-62.

Harvie, A.E. "Ambasz to Consult at Cummins Engine." *ID Magazine* (July/August 1982): 13.

Klickowski, H. "a/actualidad." *Ambiente* 33 (August 1982): 7-8.

"Latinoamérica en Berlín." *Clarin* (June 11, 1982): 2.

Marin-Medina, J. "Una Propuesta de Cultura Arquitectónica." *Informaciones* (November 4, 1982): 26-27.

Mazzocchi, G. "Bank Landscape." *Domus* 629 (June 1982): 56-57.

Morozzi, C. "La Finta Pelle del Progetto." *Modo* 55 (December 1982): 60-62.

Pallasman, J. "University of Houston College of Architecture Honors Studio." *Explorations—Löytöretkiä: Houston Arkkitehtskoulun Opilastöitä* (December 1982): 13, 16-17.

Penney, R. "Diversity and Human Factors Emerge in Furnishings Design." *ID Magazine* (September/October 1982): 24-29.

Petrina, A. "Reportaje: Emilio Ambasz." *Summa* 174 (May 1982): 21-22.

Portoghesi, P. *Postmodern—L'Architettura Nella Societa Post-Industriale.* Milan, Italy: Electra, 1982: 106-107.

Pragnell, P. "Points of Interest: Up." *Skyline* (June 1982): 8.

Rawson, D. "Future Scenarios." *Gentlemen's Quarterly* (October 1982): 240-243.

Searing, H. *New American Art Museums.* New York, NY: Whitney Museum of American Art: 12.

Sisto, M. "Il Cubo Assente." *Casa Vogue* (March 1982): 208-211.

——. "Mostre: Sei Grandi Firme per Alcantara Dai Divanetti Rigidi ai Corridoi Molli." *Casa Vogue* 133 (September 1982): 384-395.

Slavin, M. "Cummins Taps Ambasz." *Interiors* (July 1982): 18.

Smith, J.M. "Maker of Myths and Machines: An Interview with Emilio Ambasz." *Crit* 11 (Spring 1982): 21-24.

Viladas, P."Mainly on the Plain—Banque Bruxelles Lambert, Lausanne, Switzerland." *Progressive Architecture* (April 1982): 72.

Wagner, W. "New York's Museum of Folk Art Introduces a Well Mannered Tower." *Architectural Record* (July 1982): 53.

Zevi, B."Dal Barocco alle Ande." *L'Expresso* (August 29, 1982): 75.

1981

ADI (Associazione per il Disegno Industriale). "Comune di Milano." Milan, Italy: Electa: 33.

An Exhibition of Architectural Drawings and Models by Emilio Ambasz, Michael Graves, Leon Krier, Aldo Rossi. Boston, MA: Vesti Corporation, Fine Arts Management, 1981.

Belloni, A. "Prömiertes Design aus Italien Österreich Japan." *Moebel + Decoration* (December 1981): 65.

Blau, D. "Emilio Ambasz." *Flash Art* 101 (January/February 1981): 51.

Brown, T. "An Architect's Dream: Ancient Simplicity Meets Modern Art." *Home Energy Digest* (Spring 1981): 32-34.

Buchanan, P. "Reconaissance: Houses for Sale." *The Architectural Review* 1007 (January 1981): 5-8.

Carlsen, P. "Designing the Post-Industrial World." *Art News* (February 1981): 80-86.

Casati, C. "Columbus Il Mito." *La Mia Casa* 141 (October 1981): 106-107.

Davidson, S. "Cover Story: Land of Miracles." *Time* (August 17, 1981): 15.

Della Corte, E. "Product Review: Back to Economics." *Interiors* 12 (July 1981): 60-61.

Diffrient, N. "Top Award: Logotec Spotlight Range." *Industrial Design Magazine, Designers Choice* (1981): 27.

Elquezabal, E. "Compasso d'Oro 1981." *Summa* (December 1981): 19.

Filler, M. "Harbinger: Ten Architects." *Art in America* (Summer 1981): 114-123.

Furniture by Architects: Contemporary Chairs, Tables, and Lamps. Cambridge, MA: Hayden Gallery, Massachusetts Institute of Technology, 1981.

Glusberg, J. "Emilio Ambasz en Buenos Aires." *Clarin Arquitectura, Ingenieria, Planeamiento y Diseño* (December 18, 1981): 1.

Goldberger, P. "A Meeting of Artistic Minds." *The New York Times Magazine* (March 1, 1981): 70-73.

Grossman, L.J. "Emilio Ambasz o la Inefable Presencia de la Arquitectura." *La Nación* (December 20, 1981): 1.3a.

Irace, F. "Museum as Work of Art." *Domus* 615 (March 1981): 13-16.

Lewin, S.G. "Art and Antiques: Drawing Towards a

New Architecture." *Town and Country* 5010 (February 1981): 172-174.

Maerker, C. "Wohnhäuser Wie Skulpturen-Wer Will Sie? Erdloch Vom Wunderkind." *Art* (February 1981): 90-91.

Morton, D.A. "Innovative Furniture in America." *Progressive Architecture* 5 (May 1981): 36.

Portoghesi, "L'Architettura: Ma la Casa è Finita Sottoterra." *Europeo* 43 (October 26, 1981): 103.

Querci, A. "Il Momento e le Opinioni: Diece Anni Dopo, il Design Italiano negli USA." *Architectural Digest* (September 1981): 40.

Russell, B. "The Editor's Word: Winners." *Interiors* (December 1981): 61.

Schultz, G. "Preiswert und Trotzdem Beweglich." *Moebel + Decoration* (February 1981): 36-37.

Smith, P. "A Millenarian Hope: The Architecture of Emilio Ambasz." *ARTS* 6 (February 1981): 110-113.

——. "Books." *Manhattan Catalogue* 14 (April 1981): 41.

——."Viewpoints Architects and Architecture: The Underground Activity of Emilio Ambasz." *Gentlemen's Quarterly* 4 (April 1981): 30.

Sorkin, M. "Il Principio Portico." *Gran Bazaar* (May/ June 1981): 112-114.

——. "The Odd Couples." *The Village Voice* (March 18-24, 1981): 78.

Terra-2: The International Exposition of International Architecture. Wroclaw, Poland: Museum of Architecture, 1981.

1980

Archer, B.J. , ed. *Houses for Sale.* New York, NY: Rizzoli International Publications Inc., 1980: 3-16.

——. "Houses for Sale." *Architecture and Urbanism* (December 1980): 81-112.

Arditi, F."Che Bella Casa!L'Appendo al Chiodo." *Europeo* 44 (October 27, 1980): 117-118.

Barre, F. "Aménagement de Banque, Milan." *L'Architecture d'Aujordhui* 210 (September 1980): 70-73.

Blake, J.E. "Look Who's Lighting Up Britain." *Design* 379 (July 1980): 40-43.

Blumenthal, M. "Projet d'une Maison pour un Couple, a Cordobe, Espangne." *Techniques et Architecture* 331 (June/July 1980): 118-119.

"Castelli's Vertebra Chairs." *Form* 111 (1980): 54.

Crossley, M. "Review: 'City Segments'" *The Houston Post* (November 30, 1980): 16AA.

Davis, D. "Selling Houses as Art." *Newsweek* (October 27, 1980): 111.

——."The Solar Revolution." *Newsweek* (April 7, 1980): 79-80.

Dean, A.O."Luis Barragán, Austere Architect of Silent Spaces." *Smithsonian* 8 (November 1980): 152-156, 158 and 160.

Dixon, J.M. "Milan Bank: Correction." *Progressive Architecture* 4 (April 1980): 4.

Doubilet, S. "Castelli: It Ain't Necessary So." *Progressive Architecture* 12 (December 1980): 32.

"Emilio Ambasz: House for a Couple, Cordoba, Spain, Award." *Progressive Architecture* 1 (January 1980): 94-95.

Esterow, M."The Utopian and the Pragmatic." *Art News* 9 (November 1980): 14-15, 161.

Filler, M. "Eight Houses in Search of Their Owners." *House and Garden* 12 (December 1980): 104-105.

Foster, D. "Images and Ideas: 'City Segments' Exhibition." *Architecture Minnesota* (November 1980): 68-70.

Garner, P. *Twentieth-Century Furniture.* New York, NY: Van Nostrand Reinhold Company, 1980: 219.

Gehig, F. "The 27th P/A Awards, Architectural Design: Emilio Ambasz." *Progressive Architecture* (January 1980): 94-95.

Goldberger, P."Exhibition Dream Houses that Can Really be Built." *The New York Times Magazine* (October 12, 1980): Six 117, 129-130.

Horsley, C.B. "N.Y. Show Turns Spotlight on Custom Single-Family Dwellings." *International Herald Tribune* (November 24, 1980): 165.

——"Shop for a Custom House in an Art Gallery." *The New York Times* (August 24, 1980): C-8.

Houses for Sale. New York, NY: Leo Castelli Gallery, October 1980.

Huxtable, A. L. "Focus on the Museum Tower." *The New York Times* (August 24, 1980): C27-C28.

Irace, F. "Poetics of the Pragmatic: The Architecture of Emilio Ambasz." *Architectural Design* (December 1980): 154-157.

——."The Poetics of the Pragmatic." *Architecture and Urbanism* 116 (May 1980): 55-60.

Johnson, M.J. "Architecture for Sale at New York's Leo Castelli Gallery." *Architectural Record* (October 1980): 33.

Kosstrin, J. "Bad Press is Better than No Press at All, or So Speak the Wise Men of the Media." *Fetish* (Fall 1980): 4.

Larson, K. "Art: Architecture Invitational." *The Village Voice* (July 2-8, 1980): 48.

Maack, K. J."'High Tech'—eine Chance für das Design? " *Form* 89 (January 1980): 7-8.

——. "Logotec-Design: Emilio Ambasz and Giancarlo Piretti." *ERCO Lichtbericht* (April 1980): 12-13.

Mendini, A. "Elliptical Section Spot." *Domus* 605 (April 1980): 40.

——."Houses for Sale." *Domus* 611 (November 1980): 30-32.

——."Museo in Torre." *Domus* 612 (December 1980): 33.

Miller, N. "Black Ribbons and Lace." *Progressive Architecture* 3 (March 1980): 98-101.

Minardi, B. "The Myth of the Cave." *Domus* 608

(August 1980): 20-23.

Mosquera, L.M. "Diseño de Interiores, Línea Vértebra." *Summa* 157 (December 1980): 93-95.

Nakamura, T. "Special Issue: Emilio Ambasz." *Architecture and Urbanism* (May 1980): 33-60.

Papademetriou, C. "Inside 'Inside Outside'." *Texas Architect* 4 (July/August 1980): 79-81.

Pasta, A. "Ristrutturazione della Banca Bruxelles Lambert a Milano/Interior Alterations for a Bank in Milan." *L'Industria delle Construzione* 108 (October 1980): 5-8.

Pietrantoni, M. "Fairy-Tale and Ritual." *Domus* 603 (February 1980): 33-36.

Post, H. "Good Housekeeping, or Gimme Shelter." *New York* 1 (December 29, 1980): 28.

Rense, P. "Emilio Ambasz: House for a Couple in Cordoba, Spain." *Architectural Design* (December 1980): 152-153.

Schultz, G. "Ein Stuhl der 'Lebt'." *Moebel + Decoration* (August 1980): 44-45.

Smith, C.R. "Underground Buildings." *House and Garden, Building and Remodeling Guide* 6 (November/December 1980): 106-107.

Sorkin, M. "Drawings for Sale." *The Village Voice* (November 12-18, 1980): 85-86.

——."The Architecture of Emilio Ambasz." *Architecture and Urbanism* 116 (May 1980): 36-39.

Sutphen, M. "High Finance in a Stage Set." *Interiors* (June 1980): 62-65.

Wiseman, C. "Having Fun with Classics." *New York* 39 (October 6, 1980): 35-43.

1979

Blumenthal, M. "Deux Propositions Alternatives." *Techniques et Architecture* 325 (June/July 1979): 101-104.

Carlsen, P. and Friedman, D. "The First 50 Years." *Gentlemen's Quarterly* 9 (November 1979): 146-151.

Casati, C. "Concorso pro Memoria in Germania." *Domus* 598 (September 1979): 40-41.

——."Per una Piccola Cooperativa." *Domus* 594 (May 1979): 38-40.

Constantine, E. "Artistic Alternates to Modernism Architectural Projects by Roger Ferri and Allan Greenberg Museum of Modern Art, New York, June 2-July 25." *Progressive Architecture* 5 (May 1979): 30.

Dixon, J.M. "Working the Land." *Progressive Architecture* 4 (April 1979): 142-143.

Filler, M. "Interior Design: On the Threshold." *Progressive Architecture* 9 (September 1979): 129.

——."Rooms Without People: Notes on the Development of the Model Room." *Design Quarterly* 109 (1979): 4-15.

Gregotti, V. "Le Grandi Matito Sono Spuntate." *dell'Esspresso* (March 4, 1979): 176-177.

Irace, F. "C'era una Volta un Luogo un Cliente e un Architetto." *Modo* 22 (September 1979): 31-36.

Laine, C.K., ed., "McDonalds' Competition." *Metamorphosis.* The Association of Student Chapters, American Institute of Architects, 1979

McQuade, W. "Pursuing the Poetic Artifact." *Portfolio—The Magazine of the Visual Arts* 4 (October/November 1979): 76-80.

Permar, M.E. "The Most Innovative McDonald's of the Future." *Crit* 5 (Spring 1979): 26-27.

Stephens, S. "Book of Lists." *Progressive Architecture* 12 (December 1979): 56, 59.

1978

Ashton, D. "The Art of Architecutral Drawings: A Review of a Show of Architectural Drawings and Models." *Artscanada* 218/219 (February/March 1978): 34-37.

Casati, C. "Architettura: Come Disegnano Gli 'Architetti'." *Domus* 578 (January 1978): 4.

Davis, D. "Paper Buildings." *Newsweek* (February 6, 1978): 76-77.

"Design Directions: Other Voices." *The AIA Journal* 6 (Mid-May 1978): 160.

Fitzgibbons, R.M. "Body Furniture in the News." *House and Garden* 8 (August 1978): 108-109.

Gropp, L.O. "Color Abets Form for Mexican Architect." *Decorating: A House and Garden Guide* (Summer 1978): 68-69.

Kubát, B. "Suet Nábytku." *Umenní a Remesla* (March 1978): 56-58.

Locker, F.C., ed. *1978 Contemporary Authors*, Detroit, MI: Gale Research Company, 1978: 19-20.

Masaru, K. "Emilio Ambasz and His Surrealist Obsession." *Graphic Design* 69 13-28.

Morton, D. "Emilio Ambasz: Poetic Pragmatics." *Progressive Architecture* (September 1978): 98-101.

Raggi, F. "Emilio Ambasz Una Relazione Sul Mio Lavoro." *Europa/America Architecture Urbane Alternative Suburbane.* Venice, Italy: La Biennale di Venezia, 1978: 106-111.

Rose, B. "The Fine Italian Hand." *Vogue* 4 (April 1978): 247-248, 320 and 322-323.

Scäfer, S. "Forum Unberührt." *Bauen + Wohen* (Janaury

1978): 3.

Vergottini, B. and Iliprandi, G. *New York, Inclusive Tour*. Naples, Italy: Alberto Marotta Editore S.P.A., 1978.

1977

Alexandroff, G. "Centre d'Informatique, Park 'Las Promesas,' Mexico City." *L'Architecture d'Aujourd 'hui* (September 1977): 18-21.

Apraxine, P., org. "Emilio Ambasz." *Architecture I*. New York, NY: Leo Castelli Gallery, 1977: 6-7.

Bauman, H.H. "Bürostühle aus einer Initiative." *Form* 79 (March 1977): 34-35.

Bonta, J.P., *Sistemos de Significación en Arquitectura* 69. Barcelona, Spain: Gustavo Gili, 1977: 279.

Casati, C. "Underground Farm." *Domus* 576 (November 1977): 41-43.

Dixon, J.M. "Elusive Outcome." *Progressive Architec-*

ture 8 (May 1977): 90.

"Emilio Ambasz: Le Designer comme Réalisateur." *L'Architecture d'Aujourd'hui* 193 (October 1977): 64-66.

"For Sale: Advanced Design, Tested and Ready to Run." *Design* (October 1977).

Fox, M. *Print Casebooks 2: The Best in Exhibition Design*. Washington, D.C.: RC Publications, Inc. 1977: 14-16.

Goldberger, P. "Architectural Drawings Raised to an Art." *The New York Times*, (December 12, 1977).

Hess, T. B. "Drawn and Quartered." *New York* 41 (October 10, 1977): 70-72.

Huxtable, A.L."Architectural Drawings as Art Gallery Art." *The New York Times* (October 23, 1977): D-27.

McGrath, N. "Emilio Ambasz Conjures a Calmness." *Decorating: A House and Garden Guide* (Winter 1977-1978).

Nakamura, T. "Emilio Ambasz." *Shinkenchiku*, (December 1977): 186-187.

Nydele, A., ed. *Design Review: Industrial Design 23rd Annual*. New York, NY: Whitney Library of Design (December 1977): 160.

Ponti, G. "'Vertebra' Seating System." *Domus* 572 (July 1977): 38-39.

Reif, R. "Swivel, Whirl, Rock and Roll— In Comfort." *The New York Times* (June 30, 1977): 6.

Russell, B. "How to Beat Backaches and Pains in a New Hot Seat." *House and Garden* 3 (March 1977): 130.

Stern, R.A.M. "Architects of the New '40 under 40'."

Architecture and Urbanism 77 (January 1977): 72-73.

"Vertebralement Bien Assis." *Vogue Hommes* (1977).

"Emilio Ambasz" *A View of Contemporary World Architects*. Japan: Tokyo, Japan: Shinkenchiku-sha, 1977: 186.

Waisman, M. "La Arquitectura Alternativa de Emilio Ambasz." *Summarios* 11 (September 1977): 29-32.

1976

"A Cooperative of Mexican-American Grape Growers." *Space Design* 146 (October 1976): 8-12.

Bendixson, T. "Taxi: The Taxi Project: Realistic Solutions for Today." *RIBA Journal* (December 1976).

Casati, C. "In Peru: Floating Units." *Domus* 555 (February 1976): 30-31.

"Community Arts Center." *Space Design* 146 (October 1976): 13-19.

"Crate Containers Italy: The New Domestic Landscape." *Space Design* 146 (October 1976): 28-29.

Donovan, H. "Call Me a Taxi, You Yellow Cab." *Time* 26 (June 21, 1976.): 60-61.

"Ecco il Taxi Alfa Romeo." *Corriere della* Sera (October 1976).

"Educational and Agrarian Community Centers." *Space Design* 146 (Otober 1976): 20-27.

"Emilio Ambasz A Beaux-Arts Courthouse in Grand Rapids, Mich." *Progressive Architecture* 1 (January 1976): 60-61.

"Europa-America: Architetture Urbane/Alternative Suburbane. Venice: The Venice Biennale, " *Magazzini del Sale alle Zattere* (June 20, 1976).

"Giugiaro: Proposta di un Taxi per gli tanni o Hanta!" *Il Fiorino* (1976)

Hasegawa, A. "Special Feature: Up-and-Coming Light: Emilio Ambasz—His Works and Thoughts." *Space Design* 7610: 4-44.

Huxtable, A.L. *Kicked a Building Lately?* New York, NY: Quadrangle/The New York Times Book Company,.1976: 51, 205, and 207.

"Invisible Storage." *House and Garden* 8: 64-67.

Kron, J. "The Tip off on Taxi Interactions." *New York* 25: 50.

Moore, A.C. "23rd Annual Awards—Emilio Ambasz." *Progressive Architecture*: 60-61.

Mosquera, L.M. "Distinciones a Arquitectos Argentinos: Emilio Ambasz." *Summa* 103 (August 1976): 14.

Négréanu, G. "Projet d'Équipments de Secours pour

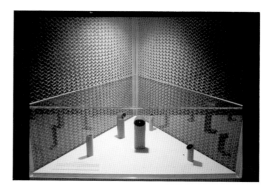

Zones Inondées." *CREE* (December 1975/ January 1976): 61-63.

"Oporta Giugiaro." *Autosprint* (July 6, 1976).

Ponti, G. "Taxi a New York." *Domus* 560 (July 1976): 40-44.

Princeton's Beaux Arts and Its New Academicism from Labatut to the Program of Geddes. New York, NY: The Institute for Architecture and Urban Studies, 1976.

Reiss, B. "I'll be Down to Get You in a Steam Taxi, Honey." *New York Magazine* 25 (January 27-February 18, 1976): 44-47.

"Seating System'Vertebra'." *Space Design* 146 (October 1976): 30-33.

Tafuri, M. "Emilio Ambasz: Village des Chicanos." *L'Architecture d' Aujourd'hui* 186 (August/September 1976): 70-72.

——."Les Cendres de Jefferson." *L'Architecture d'Aujord'hui* 186 (August/September 1976.): 53-58.

Tallmer, J. "Taxi, Mister?" *New York Post* (July 10, 1976): 32.

"The Taxi Project: Realistic Solutions for Today." *Space Design* 146 (October 1976.): 34-44.

"Un Taxi per gli USA Progettato a Torino." *La Stampa.* (June 19, 1976).

"Uno Studii Internazionale: Taxi per New York." *Stampa Sera* (June 24, 1976): 3.

Zevi, B. "Architettura:Piazza Italia è uno Stivale." *L'Espresso* (April 25, 1976): 100-101.

1975

Casati, C., ed. "Edifici Mobili Galleggianti: A Centre for Applied Computer Research." *Domus* 546 (March 1975): 1-4.

Casati, C., ed. "Recycling and Restoration." *Domus* 551 (October 1975): 8-10.

Fox, M. *The Print Casebooks: The Best in Posters.* First annual edition. Washington D.C.: RC Publications, Inc., 1975: 6.

Hasegawa, A., ed. "Center for Applied Computer Research and Programming Park 'Las Promesas,' Outskirts of Mexico City, Mexico." *Space Design* 132 (August 1975): 56-61.

Négréanu, G. "Projet pour un Centre de Calcul á Mexico." *CREE* 36 (August/September 1975): 66-67.

Ryder, S. L.. "The Art of High Art." *Progressive Architecture* 3 (March 1975): 62-67.

1974

Noblet, J. *Design.* Chêne, France: Editions Stock, 1974: 371.

1971

Portas, N. *Arquitectura: Forma de Conocimiento forma de Comunicacion.* Barcelona, Spain: Escuela Tecnica Superior de Arquitecturade Barcelona, 1971: 1 and 6.

1970

McQuade, W. "Pursuing the Poetic Artifact." *Porfolio* (October/November 1970): 76-80.

1967

Kurtz, S. A. *Wasteland: Building the American Dream.* New York, NY: Praeger Publishers, 1967.

PUBLICATIONS BY EMILIO AMBASZ

1992

"FAX" *ID* 1 (February 1992): 50-51.

"FAX: Could a Design Magazine Become the Theological Review of the 21st Century?" *ID* 2 (March/April 1992): 50-51.

"Stichliandling" *ID* 2 (March/April 1992): 74-75.

1991

"Emilio Ambasz: Works and Projects." (Zevi, R., ed.) *L'architettura.* (November 1991): 889-905.

"Luca Scacchetti Architetture." *Borrowed Lives.* Milan, Italy: IDEA Books, 1991: 42-43.

"Robertos Wilson, Luminarios (Premier Régisseur) et Maître." *Robert Wilson.* Paris, France: Editions du Centre Pompidou, 1991: 23-28.

"Visual Monologues." *Collages.* (Chermayeff, I.) New York, NY: Harry N. Abrams, Inc., 1991: 24-25.

1990

"Algunas notas sobre una correspondencia mental que mantuve a traves de los ultimos veinticinco años con Delfina Galvez de Williams sobre la obra de Amancio." *Amancio Williams.* Buenos Aires, Argentina: Gaglianone Establecimiento Grafico S.A., 1990: 13-16.

"Exhibition Recap." *SD* 2 (1990): 102-112.

Houses for the Steles. New York, NY: Ulysses Gallery, 1990: 22-23.

"Italian Radical Architecture and Design 1966-1973." (Radice, B.) Milan, Italy: *Terrazzo.* 5 (Fall 1990).

"Oficinas para una Empresa de Seguros." *Tecnologia y Arquitectura* 10 (October 1990): 34.

"Who Owns Design?" *Metropolis* 3 (October 1990): 62.

1989

(and Foscari, A.) "All the Lagoon's a Stage..." *Marco Polo* 61 (February 1989): 49.

"Dear Friends, Wish You Were Here." *Marco Polo* 61 (February 1989): 50.

Review: New Product Design. London, UK: Design Museum, 1989: 37.

1988

"Da un addetto ai Lavori: Breviario per un ..." *Modo* 108 (September 1988): 22-24.

"Elegy for Italian Design." *International Design* (November/December 1988): 55.

Emilio Ambasz: The Poetics of the Pragmatic. New York, NY: Rizzoli International Publications, Inc., 1988.

(des.) *Mimar* 27 (January-March 1988): cover/concept.

"Mycal." *Nikkei Architecture* (August 8, 1988): 94-95.

"San Antonio Botanical Conservatory. " *Deconstruction—Archite ...*3/4 (April 1988): 46-47.

"Tadao Ando." *Ando by Ando.* Bordeaux, France: Arc en Rêve Éditeur, 1988: 55.

1987

"Carrelli Elevatori a Wall Street." *l'Arca* 1 (January/February 1987).

(des. and prod.) "Design Review" *AXIS* 23 (Spring 1987): 105, excerpts 9, 18.

(des. and prod.) "Design Review" *AXIS* 24 (Summer 1987): 57, excerpts 9.

(des. and prod.) "Design Review" *AXIS* 22 (Winter1987): 105.

"Emilio Ambasz: A Decade of Architecture, Industrial and Graphic Design." *Emilio Ambasz.* (Tironi, G., ed.) Geneva, Switzerland: *Halle Sud.* Institute of Contemporary Arts, March 1987.

"Design Review: Italian Design: Requiem for Memphis." *AXIS*, vol. 22, Winter 1987: 105, excerpts 19.

"Emilio Ambasz and the Memesis of Nature." *AU: Arredo Urbano* 23 (December 1987): 72-76.

"Interior Advantage." *Brutus* 172 (January 15, 1987): 188-189.

(des.) *Mimar* 23 (January-March 1987): cover/concept.

(des.) *Mimar* 24, (April-June 1987): cover/concept.

(des.) *Mimar* 25 (July-September 1987): cover/concept.

(des.) *Mimar* 26 (October-December 1987): cover/concept.

"Nota Biografica/Textos/ Obras y Projectos." *Summarios* 109 (1987): 8-15.

"Siviglia si Riflette nel Mondo." *l'Arca*, no. 8, July/August 1987: 40-47.

1986

(ed.) "The 1986 Design Zoo." *The International Design Yearbook 1986/87.* (Sudjic, D., gen. ed.) London, UK: John Calmann and King Ltd. and Cross River Press Ltd., 1986.

"Ancient Court Music Beaten Up!" *Space Design* 8601 (1986): 57.

"Chi E Luis Barragán." *Casa Vogue,* June 1986: 94-109.

"Design Review: Italian Design: A 15 Year Perspective." *AXIS* 21 (Autumn 1986): 50, excerpts 8.

Il Giardino d'Europe. (Vezzosi, A., ed.) Milan, Italy: Mazzotta, 1986: 202-204.

"Italian Design—A 15 year Perspective." *AXIS* (Autumn 1986): 50.

"The Italian Influence." *Interior Design in the 20th Century.* (Tate, A. and Smith, R.C., eds.) New York, NY: Harper & Row, 1986.

"La Citta del Design." (Cornu, R., trans.) *Halle Sud*

Magazine (1986): 4.

"Luis Barragán." *House and Garden* (February 1986): 18-28.

(with Smith, P.) "A Millenarian Hope: The Architecture of Emilio Ambasz." *The Harvard Architecture Review.* New York, NY: Rizzoli International Publications, Inc., 1986: 96-103.

(des.) *Mimar* 19 (January-March 1986): cover/concept.

(des.) *Mimar* 20 (April-June 1986):cover/concept.

(des.) *Mimar* 21 (July-September 1986): cover/concept.

(des.) *Mimar* 22 (October-December 1986): cover/concept.

"Spain: Columbus Expo." *TWA: Ambassador* (December 1986): 9.

1985

(des.) "Contract and Residential Furniture Logotec Spotlight Range." *Industrial Design Excellence USA.* USA: The Design Foundation, 1985: 13.

"Ambasz, Emilio." *Contemporary Landscape from the Horizon of Postmodern Design.* Kyoto/Tokyo, Japan: The National Museum of Modern Art, 1985-1986.

"Design Review." *AXIS* (Autumn 1985): 3, 38-41.

"Emilio Ambasz: Botanical Pleasures." *Domus* 667 (December 1985): 14-17.

"Ensayos y Apuntes para un Bosquejo Critico." *Luis Barragán.* Mexico City, Mexico: Museum Rufino Tamayo, A.C., 1985: 23-25.

"Exhibition & Lecture Series of Work by Young Architects: Competition Winners." *Rough Drafts 85* New York, NY: Urban Center Galleries, 1985.

"Exhibition." *The Commercial Architecture* 6 (June 1985): 244-245.

(des.) "Furniture and Furnishings: Dorsal Seating Range." *Industrial Design Excellence USA.* USA: The Design Foundation, 1985: 44.

"Introduction." *Intercepting Light.* (Ando, T.) Japan: Designer's brochure, 1985.

"Manoir D'Angoussart." *The Princeton Journal* (Beeler, R., ed.) (1985): 128-131.

"La libreria nel Giardino." *Gran Bazaar* (December/January 1985): 140.

(des.) *Mimar* 15 (January-March 1985): cover/concept.

(des.) *Mimar* 16 (April-June 1985): cover/concept.

(des.) *Mimar* 17 (July-October 1985): cover/concept.

(des.) *Mimar* 18 (November-December 1985): cover/concept.

"New Work of Shiro Kuramata." *AXIS* (Summer 1985): 60-61, 63.

1984

"Dar Forma Póetica a lo Pragmático: Notas Sobre Mi Obra de Diseño." *Diario* 16 (May 11, 1984): 5 (Hogar 16).

Emilio Ambasz. Italy: Grafis Editions, 1984.

"Emilio Ambasz: The Innovator for Aiming at Utopia." *Idea: International Advertising Art* 187 (November 1984): 88-95.

"Fabula Rasa." *Via 7: The Building of Architecture.* Cambridge and London, UK: The MIT Press, 1984: 87.

"Houston Center Plaza." *AD: Architectural Design Profile (Urbanism)* 12 (January/February1984): 46-47.

"La Folly de Emilio: El Hombre es una Isla." *Follies: MOPU Arquitectura* (May/June 1984): 34-37.

"La Piazza Interminabile: Il Caffè della Città." *Domus.* 649 (April 1984): 14-19, 116.

"L'Arte Dans L'Eau: New Orleans Museum of Art." *Domus* 651 (June 1984): 30-31.

(des.) *Mimar* 11 (January-March 1984): cover/concept.

(des.) *Mimar* 12 (April-June 1984): cover/concept.

(des.) *Mimar* 13 (July-October 1984): cover/concept.

(des.) *Mimar* 14 (November-December 1984): cover/concept.

"Notes About My Design Work." *IDEA* 187 (November, 1984): 90-93.

"Notas acerca de mi labor de diseño." *Diseño* (May 1984): 71-75.

Obras y Proyectos, 1972-1984: Entre la Arcadia y la Utopia. Madrid, Spain: Colegio Oficial de Arquitectos de Madrid, 1984.

"Plaza Major, Salamanca." *Architectural Design—Urbanism* (January/February 1984): 44-45.

"Popular Pantheon." Article on James Stirling. *The Architectural Review* 1054 (December 1984): 35.

"Three Projects by Enzo Mari...." *Domus* 649 (April 1984): 14-19.

1983

"Automatisch-Dynamisches Sitzen." *MD: Moebel Interior Design* (October 10, 1983): 56-57.

Dal Cucchiaio alla Città: Nell'itinerario di 100 Designers. (Venosta, C.) Milan, Italy: Electa, 1983: 26-27.

"Emilio Ambasz: Dieci Anni di Architettura, Grafica, Design in un Multivision Ralizzato de Domus." *Centrodomus* (October 24, 1983).

"Emilio's Folly: Man is an Island." *Follies: Architecture for the Late-Twentieth Century Landscape.* (Archer, B.J., ed.) New York, NY: Rizzoli International Publications, 1983: 34-37.

"Houston Center Plaza, Houston: Metaphoric Image of the City." *Lotus International.* Venice, Italy: Gruppo Electa S.p.A. 1983: 65-69.

(ed.) "Italy: The New Domestic Landscape, Exhibit, MOMA 1972." *Domus* ???, 1983: 27.

(and Jakobson, B.) "La Casa Bifronte/Janus's House." *Domus* 635 (January 1983): 34-39.

"La Mostra 'Italy: The New Domestic Landscape' presentata...ebbe un forte e profondo impatto." *Domus*, 1983.

(des.) *Mimar* 7 (January-March 1983): cover/concept.

(des.) *Mimar* 8 (April-June 1983): cover/concept.

(des.) *Mimar* 9 (July-October 1983): cover/concept.

(des.) *Mimar* 10 (November-December 1983):cover/concept.

"Premios Kones 1982—Artes Visuales." *Diploma al Merito: Libro de Oro de las Artes Visuales Argentinas.* Buenos Aires, Argentina: La Fundacion Konex, 1983: 86.

"Review on Herbert Muschamps." *Man About Town.* Cambridge, MA: MIT Press, 1983.

"Salamanca: The Plaza Mayor. A Garden in the City, a City in the Garden." *Lotus International* Venice, Italy: Gruppo Electra S.p.A., 1983: 62-64.

"Skin and Bones." *Alcantara.* (Confalonieri, F.G., ed.) Milan, Italy: Electa, 1983: 20-29.

(des.) *The Dorsal Seating Range: Innovation.* McLean, VA: Industrial Designers Society of America 1 (Winter 1983): 23-25.

"Visual Monologue." *Collages.* (Chermayeff, I.) Vienna, Austria: Galerie Ulysses, 1983.

1982

"Ambasz: Los que Conozco Diseñan los Domingos." *Vivienda* 235 (February 1982): 8.

"Ambasz to Consult at Cummins Engine." *ID: Industrial Design Magazine* 4 (July/August 1982): 30.

"Beyond Metaphor, Beyond Form. Meanings of Modernism." *Design Quarterly* 118-119 (1982): 4-11.

Il Design Oggi in Italia Tra Produzione, Consumo E Qualcos' Altro. Italy: Museo Villa Pignatelli Giugno, 1982: 27.

"La Citta de Design." *Skyline* (November 1982): 24.

"Milano, 1920-1940." *Skyline* (November 1982): 18-19.

(des.) *Mimar* 3 (January-March 1982): cover/concept.

(des.) *Mimar* 4 (April-June 1982): cover/concept.

(des.) *Mimar* 5 (July-September 1982): cover/concept.

(des.) *Mimar* 6 (October-December 1982): cover/concept.

(et. al.) "P/A Second Annual Conceptual Furniture Competition." *Progressive Architecture* 5 (May 1982): 158-169.

(pref.) *Precursors of Post-Modernism.* New York, NY: The Architectural League, 1982.

Introduction to discussion of Architectural League Exhibition, *Precursors of Post-Modernism* (November 1982).

"Reportaje: Emilio Ambasz." *Summa* 174 (May 1982): 21-22.

Wait Until You See the Next Olivetti Machine: Memphis 82. Milan, Italy: Stampa Nava Milano S.p.A., 1982: 4.

1981

"Columbus il Mito." *La Mia Casa* 141 (October 1981): 106-107.

"Farewell, Caro Maestro." *Progressive Architecture* 5 (May 1981): 117.

"La Proposta di Ambasz." *Domus* 622 (November 1981): 49.

(des.) *Mimar* 1 (July-September 1981): cover/concept.

"P/A First Annual Conceptual Furniture Competition." *Progressive Architecture* 5 (May 1981): 150-155.

"Post Modernism, the Social Aspect." Extract:. *Performing Arts* 3 (1981): 59-60.

"The Four Gates to Columbus." *Artists & Architects Collaboration.* (Meritet, M., illus. and Diamonstein, B., ed.)New York, NY: Whitney Library of Design, 1981: 130-135.

The Return of Marco Polo. (with Vignelli, M., des.) New York, NY: Rizzoli International Publications, Inc., 1981.

1980

"A Cooperative of Mexican-American Grape Growers, California, 1976." *Design Quarterly* 113/114 (1980): 26-27.

"Ambasz." *Domus* 610 (October 1980): 20.

"Notes About My Design Work." *Architecture and Urbanism* (Special Issue: Emilio Ambasz) 5 (May 1980): 33-60.

"Imponderable Substance." *Progressive Architecture* 9 (September 1980): 138-141.

"Projet D'une Maison Pour un Couple, A Cordoue, Espagne." *Techniques et Architecture* 331 (June/July 1980): 118-119.

"Working Fables: A Collection of Design Tales for Skeptic Children." *Architecture and Urbanism* 5 (May 1980): 107-114.

1979

"CIESP: Núcleo de Desenho Industrial." *MOMA Design: Exposicão* New York, NY: The Museum of Modern Art, 1979.

"Deux Propositions Alternatives." *Techniques et Architecture* 325 (June/July 1979): 101-104.

"Favolette di Progettazione (Working Fables)." *Modo* (September/October 1979): 56.

"House & Atelier for Luis Barragán and San Cristobal." *GA: Global Architecture* 48 (1979): 2-7.

"Luis Barragán." *GA: Global Architecture* 48 (1979).

1978

"Architecture is the Reply to Man's Passion and Hunger." *The AIA Journal* (Mid-May 1978): 231.

"Ambasz, Emilio." *Global Eye '78 7 New Design Pow-*

ers. (Kamekura, Y.) Japan: Japan Design Committee, 1978.

(fore.) *High Tech: The Industrial Style and Source Book for the Home.* (Kron, J., and Slesin, S.) New York, NY: Clarkson N. Potter, Inc. Publishers, 1978.

"Views Credit: Chair Development." *Progressive Architecture* 2 (December 1978): 8.

1977

"A View of Contemporary World Architects." (December 1977): 186-187.

(des.) *Architecture I.* (Apraxine, P., org.) New York, NY: Leo Castelli Gallery, 1977.

"Centros Comunitarios Educacionales y Agrarios." *Summarios* 11 (September 1977): 8-19.

"Centro Mexicano de Cálculo Aplicado SA." *Summarios* 11 (September 1977): 17.

"Community Art Center." *Summarios* 11 (September 1977): 28.

"Conjunto de Viviendas en un Establecimiento Agrícola." *Summarios* 11 (September 1977): 26-27.

"Cooperativa de Viñateros Mexicano-Norteamericanos." *Summarios* 11 (September 1977): 20-22.

"For Sale: Advanced Design, Tested and Ready to Run." *Design* 346 (October 1977): 50-53.

"La Univerciudad (Borrador)." *Summarios* 11 (September 1977): 17.

"Le Designer Comme Réalisateur." *l'Architecture d'Aujourd'hui* (October 1977): 64-66.

"Moral: Una Condición de Prediseño." *Summarios* 11 (September 1977): 16.

"Una Declaración Sobre mi Obra." *Summarios* 11 (September 1977): 15.

"Working Fables: Sleepwalker's Dream." *Modo* 3 (September/October 1977): 56.

1976

"Commentary." *Princeton's Beaux Arts and Its New Academicism.* (Wurmfeld, M., ed.) New York, NY: The Institute for Architecture and Urban Studies, 1976: 25.

The Architecture of Luis Barragán. New York, NY: The Museum of Modern Art, 1976.

(ed.) *The Taxi Project: Realistic Solutions for Today.* New York, NY: The Museum of Modern Art, 1976.

"Up-and-Coming Light: Emilio Ambasz—His Works and Thoughts. A Statement About my Work." *Space Design* (Special feature: October 1976): 4-44.

1975

"Anthology for a Spatial Buenos Aires. A Selection from 'Working Fables'—A Collection of Schematic Design Tales for Skeptic Children." *Casabella* 389 (February 1975): 6-7.

"Coda: A Pre-Design Condition: A Selection from 'Working Fables'—A Collection of Design Tales for Skeptic Children." *Casabella* 401 (May 1975): 4-5.

"Manhattan, Capital of the 20th Century: A Selection from 'Working Fables'—A Collection of Schematic Design Tales for Skeptic Children." *Casabella,* 397 (January 1975): 4.

"Ultimately, a Flower Barge." *Progressive Architecture* 5 (May 1975): 76-79.

"The Univercity: A Selection from 'Working Fables'—A Collection of Design Tales for Skeptic Children." *Casabella* 399 (March 1975): 8-9.

(ed.) *Walter Pichler: Projects.* New York, NY: The Museum of Modern Art, 1975.

1974

"A Selection from Working Fables: A Collection of Design Tales for Skeptic Children." *Oppositions* 4 (October 1974): 65-74.

"Design im Zeitalter der Aufklärung." *Form* 68 (March 1974): 32-33.

"La Città del Design: A Selection from 'Working Fables'—A Collection of Schematic Design Tales for Skeptic Children." *Casabella* 394 (October 1974): 4-5.

"The Enlightened Client: A Selection from 'Working Fables'—A Collection of Schematic Design Tales for Skeptic Children." *Casabella* 396 (December 1974): 4-5.

1972

(ed.) *Italy: The New Domestic Landscape.* New York, NY: Museum of Modern Art, 1972.

1971

"Instituciones y Artefactos para una Sociedad Postecnolólogica." *Summa* 37 (May 1971): 30-36.

1969

"The Formulation of a Design Discourse." *Perspecta* 12 (1969): 57-71.

Photo Credits

Santi Caleca	22, 24, 32, 62	Richard Payne	8, 10
Mario Carrieri	302, 303, 304, 305	David Robinson	306
Louis Checkman	14, 16, 18, 20, 26, 28, 34, 36 ,40,	Richard Scanlan	101, 104, 105, 106, 107, 108,
	42, 44, 46, 48, 52, 60, 88, 193,		109, 110, 111, 112, 113, 118,
	194, 195,196, 197, 198, 199,		119, 144, 145, 150, 151, 153,
	200, 201, 202, 203, 206, 207,		155, 160, 161, 163, 164, 165,
	208, 209, 215, 216, 217		166, 167, 168, 169, 173, 174,
Courtesy of Cummins			175, 239, 242, 243, 251, 252,
Engine Co.	296, 297		253, 255, 257, 263, 268, 269,
Courtesy of ERCO	312		292 313, 314, 315, 324, 325,
Courtesy of La Jolla			326, 327
Museum	343, 344, 347, 348	Superstudio	70
Courtesy of MoMA	336, 337, 338, 339, 340, 341,		
	342		
Josh Haskin	136		
Wolfgang Hoyt	129, 130, 131, 132, 133, 139		
Industrial Foto	308, 309, 310, 311		
Ryuzo Masunaga	121, 122, 123, 141, 142, 143,		
	259, 260, 261, 264, 265, 274,		
	275, 277, 278, 279, 281, 284,		
	285, 290, 291, 293, 298, 299,		
	300, 301, 320, 321, 328, 329,		
	360		
Alessandro Magris	64		
Joshua Nefsky	306, 307, 316, 317, 318, 319,		
	322, 323		

PROJECT CREDITS

URBAN & BUILDING DESIGN

FUKUOKA PREFECTURAL INTERNATIONAL HALL
Client	Dai-ichi Mutual Life Insurance Co., Tokyo, Japan
Principal in Charge	Emilio Ambasz
Project Director	Hideotoshi Kawaguchi
Design Team	Humberto Cordero
	Karen McEvoy
	Rizal Oei
	Hideo Tanai
Model Maker	Peter Ydeen
Illustrator	Suns Hung

WORLDBRIDGE TRADE AND EXHIBITION CENTER
Client	Asia/USA Development Corp., Big Indian, New York USA
Principal in Charge	Emilio Ambasz
Project Director	W. Lachlan Elting
Consultant	Les Robertson
Model Maker	Peter Ydeen
Illustrators	Joaquin Carter
	Suns Hung

MYCAL CENTER SANDA
Client	Nichii Corporation, Osaka, Japan
Principal in Charge	Emilio Ambasz
Project Director	Hideotoshi Kawaguchi
Design Team	Merritt Bucholz
	Joaquin Carter
	Humberto Cordero
	W. Lachlan Elting
	Karen McEvoy
	Hideo Tanai
Consultant	Alan Henschel
Model Makers	Peter Ydeen
	Umit Koroglu
Illustrator	Suns Hung

PHOENIX MUSEUM OF HISTORY
Client	City of Phoenix, Arizona USA
Principal in Charge	Emilio Ambasz
Design Team	Daniel K. Brown
	Joaquin Carter
	Hideotoshi Kawaguchi
	Karen McEvoy
	Rizal Oei
	David S. Robertson
	Hideo Tanai
Local Architects	Langdon-Wilson Architectural Planning
Model Maker	Peter Ydeen
Illustrator	Joaquin Carter

CONVENT OF THE HOLY INFANT JESUS
Client	LKH Construction Co., Singapore
Principal in Charge	Emilio Ambasz
Project Director	Rizal Oei
Design Team	Merritt Bucholz
	Hideotoshi Kawaguchi
	Hideo Tanai
Chief Model Maker	Peter Ydeen
Assistant Model Maker	Micheal Nellini
Illustrator	Suns Hung

COLUMBUS BRIDGE
Client	Indiana Department of Transportation, Indiana USA
Principal in Charge	Emilio Ambasz
Engineers	Butler Fairman & Seufert Inc.
Chief Engineer	Stephen F. Weintraut
Project Director	W. Lachlan Elting
Design Team	Daniel K. Brown
	Joaquin Carter
	Jeff Schofield
Chief Model Maker	Peter Ydeen

Assistant Model Maker	Brad Whitermore
Illustrator	Joaquin Carter

BEAUBOURG TERRACE GARDEN
Client	Centre de Creation Industrielle CCI, Paris, France
Principal in Charge	Emilio Ambasz
Project Director	Joaquin Carter
Model Maker	Peter Ydeen
Illustrator	Joaquin Carter

MOBIPARK URBAN FURNITURE
Client	The Burelle Group, Paris, France
Principal in Charge	Emilio Ambasz
Project Director	Joaquin Carter
Design Team	Christine Morin
	Eric Williams
Model Maker	Brad Whitermore
Illustrator	Joaquin Carter

NISHIYACHIYO BUSINESS DISTRICT
Client	Nomura Real Estate Development Co., Ltd., Tokyo, Japan
Principal in Charge	Emilio Ambasz
Design Team	John Chu
	Humberto Cordero
Chief Model Maker	Peter Ydeen
Assistant Model Makers	Jim Guld
	Dimitry Samoylin
Illustrator	John Chu

HARBOR OF THE FOUR SEASONS
Client	Nichii Corp., Osaka, Japan
Principal in Charge	Emilio Ambasz
Design Team	Dwight Ashdown
Illustrator	Suns Hung

OTARU MARINE WATERFRONT DEVELOPMENT
Client	Nichii Corp., Osaka/Hokkaido, Japan
Principal in Charge	Emilio Ambasz
Design Team	Joaquin Carter
	W. Lachlan Elting
Model Maker	Brad Whitermore
Illustrator	Suns Hung

NIIGATA NEW TOWN DEVELOPMENT
Client	Nichii Corp., Osaka, Japan
Principal in Charge	Emilio Ambasz
Design Team	Joaquin Carter
	W. Lachlan Elting
Model Maker	Peter Ydeen
Illustrator	Joaquin Carter

MARINE RESORT OF THE SETO INLAND SEA
Client	Nichii Corp., Osaka, Japan
Principal in Charge	Emilio Ambasz
Project Director	W. Lachlan Elting
Design Team	Humberto Cordero
Consultant	P. Savona
Illustrator	Joaquin Carter

REALWORLD THEME PARK
Client	Real World Corp., Wiltshire, UK
Principal in Charge	Emilio Ambasz
Project Director	Joaquin Carter
Design Team	David S. Robertson
Consultant	P. Savona
Model Maker	Peter Ydeen
Illustrator	Joaquin Carter

RIMINI BEACHFRONT DEVELOPMENT
Client	Rimini City and Province, Italy
Principal in Charge	Emilio Ambasz
Design Team	Joaquin Carter

Consultant	Humberto Cordero
	W. Lachlan Elting
	Hideotoshi Kawaguchi
	Hideo Tanai
	Jun Tomita
Consultant	P. Savona
Chief Model Maker	Peter Ydeen
Assistant Model Maker	Paul Ng
Illustrator	Joaquin Carter

FOCCHI SHOPPING CENTER
Client	Focchi SpA, Rimini, Italy
Principal in Charge	Emilio Ambasz
Project Director	W. Lachlan Elting
Model Maker	Peter Ydeen
Illustrator	Joaquin Carter

PRIVATE ESTATE
Client	Name Withheld
Principal in Charge	Emilio Ambasz
Project Director	Daniel K. Brown
Design Team	Merritt Bucholz
	Joaquin Carter
	Humberto Cordero
	Hideotoshi Kawaguchi
	Dimitris Klapsis
	Hideo Tanai
	Jun Tomita
Consultants	Jay Kirby
	James Hofman
Model Maker	Peter Ydeen
Illustrator	Joaquin Carter

CASA CANALES
Client	Mr. and Mrs. Ernesto Santos Canales, Monterrey, Mexico
Principal in Charge	Emilio Ambasz
Project Director	Joaquin Carter
Design Team	Daniel K. Brown
	David S. Robertson
Consultant	P. Savona
Chief Model Maker	Peter Ydeen
Assistant Model Maker	Paul Ng
Illustrator	Joaquin Carter

INDUSTRIAL DESIGN

HANDKERCHIEF TELEVISION
Designer in Charge	Emilio Ambasz
Design Team	Masamichi Udagawa
Model Makers	Masamichi Udagawa
	Megumi Ukai
	Brad Whitermore

SOFT NOTEBOOK COMPUTER
Designer in Charge	Emilio Ambasz
Design Team	Eric Williams
Model Makers	Megumi Ukai
	Eric Williams

SOFT CASSETTE/RADIO PLAYER
Designer in Charge	Emilio Ambasz
Design Team	Eric Williams
Model Maker	Megumi Ukai
	Eric Williams

MID-RANGE ENGINE SERIES
Client	Cummins Engine Co., Columbus, IN USA
Chief Design Consultant	Emilio Ambasz
Design Team	Cummins New Product Design Staff
Manufacturer	Cummins Engine Co.

DESK SET
Client	Knoll International, (KnollExtra Division), NYC, NY USA
Designer in Charge	Emilio Ambasz
Design Team	David Robinson

Model Maker	James Gould
Manufacturer	Knoll International, USA

QUALIS OFFICE SEATING
Client	Tecno SpA, Milano, Italy
Designer in Charge	Emilio Ambasz
Design Team	Claudio Gamberini
	Salvatore Gamberini
	Emilio Generali
Model Maker	Emilio Generali
Manufacturer	Tecno SpA

AQUA DOVE WATER BOTTLE
Designer in Charge	Emilio Ambasz
Design Team	David Robinson
Model Maker	Kenneth Miller

VERTAIR OFFICE SEATING
Client	Castelli SpA, Bologna, Italy
Designer in Charge	Emilio Ambasz
Design Team	Claudio Gamberini
	Emilio Generali
Model Maker	Emilio Generali
Manufacturer	Castelli SpA

OSERIS SPOTLIGHT COMPONENTS
Client	Erco Leuchten GmbH, Ludenscheid, Germany
Designer in Charge	Emilio Ambasz
Design Team	N. Dworak
	David Robinson
Manufacturer	Erco Leuchten GmbH

JANUS WRISTWATCH COLLECTION
Designer in Charge	Emilio Ambasz
Design Team	Eric Williams
Model Maker	Eric Williams

TELESCOPIC LUGGAGE
Client	Ajioka Corp., Tokyo, Japan
Designer in Charge	Emilio Ambasz
Design Team	Salvatore Gamberini
Model Maker	Salvatore Gamberini
Manufacturer	Ajioka Corp.

WALL PANELS
Client	Sunstar Engineering, Inc., Osaka, Japan
Designer in Charge	Emilio Ambasz
Design Team	David Robinson
	Meredith Robinson
	Barbara Weston
Model Makers	Christine Morin
	Meredith Robinson
Manufacturer	Sunstar Engineering, Inc.

FLEXIBOLL PEN
Client	Pentel, Inc., Tokyo, Japan
Designer in Charge	Emilio Ambasz
Design Team	Eric Chan
	David Robinson
	Barry Scott
Manufacturer	Pentel, Inc.

MANUAL TOOTHBRUSHES
Client	Sunstar, Inc., Osaka, Japan
Designer in Charge	Emilio Ambasz
Design Team	David Robinson
	Barry Scott
	Masamichi Udagawa
	Eric Williams
Model Makers	Peter Ydeen

PERIODENT ELECTRIC GUM MASSAGER
Client	Sunstar, Inc., Osaka, Japan
Designer in Charge	Emilio Ambasz
Design Team	Barry Scott
	David Robinson
Model Maker	David Robinson
Manufacturer	Sunstar, Inc.

PROJECT INDEX

EMILIO AMBASZ

ARCHITECTURE, EXHIBITION, INDUSTRIAL AND GRAPHIC DESIGN

La Jolla Museum of Contemporary Art   June 11–August 6, 1989

Musée des Arts Décoratifs de Montréal   October 1, 1989 – January 6, 1990

Akron Art Museum   January 26 – March 25, 1990

The Art Institute of Chicago   May 1 – July 2, 1990

Laumeier Sculpture Park   September 9 – November 11, 1990

Des Moines Art Center   April 27 – June 23, 1991

The Queens Museum   October 5 – December 1, 1991

This exhibition has been organized by the La Jolla Museum of Contemporary Art and made possible by a grant from the Graham Foundation for Advanced Studies in the Fine Arts, generous contributions from Mr. and Mrs. Rea A. Axline and Dr. and Mrs. Jack M. Farris, and by grants from the National Endowment for the Arts, a federal agency, and the California Challenge Program of the California Arts Council. Additional project support was received from the San Diego Design Center.